# Knowledge Management

Springer
*Berlin*
*Heidelberg*
*New York*
*Barcelona*
*Hong Kong*
*London*
*Milan*
*Paris*
*Singapore*
*Tokyo*

Kai Mertins · Peter Heisig
Jens Vorbeck (Eds.)

# Knowledge Management

## Best Practices in Europe

With 121 Figures

 Springer

Professor Dr.-Ing. Kai Mertins
Dipl.-Sozw. Peter Heisig
Dipl.-Psych. Jens Vorbeck
Fraunhofer Institute
Production Systems and Design Technology (IPK)
Pascalstraße 8–9
10587 Berlin
Germany

ISBN 3-540-67484-5 Springer-Verlag Berlin Heidelberg New York

Library of Congress Cataloging-in-Publication Data applied for
Die Deutsche Bibliothek – CIP-Einheitsaufnahme
Knowledge management: best practices in Europe / Kai Mertins ... (Hrsg.). – Berlin; Heidelberg; New York; Barcelona; Hong Kong; London; Milan; Paris; Singapore; Tokyo: Springer, 2001
  ISBN 3-540-67484-5

Springer-Verlag Berlin Heidelberg New York
a member of BertelsmannSpringer Science+Business Media GmbH

© Springer-Verlag Berlin · Heidelberg 2001
Printed in Germany

SPIN 10724834      43/2202-5 4 3 2 1 0 – Printed on acid-free paper

# Acknowledgment

We would like to thank the following participants for their assistance in the realization of this project.

Special thanks for their contribution to the forewords: Robert C. Camp, PhD, PE (Best Practice Institute, USA), Dr. Christoph Haxel (Henkel KGaA, Germany) and Dr. Andreas Spielvogel (Continental AG, Germany).

The success of this book relies heavily on its case studies. We found very much pleasure in the inspiring interviews with knowledge management practitioners from industry. We appreciated the dedicated support and the co-authorship of the following persons: Christian Berg and Peter Drtina (Phonak), Dr. Rolf W. Habbel (Booz-Allen & Hamilton), Andrea Martin (IBM), Janet Runeson (Celemi), Dr. Peter Schütt (IBM), Dr. Frank Spellerberg (Arthur D. Little). In addition, special thanks for their cooperation to Jonathan Allen (BAE SYSTEMS), Jane Cooper (Thomas Miller) Sabine Deuschl (Booz-Allen & Hamilton), Delfried Ehlers (Roche Diagnostics), Dr. Fritz-Gernot Fehlinger (Roche Diagnostics), Mark Holford (Thomas Miller), Rudi Krcma (Hewlett Packard), Hartwig Loh (Skandia) and Uwe Romanski (Skandia).

Besides the authors many other people invested their time and effort into the completion of the case studies. Grateful thanks apply to Reinhard Arlt, Martin Carbon, Oliver Diethert, Gerd Grotenhöfer, Sönke Luck, Felix Neugart and Corinna Scholz.

For the extensive translation we would like to thank Dr. Cary Henderson, Robyne Stedwell and Elisabeth Steinbeis for their committed support and great dedication.

For the bibliography we thank Anne Brinkmann and Karin Boeck.

We would also like to thank our team members Kerstin Farchmin, Mario Görmer, Johannes Niebuhr and André Riemer for their support.

This first "German Benchmarking Study Knowledge Management" was supported by the following companies: Continental AG, Hannover; Daimler-Benz Aerospace - MTU Motoren- und Turbinen Union München GmbH; Eternit AG, Berlin; Henkel KGaA, Düsseldorf; Merck KGaA, Darmstadt; PSI AG, Berlin. We would like to thank our sponsors cordially.

The survey has been carried out with the support of the biggest German weekly business magazine "Die Wirtschaftswoche", Düsseldorf. Special thanks to Claudia Tödtmann and Barbara Bierach.

We would also like to thank our publishing partner, "Springer Verlag" especially Dr. Martina Bihn and her team for the support and patient cooperation.

The Editors

# Foreword

## By Robert C. Camp, PhD, PE

## Chairman Global Benchmarking Network (GBN),
## Best Practice Institute™,

## Rochester, NY, USA

The perception, sharing, and adoption of best practices is mostly attributed to the activity called benchmarking. Obtaining maximum value from best practices is usually attributed to knowledge management. One is an extension of the other. Knowledge management can be looked upon as the management of knowledge about best practices whether in the mind as human capital or as intellectual assets or property.

Most organizations now recognize the absolute imperative for the identification and collection of best practices through benchmarking. It can be a strategic strength when practiced and a fatal weakness if not pursued. But there is a serious disconnection in the exchange and adoption process.

Despite significant advances in the approaches and technology that pursue improvement (six sigma, process redesign, customer relationship management, etc.), organizations continue to experience great difficulty in successfully transferring leading practices. Some would say these are exemplary, proven, observed, or promising, but, in the final analysis, they are best practices - with the objective of becoming world class.

More insight is needed into how leading, or best practices are transferred and adopted - said differently, best practices for knowledge transfer or knowledge management.

The subject of knowledge management has gained considerable prominence in the United States through consortia studies, articles, and conferences. But there have been few substantive studies about the experience of knowledge management in Europe, until now. This study is commendable for its findings based on fact, for its use of definitive questionnaires, and its verifications through site visitations. It documents the recent (3-5 years), most prominent experience of organizations across all sectors in Europe.

The framework of the individual, group, and organizational sharing of best practices - from the explicit or documented to the tacit or experience-based developed through research - is very helpful in understanding the process. The many case studies in this study bring that research to life.

This is a substantive research effort. It should provide both qualitative and quantitative insight for those embarking on or pursuing knowledge management best practices for years to come. I recommend it highly for the study of its implications and the use of its findings to get results.

# Foreword

## By Dr. Christoph Haxel
## Henkel KGaA, Düsseldorf
## Henkel InfoCenter

Using knowledge in a structured and organised way is one of the key factors that determine corporate success. The goal is to share and apply knowledge faster and more efficiently than your competitors.

In Henkel's research departments, "knowledge management" has a tradition going back more than 100 years. Sharing knowledge also means publishing and protecting knowledge. Henkel applied for its first patent in 1896. Since then, thousands of inventions have been patented and many research findings have been published. In Research and Technology, we recognized early that ever the increasing speed of industrial reorganization and regrouping would require new ways of managing knowledge. In order to identify the best ways, we decided in 1997 to take part in a benchmarking study.

Within Henkel, the decision to enter a new era in information and knowledge policy within the group was made at a meeting of top managers in May 1998. Our concept for the global collection, distribution, and application of knowledge was called "The power of shared knowledge." The intention was to make the knowledge and experience of Henkel's 56,000 employees world-wide more accessible. It was not just a question of gathering facts and figures, but of making the views and experience of experts available.

We agreed that despite Henkel's modern and open information culture, a lot could still be learned from others and that our existing methods could be refined. In the benchmarking study, business consultants were of special interest, since their entire "production" capital is in the minds of their staff. We therefore asked how consultants handle knowledge management within their companies.

One business consulting firm involved in the benchmarking study particularly impressed us. We visited them to see first hand how they handle knowledge management and to discuss their experience in this area. This firm now advises our company world-wide. Henkel's Management Board also called them in, independently of the benchmarking study, to assist our Düsseldorf headquarters in knowledge management. The benchmarking study was not the only influencing factor in choosing them, but it may well have helped the decision-making process.

Knowledge management at Henkel means exchanging experience and information which is orientated to the business process. The new management tool is now being introduced and built up group-wide.

The core of the tool consists of knowledge "pieces". These are items of knowledge relating to a particular business and task. To "mine" knowledge pieces, the experience of one of our experts is skillfully tapped by an interviewer. During the debriefing process, nuggets of wisdom are entered into databases. The existing infrastructure at Henkel, where more than 25,000 employees communicate via an international information network running on the Lotus Notes platform, eliminated the need for any major investments in hard- or software. Push and pull information technologies now help to transport these valuable pieces of knowledge around the world to the right place at the right time.

Five pilot projects - 'Technology', 'Product Launches', 'Brands', 'Systems' and 'Suppliers' - are now almost complete. The task ahead is to distribute this new management tool throughout the group and to develop it further. Knowledge management has become an established feature of management practice at Henkel.

Topics such as 'e-commerce', 'innovation' and 'time to market' are the new focal points. In meeting these challenges, our experience with knowledge management and its tools is enormously valuable.

With the results already achieved in knowledge management, Henkel is well equipped for the future and on the road to becoming a model of best practice.

# Foreword

**By Dr. Andreas Spielvogel**

**Director Development Processes & Tools**

**Business Unit Original Equipment**

**Continental AG**

Tire engineering is not a classical engineering discipline and lies on the borderline between mechanical engineering and chemistry. Few books have been published on tires. Even publications are not seen very often compared to other disciplines, and I have never seen documentation describing how to design a modern tire.

It is therefore crucial that a tire engineering company does its own research and knowledge documentation. Nevertheless, the documentation of know-how had at one time low priority when compared to other R&D activities. When we started with knowledge management, most know-how was located in the minds of people who have been with the company for many years.

But what happens when R&D is relocated and undergoes significant restructuring? Older engineers and chemists retire. Younger ones quit or move into other functions and hopefully the majority stays.

In our case, the threat was so great that preventative action against loosing know-how seemed necessary.

So we started in 1995 with knowledge management without knowing that it would be so popular in the near future. Even before 1995, a lot of activities existed that nowadays have the attribute "knowledge management". Most of our approaches have been derived from in-house research and use "simple" technology. The basis was our culture, processes, and procedures. We had very little advice from outside the company.

It was therefore a challenge for us to participate in the benchmark with Fraunhofer Gesellschaft. We had no idea what our performance would be. Nevertheless we found ourselves in the upper third.

Our greatest expectation was to get into contact with other companies and to learn from best practices. The major benefits for us were our improved sensitivity to the need for knowledge management, faster implementation of new ideas, the ability to avoid of mistakes, and better overall performance. We also got a lot of attention for our approach from the public. This was more than we had expected.

Now, in the year 2000, knowledge management is one of the key elements in corporate basics (http://www.conti-online.com) and we are proud to be mentioned as a case study in the recent literature.[1] We are continuously striving for improvement.

I recommend this book for practitioners, specialists, and managers who are looking for ideas and examples of how to implement or improve knowledge management. The book gives a broad overview and best practices from well known European companies in a variety of branches. It emphasizes the important role of culture, motivation, and skills. A review of tools that support knowledge management has also been included.

---

[1] Edvinsson, Brünig (2000).

# Brief Contents

## Part 4: KM in Europe

# Contents

## Part II: Survey

## Part III: Case Studies

## 7      Knowledge Management: The "One Company Platform" - Arthur D. Little, Inc.
*Peter Heisig, Dr. Frank Spellerberg*...................................................... 127

## 8      Cultural Change Triggers Best Practice Sharing - British Aerospace plc.
*Peter Heisig, Jens Vorbeck* ................................................................... 138

# Part IV: KM in Europe

# 1   Introduction

*Prof. Dr.-Ing. Kai Mertins, Peter Heisig, Jens Vorbeck*

## 1.1   How it all started

In 1990, just after the unification of Germany, Fraunhofer IPK started two research projects partly funded by the German Federal Ministry of Research and Technology, with companies, universities and research institutes from both parts of Germany.[2] The aim of the projects was to discover and to describe the tacit knowledge of skilled mechanical workers, to develop processes and the task environments and technical prototypes to support the creation, sharing and use of tacit knowledge and to implement and test these solutions with the workers on the shop floor. With the introduction of CNC-Machines in the mechanical workshops, experienced and highly skilled workers often felt insecure about their ability to control the process. They missed the 'right sound' of the metal and the 'good vibrations' of the machine. These signals were absorbed by the new CNC-Machines and hence workers were not able to activate their tacit knowledge in order to produce high quality products. Within a second project[3] we observed similar problems with the introduction of other CIM-Technologies, such as CAD/CAM in the design and the process-planning department and with MRP systems for order management. The information supply chain could not fully substitute the informal knowledge transfer chain between the different departments.

Some years later, in spring 1997, the book by Nonaka and Takeuchi "The Knowledge-Creating Company"[4] helped us to look at our results from a different angle. We discovered that we had to bundle our research capabilities coming from engineering, computer science, psychology, business administration and social science in order to create a powerful team addressing all issues of knowledge management.

Two events set the ball rolling: The newly-founded Competence Center Knowledge Management, a profit center at the Fraunhofer IPK in Berlin, and the concept for a benchmarking study on the state of the art of knowledge management in Europe.

---

[2]   Martin (1995); Carbon, Heisig (1993).
[3]   Mertins et al. (1993); Fleig, Schneider (1995).
[4]   Nonaka, Takeuchi (1995).

We contacted the 100 largest German companies to inquire about their interest in research about knowledge management. The feedback was overwhelming. One out of two companies realized the significance of this topic and joined a founding team. Today, these companies still contact Fraunhofer IPK for further research and support in knowledge management projects. However, three years ago, we had to convince parties from this team to invest money in applied research. Despite the fact that some authors track knowledge management activities back to the early 80s[5], we realized that the awareness of this topic still had to be advanced and that the solutions propagated lacked industrial relevance. Six dedicated companies made the first move and co-financed the "First German Benchmarking Study on Knowledge Management in Europe" conducted by the Competence Center Knowledge Management.

## 1.2 The Benchmarking Study Knowledge Management: the cornerstone of our success

The Competence Center Knowledge Management at Fraunhofer IPK in Berlin has conducted the first comprehensive German benchmarking study at the level of knowledge management, in cooperation with the Information Center Benchmarking (IZB). The study focused on German TOP 1000 and European TOP 200 companies. Previous studies on knowledge management had almost exclusively focused on North America and the UK. When European companies were included, the results indicated that knowledge management in North America was at a much more advanced level of development. It was therefore the goal of this study to get an adequate picture of the level of knowledge management in large European corporations. In accordance with the benchmarking method, we also identified the best companies ("company with best practices"), and studied their methods and cultural and technological basis in detail.

Within the framework of knowledge management as discussed in the following section and the benchmarking method, the approach to business processes facilitates a comparison of best practice companies. It also allows a company to optimize its own performance. We based our study on the widely recognized business process classification of the American Productivity and Quality Center (APQC).[6]

The scientifically-sound execution of our study required a theoretical approach, a model to guide our actions. Our industrial partners on the other hand were very attentive regarding the applicability of our results. One major characteristic of our model is thus based on their input and their need for added value: The Fraunhofer

---

[5]    Wiig (1997).

[6]    Camp (1995), pp. 437.

IPK model and the study both focus on the business processes practised by a company that create its value. In this context, a core process of knowledge management and related supporting design fields are the topics of our study (Fig. 1.1).

### 1.2.1 The approach: Fraunhofer IPK Berlin models knowledge management as a core process

The connection of the above-mentioned aspects, led to the following definition of knowledge management at Fraunhofer IPK:

"Knowledge Management describes all methods, instruments and tools that in a holistic approach contribute to the promotion of the core knowledge processes - to generate knowledge, to store knowledge, to distribute knowledge and to apply knowledge supported by the definition of knowledge goals and the identification of knowledge - in all areas and levels of the organization."

The two main design criteria of our approach to knowledge management are characterized by practical considerations requiring us to develop an approach...

- ...that is easy to understand, communicate, and apply to the entire company, from the shop floor up to the top management levels.

- ...in which all actions are directed towards the value-adding core processes of the company.

This directed us to the design of an integrated core process in which all activities are supported by organizational, motivational and technical aspects. The core process can be further broken down into the core activities "define the goals of knowledge", "identify knowledge", "create (new) knowledge", "store knowledge", "distribute knowledge", and "apply knowledge." The quality of these stages is guaranteed by certain design fields for knowledge management. These fields include a company's process organization, available information technology, management systems, corporate culture, the management of human resources, and controlling.

### *1.2.1.1 The core process of knowledge management*[7]

- Create (new) knowledge: Measures and instruments that promote the creation of knowledge are, for example, the acquisition of external knowledge (mergers, consultants, recruiting, patent acquisition), the setting-up of interdisciplinary project teams that include the customers, and the application of 'lessons learned' and methods to elicit tacit knowledge.

---

[7] Heisig (1998).

4

- Store knowledge: The stored knowledge in manuals, databases, case studies, reports and even corporate processes and rules of thumb makes up one column of the other core activities. The other column consists of the knowledge stored in the brains of thousands of employees who leave their respective organizations at the end of each working day.

- Distribute knowledge: Provision of the right knowledge to the right person at the right time is the aim of the core task 'distribution of knowledge'. The methods and tools are dominated by IT applications such as the Internet or Intranet. However, these tools only provide added value if trust and mutual understanding pervade the atmosphere of the entire company as well as projects teams. The development of a common language is an important task. Other aspects of the distribution of knowledge are the transfer of experiences to new employees by training-on-the-job, mentoring or coaching techniques.

- Apply knowledge: According to our survey, the application of knowledge is the most essential task of knowledge management. Knowledge management mainly provides methods to overcome the barriers of the 'not-invented-here' syndrome: the one-sided thinking and the development of preferred solution by existing information pathologies.

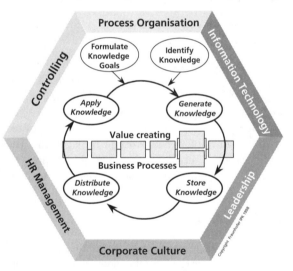

**Fig. 1.1:    Core Process and Design Fields of Knowledge Management**

## *1.2.1.2 Design fields of knowledge management*

The second important step is to set up the link between knowledge management and the general organizational design areas, such as business processes, information systems, leadership, corporate culture, human resource management, and controlling

- The business processes are the application areas for the core process of knowledge management. Existing knowledge has to be applied, and new knowledge has to be generated to fulfill the needs of internal and external customers. The core activities have to be permanently aligned with the operating and value-creating business processes. Furthermore, knowledge management activities could be linked with existing process documentation programs (for example, ISO certification), and integrated into business process reengineering approaches.

- Information technology is currently the main driving factor in knowledge management. This is due to considerable technological improvements in the field of worldwide data networking through internet/intranet technologies. IT builds the infrastructure to support the core activities of storing and distributing knowledge. Data warehouses and data mining approaches will enable companies to analyze massive databases and therefore contribute to the generation of new knowledge.

- The success of knowledge management strategies is to a large degree determined by the support through top and mid-level managers. Therefore, leadership is a critical success factor. Each manager has to promote and personify the exchange of knowledge. He has to act as a multiplier and catalyst within day-to-day business activities. Special leadership training and change programs have to be applied to achieve the required leadership style.

- If the knowledge management diagnosis indicates that the current corporate culture will not sustain knowledge management, wider change management measures have to be implemented. The required company culture could be characterized by openness, mutual trust and tolerance of mistakes, which would then be considered necessary costs of learning.

- Personnel management measures have to be undertaken to develop specific knowledge management skills such as the ability to develop and apply research and retrieval strategies as well as adequately structuring and presenting knowledge and information. Furthermore, incentives for employees to document and share their knowledge have to be developed. Career plans have to be re-designed incorporating aspects of knowledge acquisition of employees. Performance evaluation schemes have to be

6

expanded towards the employees' contribution to knowledge generation, sharing and transfer.

- Each management program has to demonstrate its effectiveness. Therefore, knowledge-controlling techniques have to be developed to support the goal-oriented control of knowledge creation and application with suitable control indicators. While strategic knowledge control supports the determination of knowledge goals, the operative knowledge control contributes to the control of short-term knowledge activities.

## 1.2.2 Empirical results and case studies

With this conceptual model in mind, we developed a comprehensive questionnaire that initially deals with the company as a whole and then focuses on a selected business process (Fig. 1.2). This business process acts as the "candidate" of the participating company for the selection of best practices. Several categories in both parts of the questionnaire were left open so that the people interviewed could include new methods used by their company. This approach takes the rapid rate of innovation in the field of knowledge management into account. The questionnaire was sent to the CEO of the German TOP 1000 and the European TOP 200. Organizationally, knowledge management is located in many different corporate areas. Still, if a company claims a best practice, at the very least the CEO should know. We therefore chose to contact top management as our central coordinators.

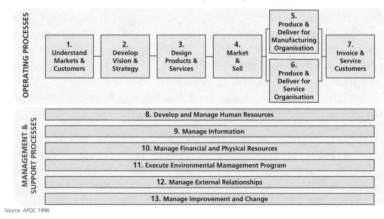

Source: APQC 1996

**Fig. 1.2:** **Scheme for the Classification of Processes Developed by the APQC**

The procedure for the execution of the survey and the selection of best practice candidates and the detailed results of the survey are presented in chapter 6. Nevertheless, the following figure may as well be offered right away to motivate the interested reader to proceed.

The results of our study confirmed the great potential for savings and improvements that knowledge management offers. Over 70% of the companies questioned have already attained noticeable improvements through the use of knowledge management. Almost half of these companies have thus saved time and money, or have improved productivity (Fig. 1.3). Around 20% of these companies have either improved their processes, significantly clarified their structures and processes, increased the level of customer satisfaction, or facilitated decisions and forecasts through the use of knowledge management.

However, some differences were apparent between the answers provided by service and those provided by manufacturing companies. 28% of the service firms indicated an improvement in customer satisfaction due to knowledge management as compared with only 16% of the industrial companies. The latter stressed improvements in quality with 23%, while only 15% of the service companies noted qualitative improvements. Answers to questions about the clarity of structures and processes showed yet another difference. 26% of the service companies indicated improvement with the use of knowledge management as opposed to only 14% in industrial concerns.

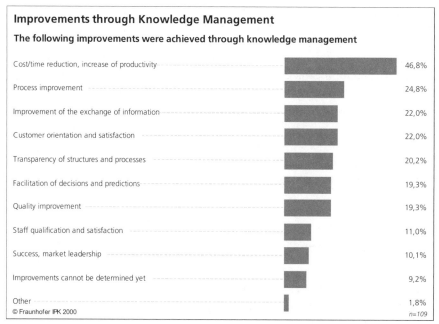

**Fig. 1.3:    Improvements through Knowledge Management**

The case studies complement the empirical results with qualitative decriptions of best practices. These best practices were gathered in those companies that evaluated themselves as professional knowledge management practitioners. All ten case studies are contained in Part III "Case Studies".

8

## 1.3 Recent developments

The acid test of applied research is the acceptance of its results in industry. As a consequence of the study the Competence Center Knowledge Management had the pleasure and the opportunity to demonstrate the value of our approach in several industry projects. These projects ranged from the conceptual design of knowledge management to its implementation and from knowledge management audits to short-term workshops.

During the past year we (as well as our sponsors) had the opportunity to exploit the findings of our study, which is the reason why we have not published until now. Furthermore, we acquired new knowledge on potentials and barriers and developed new solutions.

Part I "Design Fields" integrates both our results from the benchmarking study as well as our experience from industry and further readings of the current literature. The entirety of the individual sections reflects once more our integrated approach to knowledge management.

The chapter "Business Process Oriented Knowledge Management" by Peter Heisig describes links between business processes design and knowledge management. Various related approaches are presented and discussed briefly. A method for the analysis of business processes from a knowledge management perspective and for the integration of knowledge management activities into daily business is presented. An example for the improvement of a knowledge-intensive business process in a service industry company is described briefly. The chapter concludes with some best practice building blocks for knowledge management and with an outlook on the future of knowledge management.

The chapter "Motivation and Competence for Knowledge Management" by Jens Vorbeck and Ina Finke addresses knowledge management from the perspective of human resource management. The issue about the effects of human resource management on supporting the different core process activities focusses on two approaches: On the one hand, HRM can approach work and task design with motivating effects. On the other hand, a neglected area of knowledge management – the necessary competencies – is highlighted. The relevant competencies are broke down according to the core activities of knowledge management. The chapter closes with the presentation of a tool that allows the measurement and controlling of the development of competencies.

The chapter "Intellectual Capital" by Peter Heisig, Jens Vorbeck and Johannes Niebuhr introduces the emerging concept of intellectual capital, which has been used and supported by a wide range of companies and even government institutions. The leading approaches are delineated and measuring methods as well as indicators are presented briefly.

The chapter "Knowledge Management Tools" by Ingo Hoffmann presents the practical means that can be acquired by technical or information-technological support. The relevant basic technologies for the support of knowledge management are described, as well as a classification of the various knowledge management tools. The IPK model, which is primarily an orientation aid, is of central importance. The aspect of facilitating work tasks for the knowledge worker is emphasised here and is taken into account in the classification of the more than 50 analyzed tools. The model provides a great deal of clarity on functionally similar applications. These are sorted in relation to the core activities of knowledge management and a list of the market leaders is provided, with current internet addresses.

## 1.4   Knowledge

The term knowledge is a difficult one and the authors of this book recognize that they will not contribute to a further definition of this term. Still, a publication on knowledge management requires a clarification of the matter. Therefore, we would like to discuss our approach which is far from being exhaustive but has proven beneficial nevertheless.

The most common association with the term knowledge is scientific knowledge. Knowledge which comes from the laboratories and study rooms of universities. This knowledge is developed by using scientific methodologies and standards. It is tested and validated by the scientific communitiy. It is explicitly described in research papers, reports and books. It is stored in huge libraries, which looks like old "cathedrals of knowledge". Online knowledge supermarkets will complement these places in the future. Nearly the same association is linked with the knowledge produced by the research and development departments of companies.

The other association we have with the term knowledge is the knowledge an experienced person posesses. During our research at the beginnings of the 90ies we heard from experienced lathe operators that they feel and hear if the process is going right. A similar observation is quoted from a worker at a paper manufacturing plant:"We know the paper is right when it smells right."[8] However, you do not only find this kind of knowledge in craft work settings, you find it in high tech chip production[9] environments as well as in social settings too. From the noise of the pupils, experienced teachers can distinguish what they have to do in order to progress.[10]

The importance of knowledge for the competitiveness of companies, organizations and even economies is always mentioned to support arguments around knowledge

---

[8]   Victor, Boynton (1998), p. 43.

[9]   Luhn (1999).

[10]   Bromme (1992).

10

management. Unfortunately the term knowledge is not easy to define. There are numerous descriptions and definitions of knowledge. Romhardt [11] found 40 dichotomies of knowledge like explicit versus implicit or tacit, individual versus collective. Von Krogh/Venzin [12] created seven categories of knowledge to be used in management and organization theory: tacit, embodied, encoded, embrained, embedded, event and procedural. These definitions or descriptions are often used by academics.

The discussion about knowledge has a very long tradition. At least more than two thousands years ago Socrates[13] asks his students these questions: "Why do we have to know what knowledge is? How can we know, what knowledge is? What do we know about knowledge?"

A very popular classification of knowledge distinguishes between signals, data, information and knowledge. Some even add wisdom to this hierarchy. This classification, if not properly understood and used, could lead to a philosophical discussion of the 'right' distinction between the categories. The next difficulty arises from the often conflicting definitions of information and knowledge. In practice these distinctions are often only marginal.

Instead of a hierarchy, we found that the understanding of a continuum ranging from data via information to knowledge proved to be the most practical scheme for knowledge management.[14] Typical questions for data and information are: Who – what – where – when? etc. while typical questions for knowledge are: How? And Why?[15]

If we talk to people in charge of knowledge management in companies they rarely have problems with the ambiguity of the term knowledge. They know which kind of knowledge is relevant for their job. They value the contribution of the knowledge to their companies' success.

---

[11] Romhardt (1998), pp. 28.
[12] Von Krogh, Venzin (1995).
[13] Platon (1981).
[14] Heisig (2000).
[15] Eck (1997).

Part I

**Design Fields**

# 2 Business Process Oriented Knowledge Management

*Peter Heisig*

It seems logical that knowledge is an extremely important resource for business success. Therefore, the lack of theoretical understanding of knowledge and practically proven methods for efficient knowledge management is surprising. Only recently have academics and practitioners begun publishing their approaches and experiences under the concept of knowledge management.[16]

Our approach to business process oriented knowledge management is based on the following assumptions:

- The operative methods and procedures used to generate, store, distribute and apply knowledge differ according to particular business processes. These specific methods have to be integrated into a knowledge management approach that is oriented towards business processes.

- Aspects of corporate culture are the most frequently mentioned success factor for knowledge management. However, corporate culture is not a homogenous entity. It is an interwoven network of different professional cultures[17] (e.g. Engineer, Economist, Lawyer), functional cultures (e.g. Sales, R&D, Production) as well as underlying corporate traditions and values. A knowledge management approach focused on business processes has to consider these specific cultural conditions.

- We use our knowledge and the know-how of our colleagues, suppliers, clients, competitors and other resources on a daily basis to solve problems and get our work done. "Knowledge Management is nothing new."[18]

- "I have no time" or "My team has no time" is one of the most commonly mentioned barriers[19] for knowledge management in organizations. Therefore, knowledge management tasks have to be combined with daily work tasks and integrated into the daily business processes.

---

[16] Skyrme, Amidon (1997); Probst, Raub, Romhardt (1998); Willke (1998); Davenport, Prusak (1998).
[17] Davenport et al. (1996), p. 60.
[18] Hansen et al. (1999).
[19] Bullinger et al. (1997).

## 2.1    Knowledge management is business and process oriented

The concept of knowledge management has been used in different disciplines, mostly in knowledge engineering[20] and artificial intelligence[21] AI research often reduced the concept of knowledge management to the description of the development and use of expert systems.[22] Our analysis of approximately 100 case studies published before February 1998 shows that IT-based approaches towards knowledge management are dominant. IT-based KM-approaches focus mainly on the storage (data bases, DMS) and distribution (Intranet and Internet applications, Push and/or Pull) of explicit, electronically documented knowledge, thus ignoring the tacit dimension of knowledge.

In contrast to those conceptions, the results of our survey show that knowledge management is mainly understood by practitioners from manufacturing and the service industry as part of corporate culture and a business-oriented method: "The sum of procedures to generate, store, distribute and apply knowledge to achieve organizational goals" (see chapter 6).

The Cranfield survey[23] supports this interpretation with 72 percent of selected European managers claiming that knowledge management is 'The collection of processes that govern the creation, dissemination, and utilization of knowledge to fulfill organization objectives'.

Nearly all approaches to knowledge management emphasize the process character with inter-linked tasks or activities. The wording and the number of knowledge management tasks mentioned by each approach differ markedly. Probst et al. [24] have proposed the most common approach in German with eight building blocks: The identification, acquisition, development, sharing, utilization, retention and assessment of knowledge and knowledge goals. Another difference is the emphasis given by authors to the steps of the process or knowledge management tasks. Processes for the creation of knowledge are described by Nonaka and Takeuchi[25] while Bach et al.[26] focus on the identification and distribution of the explicit, electronically documented objects of knowledge.

The close relationship between processes and knowledge management is underscored by the critical success factors named by the companies in our survey. Nearly one out of four companies (24 %) mentioned aspects of the design of

---

[20]    De Hoog (1997); Schreiber et al. (2000).

[21]    Göbler (1992); Forkel (1994).

[22]    Gödicke (1992), p. 68; however Davenport et al. (1996) found only one expert system application within 30 knowledge work improvement projects.

[23]    Cranfield School of Management (1998).

[24]    Probst et al. (1998).

[25]    Nonaka, Takeuchi (1995).

[26]    Bach et al. (1999).

structures and processes as a critical factor for the success of knowledge management (see chapter 6).

Furthermore, our results indicate that companies focus on specific business processes to implement knowledge management (Fig. 2.1). One out of every two companies start their KM initiatives in the R&D area. Two out of five enterprises focus on the processes of "Understanding Markets and Customers" and more than one third of the companies begin in the area "Production and Delivery of Products and/or Services." The process "Manage Information" is ranked fourth in our overall sample and second in the service industry sample. We used a business processes classification scheme, which distinguishes between seven operative and six management and support processes on the first level.[27]

### Start with KM             Core Competencies

| OPERATING PROCESSES | Start with KM | | Core Competencies |
|---|---|---|---|
| | 40 % | 1. Understand Markets & Customers | 62 % |
| | 23 % | 2. Develop Vision & Strategy | 38 % |
| | 53 % | 3. Design Products & Services | 63 % |
| | 23 % | 4. Market & Sell | 43 % |
| | 37 % | 5. Produce & Deliver for Manufacturing Organisation | 60 % |
| | 36 % | 6. Produce & Deliver for Service Organisation | 60 % |
| | 6 % | 7. Invoice & Service Customers | 5 % |
| MANAGEMENT AND SUPPORT PROCESSES | 16 % | 8. Develop and Manage Human Resources | 18 % |
| | 32 % | 9. Manage Information | 23 % |
| | 10 % | 10. Manage Financial and Physical Resources | 15 % |
| | 8 % | 11. Execute Environmental Management Program | 10 % |
| | 10 % | 12. Manage External Relationships | 15 % |
| | 19 % | 13. Manage Improvement and Change | 24 % |

**Fig. 2.1:** **Where Companies Start with Knowledge Management and where they Locate their Core Competence**

The experiences of our best practice companies stress this focused approach towards knowledge management. Two companies launched a company-wide, technology-based KM initiative. After six to ten months, these initiatives were abandoned and then re-launched with a focus on the R&D area in one case and on a specific industry branch in the other.

A comparison between the business processes in which knowledge management is most commonly started and the processes in which the questioned companies

---

[27]    Camp (1995) Appendix E.

16

locate their core competence shows that knowledge management follows core competence (Fig. 2.1).

## 2.2 Approaches to the design of business process and knowledge management

One primary design object in private and public organizations are the business processes which structure work for internal and external clients. Known as Business Process Reengineering[28] (BPR) or Business Process Optimization[29], the design of business processes became the focus of management attention in the 90's. Various methods and tools for BPR have been developed by research institutes, universities, and consulting companies. Despite these developments, a comparative study of methods for business process redesign completed by the University St. Gallen (Switzerland) concludes: „To sum up, we have to state: hidden behind a more or less standard concept, there is a multitude of the most diverse methods. A standardized design theory for processes has still not emerged."[30]

"BPR`s focus is typically on studying and changing a variety of factors, including work flows and processes, information flows and uses, management and business practices, and staffing and other resources. However, most BPR efforts have not focused much on knowledge, if at all. This is indeed amazing considering that knowledge is a principal success factor – or in many judgment, the major driving force behind success. Knowledge-related perspectives need to be part of BPR."[31]

Nearly all approaches to knowledge management aim at improving the results of the organization. These results are achieved by delivering a product or/and service to a client. This again is done by fulfilling certain tasks, which are linked to each other thereby forming processes. These processes have been described as business processes. Often, knowledge is understood as a resource used in these processes. Nevertheless, only very few approaches to knowledge management have explicitly acknowledged this relation. And even fewer approaches have tried to develop a systematic method to integrate knowledge management activities into the business processes. Some selected approaches are presented and discussed briefly below.

---

[28] Hammer, Champy (1993).
[29] Diebold GmbH (1993).
[30] Hess, Brecht (1995), p. 114.
[31] Wiig (1995), p. 257.

## 2.2.1 The CommonKADS methodology[32]

The CommonKADS methodology, which has been developed since the beginning of the 80ies, claims to support the development of knowledge management solutions. Originating from the knowledge engineering background, its application in practice has shown that many projects dealing with the development of knowledge systems fail due to a technology-push approach. Therefore, the CommonKADS methodology tries to broaden its focus of development by integrating an organizational model, which tries to describe critical success factors such as "General Context (Mission, Strategy, Environment)", "Structures", "Processes", "People", "Culture & Power", "Resources" and "Knowledge Assets".

The main focus of the CommonKADS methodology is still on the development of knowledge systems as tools to support knowledge intensive tasks. Therefore, the methodology to describe knowledge assets within the "knowledge model" is well developed and has shown their advantages in the development of knowledge systems.[33]

Knowledge management itself is seen as a meta-level activity that acts on the knowledge object level. This meta-level activity consists of a cyclic exertion of three main activities: conceptualize (identify knowledge, analyze strengths/weaknesses), reflect (identify improvements, plan changes) and act (implement changes, monitor improvements). Three objects define the knowledge object level: (1) agents as persons or software that possess (2) knowledge assets and participate in (3) business processes.

The authors present the knowledge management cycle with seven activities covering the complete life cycle of knowledge within the organization. These activities are common within many other frameworks: Identify, plan, acquire and/or develop, distribute, foster the application, control and maintain, dispose.

They emphasize the value and process view of knowledge management: "As outlined previously, knowledge is a prime enabler to successfully carry out the business processes within the organization, which in turn create value for the recipients of its products and services."[34] However, the method could not show how to integrate these knowledge management activities within the business processes. The knowledge assets analysis addresses typical questions of knowledge logistics ("right place" and "right time") and quality ("right form" and "right quality"), though without covering the cultural aspects influencing these items.[35] Therefore, the main advantages provided by the CommonKADS methodology for knowledge management are the techniques for knowledge-

32   Schreiber et al. (2000).
33   De Hoog (1997).
34   Schreiber et al. (2000), p. 72.
35   Lullies et al. (1993).

oriented task analysis, and the methods to enhance knowledge sharing and reuse.[36] The method does not support the design of processes to deal with tacit knowledge. The elicitation methods help to make explicit the knowledge concepts and reasoning requirements of a prospective system. The proposed meta-level activity of knowledge management addresses process improvement aspects of the life cycle of knowledge. This link has to be made more explicit to cover all knowledge management activities and not only the sharing and reuse activities.

## 2.2.2   The business knowledge management approach

Bach et al.'s approach, so-called business knowledge management, tries to relate knowledge management activities to business objects and business processes: "a process-oriented, systematic knowledge management based on multimedia document processing".[37] Their approach distinguishes between business processes, the knowledge structure, which represents the knowledge domains, and the knowledge base, which includes knowledge management processes, roles and responsibilities as well as systems and documents. Some indicators are proposed to help the management control knowledge management processes.

One limitation of their approach is that it does not take the tacit dimension of knowledge into account. Their methodology PROMET®I-NET[38] for intranet-based knowledge management focuses on explicit, electronically documented data and information (similar approaches which also advocate intranet-based knowledge management are commonly found under the term "Content Management"). The knowledge management process named "Development"[39] is limited to the identification of unknown knowledge and the improvement of existing objects of information. Furthermore, the process does not involve the aspect of the generation of new knowledge even though the term "Development" might lead to this understanding.

## 2.2.3   The knowledge value chain approach

The importance of the combination of business processes with knowledge management tasks is also underscored by Weggeman.[40] His knowledge value chain is a continuously repeated process which is composed of six knowledge management tasks on the operational level: identify the required knowledge, document the available knowledge, develop, share, apply and evaluate knowledge. These tasks are linked to the strategic level (Mission, Vision, Goals, Strategy) and

---

[36]  Schreiber et al. (2000), p. 72.
[37]  Bach et al.(1999).
[38]  Kaiser (1999).
[39]  Bach et al. (1999).
[40]  Weggeman (1998).

the business process named primary process such as order handling, for instance. Nevertheless, his approach does not provide a well-developed method of how to integrate the mentioned knowledge management activities into the primary process either.

## 2.2.4 The building block approach

Probst et al.'s approach, which specifies eight building blocks to manage knowledge - knowledge goals, knowledge identification, acquisition, development, sharing, utilization, retention and assessment - received the broadest attention in Germany and Switzerland. Knowledge as a resource is considered the only integrative pattern of their approach, which follows no other external logic than the inherent logic of knowledge. Furthermore, they do not systematically include categories such as leadership, culture and technology within their concept[41], which has already been criticized by practitioners as a deficit.[42]

The idea of building blocks for knowledge management has been proposed by Wiig with examples of building blocks for knowledge creation and dissemination.[43] While Wiig emphasizes the connection of these building blocks with the (re-)design of business processes, the approach of Probst et al. does not provide any hints of how to integrate the proposed building blocks into the business processes.

## 2.2.5 The model-based knowledge management approach

The model-based knowledge management approach proposed by Allweyer[44] adds a new perspective to the modeling of existing business processes, especially of knowledge-intensive processes. Knowledge-intensive processes are less structured, not exactly foreseeable and, in most cases, not repeatable. Moreover, knowledge generation and application play an important role. Knowledge management activities are considered as an integral part of existing business processes. The four level architecture of business process management is adopted for knowledge management and the method is renamed knowledge process redesign.

The approach is limited to the description of required and used knowledge as well as generated and documented knowledge. Knowledge is understood as information in context with value for the owner of this information, which allows him to act. Moreover, the approach claims to support the structuring of knowledge into categories and the construction of a knowledge map to locate who knows

---

41   Probst et al. (1998).
42   Vogel (1999), p. 124.
43   Wiig (1995), p. 291.
44   Allweyer (1998).

what inside the organization. Easy-to-understand pictograms are proposed to help users describe the use of documented and tacit knowledge within their business processes. The approach does not make explicit how to integrate the knowledge management activities into business processes and the criteria to analyze and improve the knowledge processing within the business process.

### 2.2.6 The reference-model for knowledge management

An approach of a model-based design of knowledge-oriented processes proposes a reference model for knowledge management.[45] The reference model consists of an object model with system elements and activities, a process model and an implementation model. The two most important elements of the object model are (1) knowledge defined as a specialization of information or sub-class of the object class information and (2) knowledge sources separated in person-independent and person-bound sources. The definition of five basic knowledge management activities - identify, make explicit, distribute, apply and store - with two to four sub-activities implies no sequencing. Nonetheless, experience shows that there is a certain sequence, starting with the identification and ending with the storage of relevant experience.

The lack of emphasis on the importance of the sequencing of the basic knowledge management activities overlooks the fact that one important weakness in existing business processes is the lack of connectivity between these basic activities. A possible barrier for the application of the reference model is the translation of real world tasks into the specific notation of the model. This might lead to additional effort and misunderstandings between the modeling expert and the process owner. The redesign is carried out by contrasting the current process with the reference model. The relevant criteria for the design are not explicitly stated in this approach.

### 2.2.7 Summary

None of the presented approaches to knowledge management have been developed from scratch. Their main origins range from KBS development and information systems design to intranet development and business process re-engineering. Depending on their original focus, the mentioned approaches still show their current strengths within these particular areas. However, detailed criteria for the analysis and design are generally missing.

Due to their strong link to information system design, all approaches focus almost exclusively on explicit and documented knowledge as unstructured information. Their design scope is mainly limited to technology-driven solutions. This is surprising as the analysis of thirty knowledge work improvement projects suggests

---

[45]    Warnecke et al. (1998).

a modified use of traditional business process design approaches and methods including non-technical design strategies.[46] Only the business knowledge management approach [47]covers aspects such as roles and measurements.

## 2.3 A method for business process oriented knowledge management

This section introduces the method of integrated enterprise modeling as a methodological basis for analyzing and designing knowledge-intensive business processes. The steps to select, describe, analyze and design business processes in order to improve the generation, the storage, the distribution and the application of knowledge within the processes are outlined. For the improvement of business processes, the building block approach, which makes use of best practice methods and tools, is suggested.

### 2.3.1 Integrated enterprise modeling for knowledge management

Since the late 80's, the division of Corporate Management at the Fraunhofer Institute for Production Systems and Design Technology (Fraunhofer IPK) has developed the method of Integrated Enterprise Modeling (IEM) to describe, analyze and design processes in organizations.[48] Besides projects of traditional business process design, this method has been used and customized for other planning tasks such as quality management[49] (Web and process-based quality manuals for ISO certification) for the design and introduction of process-based controlling in hospitals and benchmarking (Fig. 2.2). The IEM-method is supported by the software tool $MO^2GO$ (**M**ethode zur **O**bjektorientierten **G**eschäftsprozessoptimierung = Method for Object-Oriented Business Process Optimization).

The method of integrated enterprise modeling (IEM) distinguishes between the three object classes "Product", "Order" and "Resource." These object classes are combined by the construct "Action" within a generic activity model. Five elements are provided to link the objects to the actions (Fig. 2.3). The IEM approach offers the possibility to describe knowledge as an object within the process model. According to the overall modeling task, knowledge can be modeled as a sub-class of the superordinated class "Resource" and broken down into different sub-sub-classes in the form of knowledge domains. The sub-class "Knowledge" can be linked to other "Resource" sub-classes such as "Staff",

---

[46]   Davenport et al. (1996).

[47]   Bach et al. (1999).

[48]   Spur et al. (1993).

[49]   Mertins, Jochem (1999).

"EDP-Systems", "Databases", "Documents", etc. which are relevant for the analysis and improvement of the business process. The final objective of every business process consists of the fulfillment of the internal or/and external customer demand with a product or/and service. Knowledge is required to produce or/and deliver this service or/and product and thus becomes implemented in the object "Product."[50] This implemented knowledge could be divided into sub-classes as well. The object "Order" which triggers the actions could be translated into knowledge goals if appropriate.

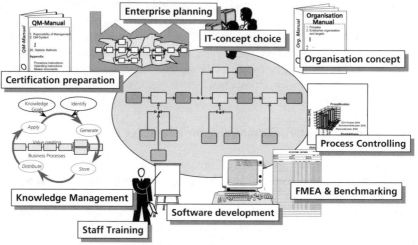

**Fig. 2.2:    Application Fields of the IEM Business Process Models**

With the assignment of attributes to objects, it is possible to describe and analyze the resources, orders, tasks and products according to the specific design goal. For instance, the classification of the product according to the degree of standardization or customization supports the definition of the appropriate strategy for knowledge management.[51]

Since process modeling has been used as a method for analysis and design in several projects during the past years, and companies are thus familiar with the methodology, the integration of knowledge management into business process modeling should not cause any practical problems. The ISO 9000 certification requires the description of processes as well. These process models could be reused and enhanced in order to save effort and costs.[52]

---

[50]    Hedlund (1994); Wilke (1998).

[51]    Hansen et al. (1999).

[52]    Allweyer (1998).

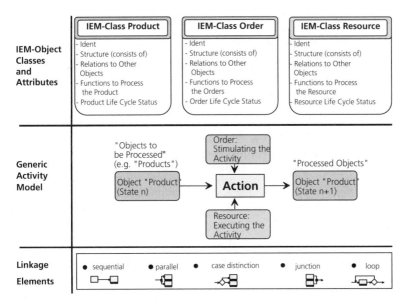

**Fig. 2.3:** **The Objects Classes, the Generic Activity Model and the Linking Elements of the IEM**

The business-oriented knowledge management approach starts with the selection of the business process to be improved. Different approaches and criteria of how to select a business process are presented. After the description of the real world business process, the analysis starts with the evaluation of each single business task. The scope is extended towards the analysis of the relations between the knowledge-processing tasks within the business process. Within the last step of the analysis the focus shifts from the actions towards the resources used and the results produced within the process. The identified weaknesses and shortcomings in the business process will be improved by knowledge management building blocks consisting of process structures.

## 2.3.2   Selection of business area and business process

As our research findings[53] suggest, most companies start with knowledge management initiatives within the business areas they consider to be their core competence.[54] Alternatively, the corporate strategy could be used to derive the appropriate business area in which knowledge management should be initiated. As already mentioned, we have observed two multinational companies, which failed with their initial corporate-wide knowledge management initiative. Both

---

[53]   see chapter 6.

[54]   Also Weggeman (1999), pp. 68.

companies recommenced with a more focused, though still global approach, one in the R&D area, and the other in two product divisions.

Finally, for a pilot project, a process or area should be selected where improvements can be achieved fast. These "quick wins" could be used as success stories for the roll out of knowledge management throughout the whole organization.

Another approach[55] to determining the appropriate business process in which to start knowledge management uses the two categories *knowledge intensity* and *process complexity* with the following attributes used for the selection:

- *Knowledge intensity* (Scale: strong – weak) – attributes:
  Contingency, decision scope, agent innovation, knowledge half-life, agent impact, learning time;

- *Process complexity* (Scale: high – low) – attributes:
  process steps, involved agents, interdependency between agents and process steps, process dynamic;

Agents are persons and/or software programs which process knowledge. The evaluation process should start with each activity first and should then take the entire process into consideration. This approach distinguishes four classes and only processes with high process complexity and stronger knowledge intensity (class 3) should be improved by knowledge management methods (Fig. 2.4).

This understanding is similar to that of knowledge work processes, which are "characterized by variety and exception rather than routine" and "performed by professional or technical workers with a high level of skill and expertise. Knowledge work processes include such activities as research and product development, advertising, education, and professional services like law, accounting, and consulting. We also include management processes such as strategy and planning."[56] Eppler et al. differ from Davenport et al. in their consideration of processes such as advertising, law and strategic decision-making, which are less suitable for improvement through knowledge management methods (Fig. 2.4).

The CommonKADS method suggests in the first process breakdown worksheet the "boolean indicating whether the task is considered knowledge-intensive." However, the presented example and the later description of knowledge-intensive tasks are of limited help for non-knowledge engineering experts.[57]

---

[55]  Eppler et al. (1999).

[56]  Davenport et al. (1996), p. 54; similar also Allweyer (1998), p.39.

[57]  Schreiber et al. (2000), p.33: process breakdown, p.56: example with scale: Yes – medium – high – very high, p. 125: 11 types based on the type of problem being solved.

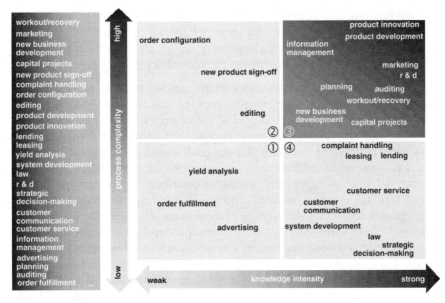

**Fig. 2.4:** **Knowledge Oriented Classification of Business Processes** [58]

For the selection of a business process, the criteria given by Davenport et al., i.e. variety, exception, level of skill and expertise with a scale ranging form low to high, are quite sufficient for practical use.

### 2.3.3 Modeling of knowledge-intensive business process

Starting from our assumption that we use knowledge to perform our daily work tasks within the business processes and the empirical result that lack of time is one of the biggest barriers, a solution for knowledge management has to focus on tasks, performed by people or departments. The level of detail should not be exaggerated, though.[59]

For the modeling of the work process we have to identify the relevant knowledge objects. These are the resources since they represent the knowledge used to perform a certain task. The task itself has to be considered as the action, which transforms the required knowledge. The output of this transformation is the product with the implemented knowledge. The explicit or logical order, which triggers the action, could be regarded as a knowledge goal.

---

[58] Eppler et al. (1999).

[59] Davenport, Prusak (1998), p. 157 mentioned a firm which decribed "one "organiational learning" process, four subprocesses, fifteen sub-subprocesses, and fifty-three sub-sub-subprocesses."

We start focusing on a representative product or service as a result of the business process. A product or service is representative if more than 30 to 40 per cent of the capacity is spent on producing the product or service and if its contribution is of high value to the final product offered to the internal or external client.

The products, activities and resources of the selected business process will be described using the IEM methodology. Existing process descriptions could be used to save time and effort. The level of the description should be the level on which the operational tasks are performed and the knowledge is used. From a knowledge perspective, not only the required knowledge domains should be named as a resource but all the relevant resources such as documents, databases, internal and external experts etc. should be described. The objects ought to be named with the company-specific concepts as this helps to create a common language and common understanding of the process. Our experience also shows that this facilitates the participation of the people involved in the process itself. Due to the high autonomy required by knowledge workers, Davenport et al. stress the importance of their participation for successful improvement of the process.[60] The IEM methodology has been used in a wide range of projects in industry such as telecommunications and automobile, as well as in public organizations such as hospitals and the police. Managers and employees from nearly all organizational levels have been involved in describing their work processes using the four elements of the IEM methodology.[61]

A first idea about the kind of knowledge needed to produce the service or product results from the assessment of the process owner concerning the degree of standardization of his product or service. Standardized products and services are mainly based on the reuse of explicit, codified knowledge while customized products rather tend to incorporate tacit knowledge.[62] The codification of knowledge leads to a higher emphasis on processes and IT whereas customization requires more emphasis on people and face-to-face sharing methods.

Some knowledge management approaches consider these business process models as knowledge assets, which represent the important process knowledge of a company.[63] Generally this notion is correct. However, a web-based documentation of this process knowledge is not sufficient for extracting value from this asset for the company, not even for a knowledge-based company. "Similarly, many firms viewed the commitment to implementing new knowledge work designs as persuasion rather than mandate. They offered, marketed, or communicated the new designs through education rather than forcing them on those who performed

---

60 Davenport (1996).
61 Tünschel et al. (1998).
62 Hansen et al. (1999).
63 Allweyer (1998), p.45.

the knowledge work."[64] Often knowledge management approaches with a strong business process reengineering background do not consider this important task of actively marketing and distributing their own modeling results. One of our best practice companies showed how this process knowledge could be trained and transferred with a tool called "Process Rally." Moreover, this tool supports the elicitation and sharing of tacit knowledge of the involved process owners.[65]

The outcome of the modeling step is the mapping of the business process with the produced products, the performed real tasks and the required knowledge resources. Within the next step we will assess the real world tasks.

### 2.3.4 The knowledge activity profile

Our basic assumption suggests that we are permanently using knowledge to fulfill our tasks in order to achieve some specified goals. Therefore, each task might be considered as a knowledge-processing task. This should not imply, however, that we are looking for more or less rigid rules. Rather, we attempt to create awareness for the inherent knowledge character of each single task. Furthermore, we suggest that the common language used by the process owners to describe their process be maintained and their tasks not be translated into a specific knowledge management notification as suggested by Warnecke et al.[66]

The first step of our analysis focuses on the actions of the business process model. These actions are the tasks performed within the process by the department or by individuals. They are assessed through their function and contribution to the core activities of knowledge management in detail. Two main questions have to be answered: (1) Does the action in its essence represent one or more core tasks of knowledge management: – generate – store - distribute – apply knowledge? (2) How do we estimate the current contribution of this work task to the core activity of knowledge management? Resulting from this assessment, the knowledge activity profile of the business process emerges. We use four core activities of knowledge management, which have been identified as "essential" and "important" in our survey.[67] Furthermore, we think that these activities are sufficient in order to analyze the business process and to assure the involvement of process owners from all organizational levels (Fig. 2.5).

---

[64] Davenport (1996), p. 60.
[65] see chapter 14.
[66] Warnecke et al. (1998), p. 28.
[67] see chapter 6.

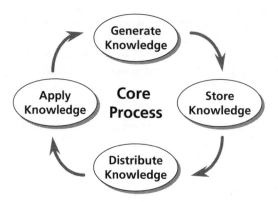

Fig. 2.5:    Core Process of Knowledge Management

The figure (Fig. 2.6) demonstrates a short process example of a problem solving process on level 0 with the software tool MO²GO according to the IEM methodology. The first task "Problem solving" contributes to the knowledge management core tasks "Apply" and "Generate" knowledge. The codification of the solution within the minutes fulfils the task "Store" knowledge. "Send minutes" and "Tell solution" represent the "Distribution" of the explicit knowledge within the minutes and of the implicit knowledge within the verbal explanations during the conversation with a colleague. The operational task "Perform solution" represents the "Apply" core task of knowledge management. The application of the solution generates experiences and thus additional knowledge since knowledge is the only resource, which increases with its use.

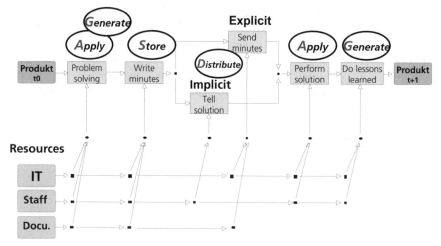

Fig. 2.6:    Operational Tasks with their Contribution to Generic Knowledge Tasks

In some best practice companies, we have observed a wide range of operational tasks to perform "lessons learned." In a financial service company, for instance, a short description of the lessons learned with the current underwriting case was required to finalize the case, additionally supported by a workflow application. In a different company, an interview-based debriefing approach was used to extract the lessons learned from a new product launch. Moreover, a team-based approach to discussing different evaluations of the outcomes in order to gather "Do's and Don'ts" for further improvements was found in product development processes and a project work environment.

With the second evaluation, we will assess, for instance, whether the current performance of the operational task "Write minutes" sufficiently covers the generic knowledge task "Store" knowledge.

The result is a knowledge activity profile, which shows the level, and the quality of support provided by the current operational task towards the core process of knowledge management.

### 2.3.5    The degree of knowledge connectivity

The next step contains the evaluation of the degree of connectivity inherent in the core process activities of knowledge management within the selected business process. As we often perform knowledge management activities implicitly, the core process lacks the appropriate degree of integration or connectivity. For instance, new knowledge is generated, though not explicitly, documented in a database; a database is built but is not used by the targeted user group; knowledge is distributed by the Intranet though not applied by the staff; knowledge is applied but lessons learned are not generated. These are examples of the successful performance of some individual core activities without these single activities being connected, however. The core process itself is therefore not closed or integrated.

The main questions are: How is the generated knowledge stored? How is the stored knowledge distributed? How is the distributed knowledge applied? How is new knowledge generated? The result of this analysis is a profile demonstrating the strong and weak points of the business process depending on the degree of interconnection between the identified core activities. The following figure (Fig. 2.7) shows an example of a business process with 13 operational tasks classified according to their contribution to the core knowledge activities. The focus of the analysis now shifts from the single operational task towards the sequence of tasks. A strength of this business process is the sequence "Generate" (no. 3) and "Store" (no. 4), since the generated knowledge is immediately stored. A weak aspect, on the other hand, is the absence of lessons learned, thus the neglected opportunity to generate new knowledge, after the "Apply" activities (no. 8 and no. 11). Moreover, the late distribution of knowledge (no. 9) should be avoided.

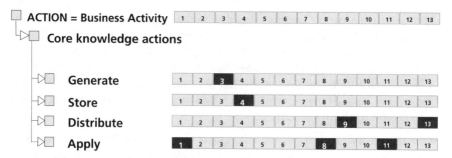

Fig. 2.7:   Analysis of Connectivity of Knowledge-Oriented Task in a Business
            Process

The optimization and the new design of business processes aim at closing the
identified gaps within the underlying core processes and at sequencing the core
tasks of knowledge management. One design principle is to use available
procedures, methods, tools and results from the process to design the solution. As
our projects with different companies have demonstrated, there are already many
worthwhile attempts aimed at improving the handling of knowledge. However,
these approaches are neither considered nor dealt with as systematic and
structured knowledge management.[68] Therefore, in most cases, they have to be
discovered and reused from a knowledge management perspective. This is due to
the fact that one important barrier of knowledge management is the lack of time of
staff and managers. If the gap cannot be closed with existing methods, a new
solution has to be developed in compliance with the missing core activity of
knowledge management. The overall solution not only has to focus on explicit
knowledge in documents and databases but also on tacit knowledge of the
employees. The latter aspect is overlooked by most of the existing knowledge
management approaches.

### 2.3.6   From actions to resources: analysis of their relations

Many knowledge management approaches recommend to start with the
identification of existing knowledge in the firm or organization first. This step
leads to the so-called knowledge map. The knowledge map with its connection to
city maps or other geographical maps is a very helpful tool to provide orientation
and to support the discovery of available knowledge. The existing knowledge
domains could be visualized in an easy-to-understand manner. However, the
potential of modern tools and techniques is rarely utilized for the visualization of
knowledge in maps. Frequently, existing knowledge maps do not overcome
hierarchical trees typical of Microsoft Explorer or Lotus Notes applications. There
is clearly a need for information architects as Wurman suggests: "1) The

---

[68]   Heisig (1998a); Heisig (1998b).

individual who organizes the patterns inherent in data, making the complex clear. 2) A person who creates the structure or map of information, which allows others to find their personal paths to knowledge. 3) The emerging 21st century professional occupation addressing the needs of the age focused upon clarity, human understanding, and the science of organization of information."[69] Some helpful tools are the Tool MindMan and the search, retrieval and indexing tools, for instance.[70]

However, a more problematic disadvantage, which results from the identification step, is the static nature of most knowledge maps. In reality, the knowledge needs are dynamic depending on the tasks to be performed or the problem to be solved. Therefore, the static view has been enhanced by the process view. The process view helps to identify more precisely whether the knowledge is available, which kind of knowledge is needed, whether this knowledge exists in documents or brains, etc. Furthermore, it is possible to describe the existing tools, people and organizational units etc. as other sub-classes of the object class resource (Fig. 2.8).

The focus of the analysis of our approach shifts towards the evaluation of the resources required to perform the task. The questions to be asked are: 1) Which resources are used within the tasks that generate knowledge? 2) Which resources support the operative tasks that store knowledge? 3) Which resources are used by the operational tasks that distribute knowledge? 4) Which resources support the tasks that apply knowledge? The results of the analysis not only demonstrate which kind of knowledge is applied, generated, stored and distributed, they also consider the other resources such as employees, databases and documents.

### 2.3.7 Improvement of a knowledge-intensive business process in a service company

Figure Fig. 2.8 describes a knowledge-intensive business process in a service company. The products of the business process are mainly reports about the state-of-the-art in different knowledge and project fields with background information about history, strategies, partners and coalitions. These reports serve as input for meetings in international institutions and organizations. The work performed in this business process is typical of many governmental and semi-governmental associations and federations on a national and international level.

The knowledge required consists of explicit knowledge from working papers, technical project reports, strategy papers, traveling reports and meeting protocols and the knowledge about internal and external experts. The tacit knowledge, on the other hand, covers the knowledge about assessment criteria of proposed decisions and their consequences for the own strategy and the development of the

---

[69] Wurman (1996), Book cover.
[70] see http://www.mindman.com, chapter 5.

32

company, the knowledge about the position of partners and 'competitors' and the knowledge about the 'real' internal experts who are able to give valid and understandable judgments, etc.

Furthermore, the dynamics of the work are strongly event-driven as input typically arrives only some days before the scheduled international meeting. The resources used to carry out the work are represented by extremely dispersed explicit knowledge. However, this knowledge is not available for everyone at any time since it is stored both in form of paper-based as well as electronic files on different drives and without any guidelines as to how the files should be named. Knowledge about internal experts is only documented on paper if at all.

**Fig. 2.8:** **Different Sub-Classes of the Object "Resource" Are Linked to Knowledge-Related Tasks**

The aim of the project was to improve the reactivity of the organizational unit. The solution that was developed with great involvement by the employees of the unit and their internal clients consisted of four core elements in compliance with the Fraunhofer IPK reference model for knowledge management.[71] According to our design fields, we provided 1) a technical platform based on Lotus Notes Domino R5, 2) new methods to elicit and document tacit knowledge from briefing and de-briefing sessions, 3) roles and responsibilities for the development of defined knowledge themes and 4) a management tool for motivation and feedback of the involved knowledge workers. The design fields "Corporate Culture" and "Controlling" were not particularly focused upon in this specific project. An

---

[71]   see Introduction.

online intellectual capital monitoring tool to measure and control the generation and usage of the knowledge assets should enhance the Lotus Notes application.

It was observed that work within this particular service company is characterized by variety and exception rather than repetition and routine and thus that experiences are gathered on an extremely individual basis. In order to consider and benefit from these experiences, a participatory project approach[72] was chosen which emphasizes the participation and commitment of all employees of the organizational unit. We started with a joint workshop to define the goals for improvement and to explain the notion of knowledge management on the basis of best practice examples from our case studies. The description of the business process was performed with the joint participation of all employees. The defining and structuring of knowledge domains was carried out together with the internal clients of the unit. The specification of the software tool was also performed in cooperation based on design alternatives proposed by the Fraunhofer team.

Having identified the gaps within the knowledge process and the missing core knowledge activities within the business processes, we were able to look for knowledge management building blocks to improve the performance, i.e. to fill the gaps.

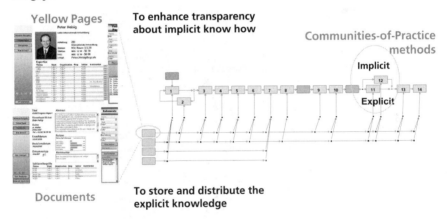

**Fig. 2.9: Improved Knowledge-Intensive Business Process**

In order to improve the information environment supporting the knowledge-intensive business process, we developed a web-based application, the so-called "Knowledge Navigator" (Fig. 2.9). The application has an intuitive user interface which shows the "top 50 knowledge-assets-per-knowledge-theme." The yellow page module increases the transparency of the "experts-per-knowledge-theme" and the document module gives direct access to the state-of-the-art documents. A

---

[72] Liedtke et al. (1995).

34

feedback feature supports direct evaluation of the knowledge piece and improvement suggestions for the authors.

In order to improve the exchange of knowledge, elements of communities of practice[73] and methods to elicit tacit knowledge[74] were jointly developed, introduced and trained. A workshop-based tool to evaluate the improvement, to provide feedback and to find an agreement on goals for knowledge development was designed and introduced.

## 2.3.8    Knowledge management building blocks

Within our benchmarking study, we identified around 30 best practice methods, which can be adopted as building blocks for improving the systematic use of the most important resources of any organization. The following figure (Fig. 2.10) shows on a continuum from explicit to tacit knowledge on the vertical axis which kind of knowledge is covered by some selected best practice methods. The horizontal axis indicates whether the method addresses a single person, a defined group of people (Department, Project Team), the whole organization or external partners like clients and/or suppliers.

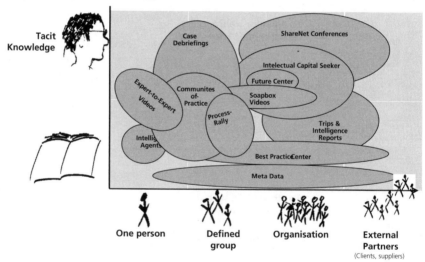

**Fig. 2.10:   Best Practice Methods as Building Blocks for Knowledge Management**

---

[73]   Wenger et al. (2000); Wenger (1998).

[74]   Baumert (1999).

Furthermore, some of the identified best practice methods can be linked to the business processes they mainly support. Figure Fig. 2.11 demonstrates where business processes are supported by some of the methods described in the case studies.

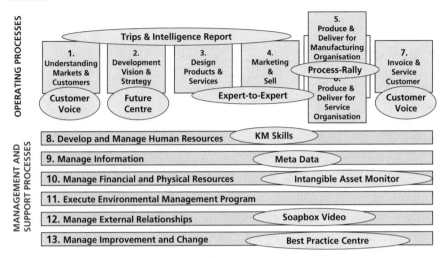

**Fig. 2.11:  Best Practice Methods Linked to Business Processes**

## 2.4    Outlook

Knowledge management is currently one main buzzword on the agenda of Top-Management and marketing and sales departments of software providers and consulting companies. Nevertheless, the awareness of the decision makers is increasing. Knowledge is regarded as one or even the main factor for private and public organizations to gain competitive advantage. First experiences from knowledge management projects show that a win-win situation for companies and employees is possible. By reducing double work, the company saves costs. Moreover, employees increase their experiences through continuous learning and their satisfaction through solving new problems and not reinventing the wheel.

Even if the buzzword knowledge management grows out of fashion, the essence of the idea of knowledge management - the systematic management of knowledge and experiences of the employees, suppliers and clients - will definitely never be superfluous. Even in the dynamic new economy, experience and know-how are still extremely important as the example of retired experts show who are very happy to pass their knowledge as 'Senior Experts' on to young start-up companies.

With business process engineering, companies have focused their attention on eliminating non-value-adding process steps in order to improve their competitiveness by means of value-adding process steps. In the future, companies regard their business processes as knowledge processing processes and enhance their ability to improve the usage of their one and only competitive advantage - the know-how of the people.

# 3 Motivation and Competence for Knowledge Management

*Jens Vorbeck, Ina Finke*

A systematic and efficient approach to knowledge, a supportive corporate culture, motivated employees who gladly share their knowledge and use external knowledge for their own business activities - the demands on employees, leadership, management and personnel departments that make up the decisive factor for the success of a knowledge management system are high. Personnel management has the task of preparing its most important resource - human capital - for the challenges of knowledge management with methods and techniques for shaping "soft factors."

"The mastering of intelligent knowledge does not result from passive, mechanical, or pre-programmed learning. Instead, intelligent knowledge requires an active, constructive, and increasingly self-motivated perspective on the part of the learner."[75] To build, organize, activate, and utilize knowledge is not a procedure in which learners passively and receptively process something offered to them.[76] This means that an approach to the management of knowledge in organizations should view learners and the conditions that support them as an integrative component of its contents.

Both industrial and service corporations name the factors personnel, corporate culture, and leadership as the most important factors for success in knowledge management. Surveys of the top 1000 German and the top 200 European firms[77] confirm that the relevance of these aspects is well appreciated. At the same time, discussions and workshops with the representatives of companies underscore the enormous need for integrated solutions to problems and praxis-oriented research.

"How do I motivate my colleagues to share knowledge?" "How do I construct a supportive knowledge culture?" "Knowledge is power!" "If I share my knowledge, I will be replaceable!" These are only some of the statements that describe the human factor as a central factor in a system for knowledge management. While investment in innovative information technology is growing exponentially and diverse scenarios from "Chief Knowledge Officer" to "Community of Practice" have already been developed, personnel management

---

[75] Weinert (1997), pp. 31.
[76] Mandl & Spada (1988), p. 123.
[77] see chapter 6 in this book.

still operates primarily with "classical" approaches. This means that monetary incentives are still the most commonly used motivation, followed by the visualization of success and supplementary seminars. Tampoe[78] identified three main motivators: personal growth as the most important one, operational autonomy and task achievement. These factors require precise focusing. The need for creative and practical tools is obvious.

This chapter is concerned with the following questions:

- How are motivation and capabilities for knowledge management related? Which role do these factors play in successful knowledge management?

- What kind of role does personnel management play in knowledge management? What does personnel management do today and which future roles will it play?

## 3.1 Task orientation as a basis for the motivation for knowledge management

### 3.1.1 The motivational model of knowledge management

The goal of the design of a knowledge management system is to integrate all necessary procedural steps into the processes of the existing organization and to generate neither extra work nor the need for new positions.[79] It is required that employees recognize a systematic approach to knowledge to be a self-evident part of their profession, which they integrate into their everyday work.

The challenge to the designers of the system is to create tasks that will be understood by employees as sensible and meaningful. This means an intrinsically motivating design of the assignments necessary for knowledge management.

"The idea of task orientation is based on the experience that sensible work designs activate the interest of employees and promote the implementation of knowledge, capabilities, and the completion of tasks, especially when these employees are supported by their work environment."[80] This implies clearly defined concepts for the tasks that result from the demand for "sensible work designs." On the other hand, the application of capabilities and task completion requires the identification and promotion of such concepts.

Colleagues need new capabilities in order to do justice to the requirements intrinsic in the tasks of knowledge management. This new competence can be

---

[78] Tampoe (1996), pp.179.
[79] Heisig (1999), pp. 27.
[80] Frei (1996), p. 41.

supported with strategic personnel management. As the most important organizational institution in personnel development, human resource management is a design factor along with appropriate leadership and a supportive corporate culture. The statement for colleagues that is contained in this model of motivation is: "I see knowledge management as my personal task. This means that the assignments I'm supposed to carry out in knowledge management fulfill certain design criteria. This again requires capabilities that work together with the design of tasks in a motivating way. That is how knowledge management can become a part of my daily work without generating additional work."

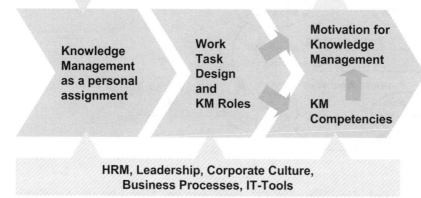

**Fig. 3.1:** Enabling Factors for the Motivation of Knowledge Management

Fig. 3.1 summarizes the necessary enabling factors for the motivation for knowledge management. The particular elements will be described below.

### 3.1.2   The task as an integrating element of knowledge management

"As opposed to a dichotomous conceptualization to knowledge management, truly comprehensive approaches start with a holistic knowledge management that connects aspects of technological and human orientations."[81]

A focus on technical solutions overemphasizes data and information management. A focus on human aspects with the initiation of training that motivates employees to share knowledge is an approach for personnel development, not for knowledge

---

[81]   Schüppel (1996), p.189.

40

managers. A holistic system for knowledge management means that all components of the system must be equally considered.[82]

Accordingly, a knowledge management system is determined by the design of the dimensions process organization, information technology, controlling, human resource management, corporate culture and leadership. From a psychological perspective, the connecting element of such a system is the task with its characteristic qualities: "... the task must be the point of articulation between the social and technical systems – linking the job in the technical system with its correlated role behavior in the social system" (see Fig. 3.2).[83]

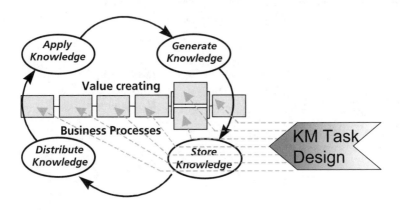

**Fig. 3.2:** **Task Orientation as the Basis for the Motivation of Knowledge Management in the Value Creating Business Processes**

The definition of a work task as a connecting element gives the members of a firm a departure point for the design of knowledge management. Strategic thinking in personnel management is necessary for the perception of this design assignment. It is then possible to think about the contents of tasks and the concrete support of personnel management, leadership, and a supportive culture.

## 3.2   Tasks of human resource management

The central goal of human resource management is to increase the capabilities of the personnel of a firm. The business capabilities of personnel are "the potential accumulated in employees, their knowledge and abilities, and their desire to get involved and achieve."[84] The relationship of these components, the desire to

---

[82]   Reinmann-Rothmeier, Mandl (1999), pp. 5.

[83]   Blumberg (1988), p.56.

[84]   Mroß (2000), p.36.

achieve (motivation) and knowledge/abilities (qualification), can be characterized as follows: highly motivated employees add nothing to the firm if they don't have the necessary abilities. This is also true when employees have no desire to apply their abilities. The task of human resource management is to qualify and motivate employees for the more efficient utilization of a corporate knowledge management approach. This comprises on the one hand the identification of relevant competence and respective training and on the other hand the design of stimulating jobs (motivational aspect). These are the constituting factors of human intellectual capital (see Fig. 3.3).

A rethinking of classical personnel management is necessary in order to do justice to this assignment and systematically utilize the knowledge of a firm's employees. The "chronic delay in measures for qualification"[85] is a common complaint about today's personnel departments. Educational and learning measures are not initiated until the need for qualification is apparent, such as after the introduction of technical changes. Instead of reacting only to the need of the moment, a new perspective could anticipate qualifications and conditions that will be relevant in the future.

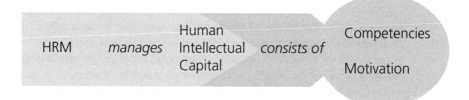

**Fig. 3.3:    Main Objectives of Human Resource Management**

Adequate personnel management implies a new definition of human resource management: "Strategic human resource management is the implementation und initiation of a company's business strategies by means of the identification, growth, remuneration, and retention of the necessary human capital."[86]

As a consequence, this means that the management of knowledge influenced by human resource management should increase intellectual capital, i.e., the abilities and motivation of employees. In this context, personnel management has the chance to strategically re-orient itself with knowledge management. But, at which point of knowledge management can the personnel department get involved?

We focus on these two objectives: on the one hand, the design possibilities to increase motivation and on the other hand, the identification of competence

---

[85]    Pawlowsky (1994), p. 339.
[86]    Sattelberger (1999), p. 44.

relevant for knowledge management in order to qualify them by meeting the specific demands.

### 3.2.1 Design criteria for tasks in knowledge management

Let's assume that a personnel department accepts the challenge of a design role in the process of knowledge management in order to create structures for the conscientious development of employees. There are concrete departure points for these changes.

To understand knowledge management as a work assignment means to incorporate it into daily business without significantly increasing the workload of employees. Theories about the structuring of jobs suggest that a task must be characterized by certain qualities in order to motivate employees effectively. These elements include: unity, sense, diversity in requirements, possibility for social interaction, and educational and developmental possibilities.[87]

We will now describe these qualities more closely in their relationship to knowledge management:

- *Unity and meaningfulness:* As far as possible, the task should contain elements for planning, implementation, and control so that employees get feedback about the results of their own activities. The positive effect of each personal assignment is clearly recognizable. This task can be seen as sensible and meaningful. The value of one's personal assignment within the work process is clear. Leadership plays primarily a supportive and advisory role. Given the responsibility to complete a task, the employee's need for autonomy can be met. Studies carried out by Fraunhofer IPK of more than 17,000 employees in more than 10 firms show that an average of 75% of those questioned were dissatisfied with the feedback from their company leadership. The need for a complete task and for feedback about results is relatively high and plays a substantial role in motivation.

- *Diversity in requirements and learning possibilities*: The completion of a task should place different demands on the capabilities of employees. A task should be neither too difficult nor too simple. Moreover, it should be diversified and not be monotonous. In order to prevent too much stress for employees, it is important to identify and train the capabilities that promote knowledge management as a task. An assignment should place optimal demands on employees. These demands should be slightly higher than the employees' capabilities in order to increase motivation. With the application of existing and new qualifications, individual learning processes can be activated that help employees to develop further and improve their long-term flexibility. It is also important to have the

---

[87]    Ulich (1998), pp. 179.

opportunity to generate new knowledge while meeting the demands. The utilization of knowledge requires special competence. In various studies, checklists were developed that offer an overview of the diverse and complex capabilities required.[88] We will focus on these capabilities in a later section.

- *Possibilities for social interaction:* This design aspect is important for knowledge management for several reasons. It supports the kind of cooperation necessary for the completion of tasks. In addition, cooperative support helps employees deal better with stress. In the context of knowledge management, social interaction plays an important role in the exchange of implicit (experiential) knowledge. Studies show that at least three-quarters of all communicative acts take place through face-to-face interaction within a department.[89] The design of knowledge management should take this demand for social interaction into consideration. The support of direct exchange between employees is getting more and more attention, even in the architectural design of the workspace.

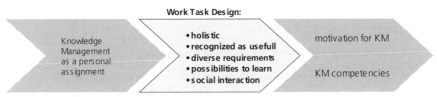

**Fig. 3.4:    Summarized Criteria for the Design of the Work Task**

Fig. 3.4 summarizes the relevant design criteria for tasks, which help developing motivation.

Employees either have to have the necessary capabilities and competence as a prerequisite or they have to develop this competence with time if they are to meet the requirements that knowledge management introduces into daily business. Methods become relevant that help to perceive the need for new training, formulate plans for personnel development, and plan further educational measures.

Besides the design possibility, which refers to every single one, there is also the possibility to emphasize the roles of specific persons. In the following, this option will be illustrated.

---

[88]    e.g. Reinmann-Rothmeier & Mandl (1998); TFPL Ltd. (1999).
[89]    Picot & Reichwald (1987), p. 36.

### 3.2.2    Roles of knowledge workers

Knowledge workers are an integral part of the process-oriented perspective on knowledge management. They will be appointed explicitly and are responsible to support the implementation of knowledge management activities. "Knowledge management is a core competence comprising of a range of skills, experience and personal attributes. The level of competence required in each individual depends on his or her role in a knowledge environment. It is critical that knowledge management as a core competence is recognized and developed – for society, the economy, the organization and the individual. The lack of information literacy skills is a major roadblock to the knowledge economy."[90] This quote describes clearly the necessity of the development of competence for knowledge management. It also demonstrates the relationship between such competence and the roles of employees in knowledge management.

The requirements placed on knowledge workers in a firm are defined by their role in knowledge management. There are different findings about possible roles in knowledge management processes.

North[91] comes to the conclusion that knowledge workers in knowledge-oriented firms can be divided into five groups:

a)    Knowledge practitioners (operative employees),

b)    Knowledge engineers and entrepreneurs (middle management),

c)    Visionaries (top management),

d)    Information managers and infrastructure managers (operative management) and

e)    Support colleagues (back office, secretary).

The roles and tasks are determined by existing organizational concepts or management approaches. North refers to the perspective of Nonaka and Takeuchi[92] who suggest a "middle-up-down" approach in which the key role in organizational knowledge management is assigned to the middle management. According to analyses of "top-down" and "bottom-up" approaches, Nonaka et al. conclude that a third way, the "middle-up-down" approach, is most appropriate for supporting the generation of knowledge. The top management develops a vision while the middle management devises concrete concepts, which the employees are able to understand and to implement. The key position lies on the middle level since here, the discrepancy between visions and reality can be solved.

---

[90]    TFPL Ltd. (1999), p.15.

[91]    North (1998), p. 126.

[92]    Nonaka, Takeuchi (1995), p.130.

The case studies in the context of our study at the IPK confirm these role definitions although our terminology is somewhat different. In brackets you find the industry branch in which special knowledge workers carry out coordination, marketing and implementation tasks.

- **Coordination**
  Knowledge Coordinator, Practice Leader (Consulting)

- **Internal Marketing**
  Knowledge Advocate (Consulting)
  Knowledge Network Program Manager (Pharmacy)

- **Implementation**
  Intellectual Capital-Seeker (Consulting)
  Knowledge Steward (Consulting)
  Intellectual Capital-Teams per Practice (Consulting)
  Customer Voice-Analyst (Electronics)

Role descriptions in our study at the IPK are consistent to a great degree with the generic descriptions of the TFPL-study[93]: An initial strategy team (Chief Knowledge Officer), a planning team (Chief Knowledge Team), an implementation team, knowledge practitioners and knowledge workers (all employees). This study goes beyond the simple assignment of names to the roles to further explaining the assignment of the new activities to existing roles and skills. At the same time, the definition of the "knowledge workers" makes it clear that knowledge management is a procedure that must be part of the daily work.

In order to support knowledge management, it is not absolutely necessary, though, to create special teams or to appoint single persons. Alternatively, it is also possible to motivate and to appoint every single employee to implement knowledge management into his everyday life. To make the employees aware of their own responsibility in creating knowledge-oriented company is one of the main tasks of human resource management.

## 3.3 Competence for effective knowledge management

After the challenge for personnel departments is formulated and the departure point for the design is outlined, the next step is the generation of the concrete capabilities and the necessary qualifications of a competent knowledge manager. This topic has so far been neglected regarding knowledge management. In the following, we refer to studies, which appeared to be the most extensive.

In order to fulfill the requirements mentioned above, it is necessary to specify the capabilities that employees should systematically acquire. In this context, a

---

[93]   TFPL Ltd. (1999), pp.59.

definition of the concept 'knowledge' is important as the relevant competence demonstrates a certain handling of knowledge.

### 3.3.1 Working definition of knowledge

From a psychological perspective, knowledge can be understood as the result of a learning process about given facts, their qualities, and relationships to other units and qualities. A kind of subjective 'lexicon' organizes knowledge and makes it available to memory. In a conceptual or figurative sense, knowledge means codified experiences that are a requirement of mental representations. A cognitive or internal/mental representation includes the organizational forms of individual knowledge and the process by which this knowledge changes. The derivation of new knowledge occurs by means of conscious or unconscious conclusions that enable the generation of plans for action (Fig. 3.5).[94]

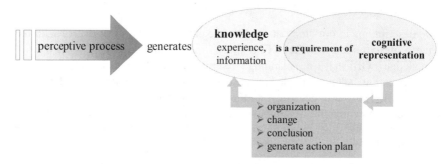

**Fig. 3.5:    The Interaction between Knowledge and Cognitive Representation**

Important aspects of knowledge make it clear that the utilization of knowledge is closely connected to the individual. Above all else, knowledge is subjective. An individual perceptive process occurs in which individual knowledge is generated. This generation is contextual, i.e., situational and is not dependent on cultural context. Knowledge arises in and by means of social relationships, through interaction with other carriers of knowledge. The close connection to action becomes apparent when practical plans are generated that enable active interaction with the environment.

As a resource, the knowledge that is stored and changed for the most part in the minds of employees influences our decisions and our behavior. The example of an employee who is supposed to take the minutes of a meeting shall illustrate this idea: If it is the first time that this employee takes the minutes, he or she must rely on previous knowledge about how minutes are taken in the company (rules, format, news lists, etc.). Certain capabilities are required in order to transform this

---

[94]    Häcker & Stapf (1998).

knowledge into action (computer skills, the ability to search for models in the Internet, etc.). In addition to the colleague's knowledge, a part of the behavioral component is the individual capabilities that are necessary for the efficient utilization of knowledge. The next section will concentrate on these relevant capabilities.

### 3.3.2    Basic competence for knowledge management

The motivational model of the Fraunhofer IPK (Fig. 3.1) assumes the development of certain basic competence so that a knowledge management system can function. The differentiation between the single capabilities and their classification into core activities is not that sharp. We mention only the most important and basic ones, which represent the main focus in the core activity. These main competences will now be defined according to the knowledge management core process.

The results of a Delphi study in a research series at the Ludwig-Maximilians-Universität München (LMU)[95] showed the following collection of capabilities that are decisive for personnel knowledge management. First, there are the abilities to critically evaluate information and knowledge, to communicate, and to learn. Additional factors are the ability to ask relevant questions in order to select information and structure knowledge, to share knowledge within a group, and motivational and emotional flexibility as well as open-mindedness and self-motivation.

The LMU came to the conclusion that knowledge management should be proclaimed a special educational goal. This means that professional knowledge managers will be trained "who take over the classical assignments of personnel development, implement special activities in the approach to knowledge, and who above all function as promoters of holistic strategies for knowledge management."[96]

One of the key results of an extensive international research project undertaken by TFPL in 1999 is a Knowledge Management Skills Map.[97] The project team contacted over 500 organizations involved in implementing knowledge management and identified the roles that they had created. The skills that were needed in those roles and the additional skills required throughout the respective organization were also identified. We are reporting the key findings of the study because they are linked to the core process of the approach to knowledge management at the Fraunhofer IPK. First, it is clear that "the dynamics of a

---

[95]    Reinmann-Rothmeier, Mandl (1998), pp. 5.

[96]    Reinmann-Rothmeier, Mandl (1998), p. 5.

[97]    TFPL Ltd. (1999), p. 78. The project was jointly funded by TFPL and the UK government's Library and Information Commission.

48

knowledge culture require a core set of 'information literacy' skills to be available throughout the organization. Without an acceptable level of information literacy, the knowledge and information processes and flows will be inefficient and ineffective. Information Literacy combines an awareness of the value of information and knowledge to the organization with the skills and competence that enable an individual to play a full, effective and rewarding role in knowledge environments."[98]

The approach to information literacy corresponds to a great degree with the concept of basic competence at the Fraunhofer IPK. "To be information literate, a person must be able to recognize when information is needed and have the ability to locate, evaluate and use effectively the needed information."[99] In addition, an informational literate person is one who: "recognizes that accurate and complete information is the basis for intelligent decision making; recognizes the need for information; formulates questions based on information needs; identifies potential sources of information; develops successful search strategies; access sources of information including computer-based and other technologies; evaluates information; organizes information for practical application; integrates new information into an existing body of knowledge; uses information in critical thinking and problem solving."[100]

In the same sense, "information literate people are those who have learned how to learn. They know how to learn because they know how knowledge is organized, how to find information, and how to use information in such a way that others can learn from them. They are people prepared for lifelong learning, because they can always find the information needed for any task or decision at hand."[101]

These definitions make it clear that the four key skills of information literacy are creating, finding, sharing and using. The analogy to the holistic core process of our model is obvious.

In the following section, the core competence discussed above will be classified according to the four core activities of knowledge management.

### 3.3.3    Create knowledge: the ability to learn and communicate

The creation of new knowledge can occur at different levels: in reproduction, through achievement, by solving problems and completing tasks, etc. Existing knowledge and experience is used in these processes, processes that always include learning processes. This knowledge and experience is applied to new contexts and questions. Therefore, the experience of employees is of great

---

[98]    TFPL Ltd. (1999), p. 11.
[99]    Burnhein (1992), p.192.
[100]   Doyle (1992), cited in the web.
[101]   American Library Association (1989), cited in the web.

importance. This might have a positive effect since new information is processed selectively. However, it might also have the negative effect that the employee is tempted to 'sleep' on knowledge that already exists. The motivation of employees to always learn more should be activated and supported.

In a firm, information and knowledge are generated in many different ways. There are many documents that are exchanged on different levels of the company. In the context of knowledge management, it is of critical importance to share information, to create connections between ideas, and to build cross-connections to other topics. Employees must also be able to express their ideas. This addresses a basic competence for communication. An adequate command of presentation techniques, such as listening and verbal and written expression, and an awareness of the rules and processes of interaction as well as their influence on human communication are also advantageous for a successful transfer of information and knowledge.

### 3.3.4    Store knowledge: structured and systematical storage capability

The ability to store knowledge effectively (for example, in a PC), allows

- A quick search for information,
- Access to information for other employees,
- The directing of colleagues to specific information and
- The effective sharing of knowledge as it is easily stored for everyone's use.

In order to be able to store existing knowledge, abstract thinking is also relevant. In regard to the documentation of experiences, the storage of the relevant inherent statements does not only require an ability to abstract, but also a capability to focus on the substantial and to word briefly and succinctly.

It is possible to make knowledge accessible to others with the unified use of indices so that everyone can reproduce storage procedures. With the help of directional signals (subject lines in e-mails, summaries, meta-data, links in the internet), everyone who is looking for information can find what they want or be directed to a specific document. This is where the ability to use media to distribute knowledge becomes relevant. This will be the subject of a later section.

### 3.3.5    Distribute knowledge: capacity of teamwork and awareness of the value of knowledge

Nowadays, when knowledge is supposed to be shared, it is often required to be able to apply the current new media in order to systematically provide others with this knowledge. Though, the motivation and readiness to share knowledge is a prerequisite for the ability to make knowledge available to others. The development of a team spirit supports the sharing of knowledge, as colleagues feel connected to each other because they follow common goals and they are dependent on each other in their activities. This is closely connected to the design of tasks. A highly interdependent assignment that can only be handled in close and cooperative teamwork promotes the cohesion of a group.

In addition to a feeling for teamwork, an understanding or awareness of the value of information and knowledge, i.e., the value of both components for the firm and the team is necessary for effective knowledge management. A corporate identity, which is oriented towards knowledge management, can motivate employees to share their knowledge with their colleagues. The possibility to identify with the company facilitates the sharing of knowledge between different locations. To ascribe value to information gives a special meaning to the exchange of knowledge among employees. Value promotes a common understanding of the system that is to be implemented, of the common procedure and common goals that are to be followed, etc.[102] Human resource management is able to support this common understanding through helping transmitter and receiver to become sensitive for each other. The employee has to understand the need for knowledge and the use of the information, which has been gathered by his colleagues. The supply of specific knowledge has to be strongly customer-oriented in order to be able to respond precisely to the demands of the receiver instead of overwhelming with unstructured information.

### 3.3.6    Apply knowledge: realization and media competence

The use of newly generated knowledge also allows new learning experiences and perceptions. It is possible to create yet more knowledge with the concrete application of new knowledge, which then closes the circle of the core process of unified knowledge management.

On the one hand, employees have to command instruments and techniques for adequate processing in order to utilize and work with information. This means that everyone must command the media that are used in a firm for the utilization of knowledge. On the other hand, knowledge of the dominant 'information culture' is very important. The employees' procedure depends on existing 'push' or 'pull' culture, for instance. An employee who solely uses the telephone to receive an important piece of information is likely to get into trouble if his company prefers the exchange of information via e-mail. A critical point for the success of a search is to decide which medium will be used to find the necessary information to communicate about which topic or which question. For example, there are cases where the telephone is preferable to an electronic message. Generally speaking, the more important the information for exchange is, the faster a sensible medium

---

[102]    Reinmann-Rothmeier, Mandl (1999), pp. 4.

(for example, personal contact with the possibility of non-verbal communication) should be chosen.[103]

The use of new media (internet, intranet) requires open-mindedness and flexibility on the part of employees that enables them to handle the continuous development of technology.

Correct use of the contents and meaning of knowledge is just as important as an adequate approach to knowledge technologies. The concept of competence in application includes the complex use of individually generated knowledge. Information must be considered, evaluated, selected and compared. It can be evaluated according to relevance, quality, and appropriateness and then integrated with other information from other sources. In addition to the ability to integrate information, it is also important to sort and/or perhaps reject information. It is just as important to be able to evaluate the comparability of information from different sources and to present results, i.e., processed information in a meaningful and sensible way. This is again related to the general ability of employees to communicate that is fore grounded in the creation of new knowledge. The ability to offer criticism and to ask appropriate questions - both of which are noted by the LMU - complete our image of competence in application.

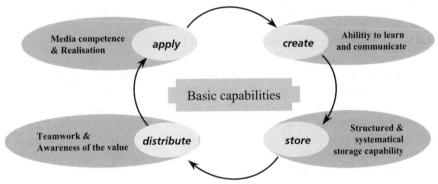

**Fig. 3.6: Basic Competencies for Knowledge Management**

Fig. 3.6 summarizes the basic competencies for the implementation of knowledge management:

Basic competence were formulated and integrated into core activities with reference to the completed core process of knowledge management. As illustrated, the adequate design of the task covers the motivational component. On the other hand, implementation is made possible by the qualifications of employees. It is imperative that basic competence is described in detail for every employee. The individual development of each and every employee can be made clear with the

---

[103]  Finke, Scholz (2000), p.73.

help of a system of indicators. A description of competence at the level of employees makes it possible for the firm to construct an overview of the employees' potential.

## 3.4 Managing motivation and competence

In order to generate and apply information, space must be created at different levels that make individual knowledge management easier for employees. This includes strategies that simplify internal communication, promote productive meetings, and solidify results as the productive output of such meetings (storage for further development). The ability to use information creatively can be supported with self-defined responsibilities. The design of the appropriate conditions is the responsibility of the leadership and the personnel department of a firm.

The case studies of the Competence Center Knowledge Management show that there are solutions that can also be implemented in other firms as best practices with little modification. For example, it is worthy of note that the approach of a British pharmacy-concern defines capabilities for knowledge management as a primary topic of personnel management.

### 3.4.1 Experiences from a pharmaceutical company

Around four years ago, a pharmaceutical company initiated an exploratory knowledge network program to identify potential approaches to and the likely benefits of knowledge management. First, an attempt was made to include all employees, which was anything but optimal. The experience the company gained through its program resulted in a realignment of its activities. One year later, a program focused on the company's research and development departments established a successful infrastructure for knowledge management.

The company tried to analyze the cause of the unsuccessful flow of knowledge by developing categories for all actual or potential barriers. The barriers were categorized in a careful and systematic analysis of discussions, anecdotes, and questionnaires. These barriers were: cultural, technological, and content oriented. These categories provided an overall framework for knowledge management in this company.

By renaming the design field "Corporate Culture" as 'Behaviors', the company took an important step towards putting knowledge into practice and influencing its corporate environment. The human factor thus became important in the exchange of knowledge.

Comprehensive programs to change its corporate culture could not even be considered by the company at such an early stage in its knowledge management program. The company therefore focused on an essential aspect of corporate culture: the behavior of staff members while dealing with the core activities of knowledge.

By focusing on this demanding but manageable aspect, the knowledge management program team expected to achieve positive, long-term changes that would lead to a supportive corporate culture. This means that the interaction between corporate culture and the individual behavior of staff members was re-discovered. The program not only focused on the positive effects of corporate culture on the staff members' behavior, but also on the influence of individual behavior that promotes the knowledge of corporate culture.

The company developed an understanding of those capabilities that help share knowledge by analyzing the requirements needed to overcome the barriers to sharing. This was done by breaking down the activities of the central process of knowledge management in order to obtain specific expectations of the staff members' capabilities. After defining these capabilities, the company took another step forward: The staff members of the knowledge networks were given via Intranet clear and concise information about their goals.

This comparison of actual and target capabilities and behaviors will be implemented by the company as a guideline in activities, promoting personnel development and in the development of new IT solutions. The model can be developed either for individual employees or for entire teams. In the future, this evaluation system may be coupled with rewards and recognition policies.

### 3.4.2 MaC-KM: A tool for the development of competence and the motivation for knowledge management

We will now outline a procedure for the development of competence and the motivation of knowledge management that is based on the theoretical points and experiences of our case studies. This procedure includes a concept for workshops and a description of the most important functions of an IT-tool.

The competence we have specified can be easily and well organized in such a model. Indicators for individual competence must be outlined on the employees' level that measure appropriate capabilities in their existing form. For example, indicators such as participation in data processing courses or type and length of use of certain applications could be used for media competence. Depending on the assignments at hand, feedback from colleagues about presentations and talks or about the evaluation of documents can help investigate relative capabilities for communication.

These values can be used as guidelines for the development of competence. The level of individual development can be derived from the self-evaluation of the employee or from "hard data" such as participation in training seminars. An objective evaluation from company leadership or from other employees in the

54

spirit of 360-degree feedback offers a control for comparison. Further thought should be given to anonymous evaluation that is not dependent on the previous praxis of a firm or its corporate culture. However, leadership or personnel management can define the comparative control factor as a target value.

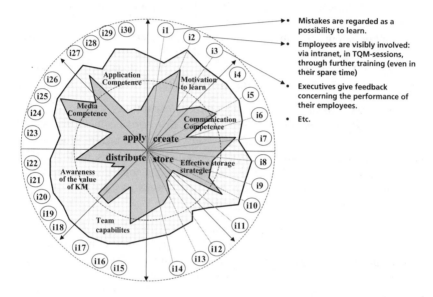

**Fig. 3.7:    MaC KM Pilot**

The figure (Fig. 3.7) presents a possible visualization of these results in the Intranet. The four activities of the core process - create, store, distribute and apply are divided respectively into two dimensions. It is also possible to divide it into more than two, but in reference to the mentioned basic competence we suggest two for every core activity. A variable number of indicators can be placed in each of these eight dimensions. The classification and content of indicators depends on the knowledge goals of the respective employee or on this employee's position in the firm.

The procedure for the adjustment and use of the "MaC KM Pilot" (Motivation and Competence for knowledge management) follows these steps:

1.  Company-wide identification of strengths and weaknesses in the approach to knowledge (knowledge audit).

2.  Construction of expert networks in which the participants are brought together due to the structure of knowledge processes.

3.  Workshop for the common definition of indicators to evaluate capabilities for knowledge management.

4. Clear decision on the part of the responsible representatives about which form (360 degree, common goals, self-evaluation) is the basis for evaluation.

5. Introduction of "MaC KM Pilot".

6. Exchange of experience and the level of achievement in real or virtual meetings of the members of the expert network.

MaC KM and the respective software tool "MaC KM Pilot" are an attempt to integrate results from positive examples in industry into a systematically unified procedure. The definition of capabilities enables employees to take active part in self-determined changes in behavior and in the development of their own competence. Thereby, continuous and systematic feedback and goals set with the participation of employees support the motivation of individuals not only to introduce their own knowledge, but also to approach knowledge in a responsible way commensurate with the spirit of the firm.

## 3.5 Summary and outlook

In the past chapter, the significance of the employees' motivation and abilities regarding knowledge management has been emphasized. Permanent motivation can be achieved through a demanding and sensitive task formation that is supposed to consider the expectations and needs of the knowledge workers. The above-mentioned design criteria such as diversity in requirements and learning possibilities assist the human resource management as the responsible constructor of systems and tasks to put the theory into practice.

In order to transform the crucial core activities accounting for knowledge management into visible action, the knowledge worker should have certain core competence. Thus, to share or store knowledge adequately, for instance, the employee is required to apply his communication abilities or his Know How in handling IT-Systems. Here, the human resource management is responsible for identifying the capabilities relevant for completing a task and to qualify these accordingly. The MaC KM Pilot allows for controlling the development of competence on a long-term basis and thus represents a personnel development tool.

In the future, knowledge oriented activities within the area of personnel management will require a new focus in order to substantially sustain and support the development of corporation-wide knowledge management. As claimed in the other chapters, it is possible to influence the core activities within the business processes from the perspective of all kinds of design fields (IT-systems, Controlling, etc.). The aim is a closed core process in which all the core activities are performed successfully.

56

Furthermore, approaches were provided for the human resource management towards finding a way of how to contribute to a successful knowledge management. Putting the theory into practice, it is crucial not to think solely in terms of one's own business, but rather to keep in mind the management system as a whole. Only an interaction of the system constructors leads to a holistic and reasonable knowledge management resolution. The responsible representatives from each design field have to pursue common goals and co-ordinate their action plans.

In practice, this implies that the knowledge worker cannot use his IT-knowledge when completing his everyday tasks if the data quality of the available media is inappropriate, for instance.

Therefore, personal goal statements and action plans have to be coordinated in order to achieve an intertwined and thus efficient functioning of all elements of the knowledge management system.

Especially in the area of personnel management, there is a lot of unused potential regarding the construction of knowledge management systems. However, an integration of the above-mentioned suggestions will lead to a constructive reorientation.

# 4 Intellectual Capital

*Peter Heisig, Jens Vorbeck, Johannes Niebuhr*

Finance and economic circles have been aware of the fact for some time that the value of a firm rests on something more than just its financial and material capital. The so-called intangible or invisible assets of a company, such as know-how, the creativity of employees, and mature relations with customers influence its value enormously. In the last few years, economic enterprises have discovered these factors for themselves in addition to knowledge and knowledge management.[104] In a survey conducted in 1999, 82.3% of the 1,300 firms questioned from various branches in Europe, North America, and Asia named intellectual capital as a critical factor for their future business success.[105]

## 4.1 The emergence of intellectual capital

In 1994, the insurance firm Skandia first published its report on intellectual capital (see our case study in chapter 15) and has since become known for its management of intellectual capital. In the meantime, innumerable companies have directed their attention to the factor intellectual capital. In many companies, such as Chevron and the oil concern Dow Chemical, the management of intellectual capital has become part of the everyday. The latter firm began to categorize all of its patents and to develop a new strategy for their use in 1993.[106] In the meantime Telecom Italia has also started to develop a report on intellectual capital.

In addition to the numerous books and articles about this topic that have been published, several studies and reports have appeared that use case studies to investigate the most up-to-date ideas and methods for perceiving and measuring intellectual capital.[107]

Intellectual capital has also been recognized by national governments as a factor. For example, a symposium took place with large investors, regulators, academics, consultants, and corporations under the auspices of the controlling body of the American stock exchange, the Securities and Exchange Commission (SEC) in 1996. The symposium looked for methods to evaluate intangible values. Shortly

---

[104] Bertels and Savage (1998), p. 7.
[105] Edvinsson and Brünig (2000), p. 136.
[106] Roos et al. (1997), p. 48.
[107] Skyrme (1998); Skyrme and Amidon (1997).

58

thereafter, New York University's Stern School of Management established the Center for the Measurement of Intangibles. The Center's purpose is to research the management, evaluation, and disclosure of intangibles.[108] In the same year, a task force was established in Denmark under the leadership of Professor Jan Mouritsen from the Copenhagen Business School and the Danish Trade and Industry Development Council that investigated how ten Scandinavian firms manage their intellectual capital. Firms such as Skandia, WM-data and Celemi (see the Celemi case study in chapter 4.4) and the savings banks Nordjylland (SparNord) , Sverige, ABB, and Telia took part in the study. The results were published in a memorandum in 1997.[109] A report on the topic of intellectual capital has also been available at the Dutch Ministery of Economics since October of 1999.[110]

In Spain, 23 companies formed the "Club intellect" in 1998, including firms like Hewlett Packard, Banco Bilbao Vizcaya, Repsol, Erricson, IBM, Renfe, Roche and Zurich. Several universities and the Spanish Association of Accountants, Asociatión Espanola de Contabilidad y Administración de empresas (AECA), are also members. Their goal is to promote the measurement of intellectual capital and to develop appropriate methods.[111]

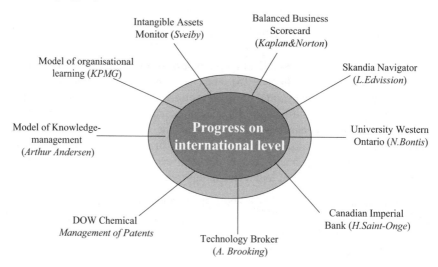

**Fig. 4.1:** **Methods and Models for the Management of Knowledge and Intellectual Capital[112]**

---

[108] Sullivan (1998), p. 300.
[109] The Danish Trade and Industry Development Council. Memorandum (May 1997).
[110] "Intangible Assets. Balancing accounts with knowledge" Published by the Ministry of Econmic Affairs (October 1999).
[111] Club intelect (1998).
[112] Club intelect (1998), p. 17.

Figure Fig. 4.1 summarizes the most widely known methods and models for the management of knowledge and intellectual capital.

Since then, the meaning of the management of intellectual capital for a modern company has been accepted everywhere and appears to be finding further resonance. This is no doubt attributable to developments in today's economic world in which knowledge has become a decisive competitive factor. However, some authors have noted that this management also makes misuse possible if, for example, management has access to better control measures through knowledge workers.[113]

## 4.2 The relevance of intellectual capital for a knowledge-based economy

The stock values of many firms in the new economy are often used to illustrate the growing meaning of intellectual capital. We mean the usual examples here, such as Microsoft, SAP, Oracle, etc., whose market value is often several times greater than their actual book value. It is the intellectual capital, the innovative capabilities, and the knowledge in the minds of their employees that makes these companies so valuable and that is reflected in the high price of their stock.

But, intellectual capital is certainly not an attribute that can be attributed just to the new economy. Corporate brands like Mercedes-Benz or Coca-Cola, patents, trademarks, or the goodwill, the respective corporate image were already considered to be important, even if unbalanced values of a company. At the very latest, these values paid off during mergers or the sale of a company. There is often more knowledge and a greater portion of intellectual capital hidden in all other products, too, than appears at first glance. This includes even the most essential goods for consumption.[114]

As opposed to the old economy with its essential product-orientation, it is clear that the knowledge basis of a firm in today's and especially tomorrow's economic world is growing in importance. This is not only true in high-tech or biotech areas. This means that knowledge and information are part of the most important resources that are at a firm's disposal today and that they often create a decisive advantage over the competition.[115] The capital of a company like Microsoft doesn't stem from production sites that can be financially written off. Instead, this capital comes to a great degree from the knowledge and abilities of Microsoft's programmers and from knowledge about customers. The source of future economic prosperity is no longer exclusively material. It lies in the knowledge that

---

[113]   Yakhlef and Salzer-Mörling (2000).
[114]   Stewart (1998), p. 30. See also Edvinsson (2000).
[115]   Roos et al. (1997), p. V.

is used to work and thus to create value.[116] The intellectual wealth of many firms now accounts for a very large part of their total wealth, especially for those firms that are knowledge intensive. There are estimates that rate the intangible value of certain firms 3, 4, sometimes even as high as 16 times higher than their material value.[117] The following quotes underscore the increasing meaning of the knowledge factor in economics:

"Knowledge is now a crucial factor underpinning economic growth. Producing goods and services with high value-added is at the core of improving economic performance and international competitiveness [...] Increasing intangible investment [...] has become a major issue for enterprises and governments."[118]

"We're very much moving into a knowledge-based economy, and the proper measuring and accounting of assets that create wealth in a knowledge-based economy is critical. It's the whole underlying foundation of our economy going forward."[119]

A modern company has to face the changes that come with a knowledge-based economy if it doesn't want to miss its connection to the future, or more drastically formulated: "in the modern business world, the business imperative is to manage intellectual capital or die!"[120]

## 4.3 The challenges of managing and measuring intellectual capital

On one hand, everyone agrees about the value of intellectual capital for today's firms. On the other hand, the difficulties in representing and managing this capital are obvious. Intellectual capital is valuable, yet invisible – or more clearly: "IC is something you can't see, you can't touch, and yet makes you rich."[121] It is therefore difficult to find and then difficult to evaluate and measure. This is why intangibles are not found in the balance sheets of most companies. Previous methods for balancing books that were primarily material and financially oriented can hardly be described as modern.[122] Such methods appear hopelessly antiquated

---

[116] Edvinsson and Brüning (2000), p. 13.

[117] Stewart (1998), p. 73.

[118] Jean-Claude Paye, Secretary general, OECD; quoted from Skyrme and Amidon (1997), p. 127.

[119] Steven Wallman, Commissioner, US Securities and Exchange Commission; quoted from Skyrme and Amidon (1997), p. 12.

[120] Roos et al. (1997), p. 5.

[121] Thomas Stewart, Fortune; quoted from Skyrme and Amidon (1997), p. 127.

[122] "The systems of accounting and financial reporting that are being used today date back more than 500 years. These systems are not only part of the old economy, they are part of the Renaissance economy." (Baruch Lev, the Philp Bardes Proffesor of

when confronted by the demands of a knowledge-based economy, especially because traditional methods look essentially at the history of a firm without making a statement about its future capabilities. These rest on intellectual capital:

"There is an over-reliance on financial measures of performance. Historic financial measures are lagging indicators: they are an unsatisfactory guide to future performance. There are many examples of apparently successful companies which have subsequently failed."[123]

"The pace and dynamism of the knowledge era brings the need for a forward perspective in managing organizational performance. Over-reliance on traditional accounting and financial data with focus on the bottom-line means that managers are having to drive their business looking through a rear-view mirror."[124]

Due to the difficulty of measuring intangibles, managing them internally is as problematic as balancing them sensibly. As indicated, knowledge, or better, the correct management of knowledge, i.e., intellectual capital has become a decisive competitive advantage for a modern company.[125] A firm that wants to evaluate and utilize its intellectual capital "needs therefore to monitor the formation and investment of intellectual capital toward evolving the firm's intellectual capital programs over time."[126]

In the middle of the 90's, Robert Kaplan from the Harvard Business School and David Norton from the Renaissance Strategy Group developed the first approach to a model that does justice to the meaning of intellectual capital. They suggested a balanced scorecard[127] that includes customer, internal and growth measures in addition to financial indicators (see Fig. 4.2). Since then, this concept has become very popular.

A balanced scorecard is primarily designed to provide management with extra indicators as instruments in addition to traditional financial figures. It is therefore less oriented towards external reporting.

On the other hand, a pioneer in reporting intellectual capital is the Swedish insurance company Skandia. Skandia first published a report on its intellectual capital „Visualizing Intellectual Capital in Skandia" as a supplement to its yearly financial report in 1994 (see the case study in chapter 15). Skandia created its own

---

Accounting and Finance at NY University's Leonard N. Stern School of Business, The International Knowledge Management Newsletter (July 2000), p. 9. As a matter of fact, the Venician monk Luca Pacioli wrote the first publication about accounting, "Summa de arithmetica, geometrica, proportioni et proportionalitá" in 1494.

[123] Skyrme and Amidon (1997), p. 138.
[124] Hubert Saint-Onge, Vice President People, Knoweldge and Strategies at Canada's Mutual Group; quoted from Skyrme and Amidon (1997), p. 128.
[125] Prusak (1998), p. IX.
[126] Klein (1998), p. 6.
[127] Kaplan and Norton (1996).

simple term for intellectual capital. First, if something was tangible and "remained" after the employees went home, it was called structural capital. Everything else, including knowledge, relationships, know-how, and other such intangibles, was called intellectual capital.[128]

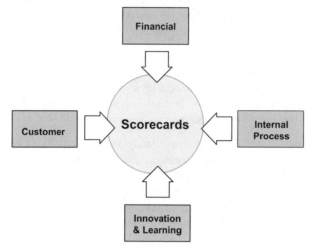

**Fig. 4.2:    The Balanced Scorecard**

The management and control of intellectual capital is certainly no longer terra incognito, although the questions that confront this management have not yet been fully answered. What is included in the intellectual capital of a firm? Which aspects of this capital are important for company and management strategies? How can these aspects be represented and finally measured? In addition to the balanced scorecard and Skandia's model, a number of different approaches for the classification of intellectual capital now exist. In the following section, we will investigate some of these more closely. We will then examine various approaches and methods for measuring intangibles.

## 4.4    The components and categories of intellectual capital

We have already mentioned several aspects of intellectual capital, such as the know-how of employees, customer relations, and the public image of a firm. Intellectual capital also includes the codified knowledge of a firm, especially patents and copyrights. Trademarks, innovative efforts, and company infrastructure mean just as much for the intangibles of some enterprises. This list can be expanded exponentially. It is therefore critical to clarify how to structure and represent intellectual capital and which of its aspects are important for a firm.

---

[128]    Edvinsson (1998), p. 279.

It is important to note that not all knowledge is intellectual capital. A terrific idea that is not documented and is therefore useless for the firm is not valuable. An idea is valuable only when it useful, i.e., when it can be used by the firm, or more precisely: "Intellectual capital is the sum of all the knowledge of employees that can give the company a competitive edge."[129]

### 4.4.1    The components of intellectual capital according to Sullivan

Sullivan created a classification scheme for intellectual capital that takes this differentiation into account (see Fig. 4.3):

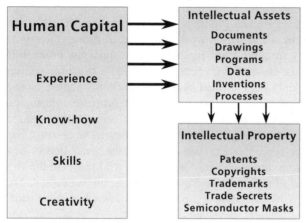

**Fig. 4.3:    The Intellectual Capital of a Firm According to Sullivan**[130]

Sullivan defines the human capital of a firm as the capabilities of employees, contractors, suppliers, and other company people to solve customer problems. The resource human capital is the entire company's know-how and information about topics of importance to the company. According to Sullivan, human capital includes the collective experience, skills, and general know-how of all the firm's workers.[131] It is important that this human capital generates the value or the wealth of a firm and in this way produces the 2nd component of intellectual capital, intellectual assets. These are the codified, tangible, or physical descriptions of specific knowledge to which the company can claim ownership rights in order to produce intellectual property such as patents, copyrights, etc. In addition to the components of intellectual capital, Sullivan also describes structural capital: "Structural Capital is the support or infrastructure that firms provide to their

---

[129]    Stewart (1998), p. 7; also Sullivan (1998): "Working definition of IC: knowledge that can be converted into profit", p. 21.
[130]    Sullivan (1998), p. 22.
[131]    Sullivan (1998), p. 22.

64

human capital."[132] It includes physical elements such as computers, desks, and telephones or even buildings, electricity, and so on. Structural capital also includes intangible elements such as information systems, computer software, work producers, marketing plans, and company know-how. Sullivan perceives that complementary business assets are a further element of intellectual capital. These assets primarily refer to new knowledge that is generated by the production or marketing of a new innovation: "complementary assets are a source of value in addition to the value created by the innovation."[133]

### 4.4.2 The difference between the extraction and creation of value

Sullivan's classification of intellectual capital is based on how intellectual capital can be profitably applied by a firm. In this case, the goal of management is to extract intellectual property from the know-how of human capital and profit from this extraction. This is known as value extraction. Value extraction focuses primarily on the codified knowledge created by an organization's human capital. Value extraction is concerned with evaluation, decision processes, databases, screening and culling, conversion mechanisms, and asset management systems and capabilities.[134] Value extraction is different than strategies to create value, strategies that have another goal: Value creation concerns the generation of new knowledge *and* its conversion into innovations with commercial value. In the area of value creation, the focus of management is people, that is, human capital. The activities of value creation include training, education, knowledge, innovation, building organizational structures, developing customer, organizational, and individual relationships, and managing values and culture.

### 4.4.3 The components of intellectual capital according to Sveiby

One of the pioneers in the area of knowledge management, Karl Erik Sveiby, follows another approach than Sullivan. Above all else, Sveiby turns his attention to the employees of a firm and their know-how. As opposed to Sullivan, he focuses more on value creation than value extraction.[135] Accordingly, he ascribes great value to the competence of employees in his classification of intellectual capital.

---

[132] Sullivan (1998), p. 23.
[133] Sullivan (1998), p. 24.
[134] Sullivan (1998), p. 20.
[135] Sullivan (1998), p. 20.

Sveiby breaks down the intellectual capital of a firm as follows: [136]

- *Competence of employees* (education, experience),
- *Internal structure* (legal form, management, systems, corporate culture, F&E, software),
- *External structure* (brands, customer relations, supply relations).

Sveiby's classification and definition of intangibles greatly influenced the management of intellectual capital of many Scandinavian firms such as Celemi (see the case study in chapter 10).

### 4.4.4 The components of intellectual capital according to A. Brooking

Another example that includes both value extraction and creation can be found in the ideas of Annie Brooking, a co-founder of Technology Broker. This company offers consultations for the management of intellectual capital. In her book "Intellectual Capital. Core Asset for the Third Millenium Enterprise", Brooking proposes the following 4 components of intellectual capital: [137]

- *Market assets* (all market related intangibles, including various brands, customers, distribution channels, repeat business, backlog ),
- *Human centered assets* (collective expertise, creative and problem solving capability, also psychometric data and indicators on how individuals may perform in situations such as in a team or under stress),
- *Intellectual property assets* (know-how, trademarks, trade secrets, copyright, patents, design rights, trade and service marks),
- *Infrastructure assets* (all the elements which make up the way the organization works: corporate culture, methodologies for assessing risk, methods of managing a sales force, financial structure, databases of information on the market or customers, communication systems [e-mail]).

These are a few examples for the classification of intellectual capital. This kind of classification or perception of the elements of intangibles is the first step towards a sensible management of intellectual capital.

---

[136] Sveiby (1998), pp. 26.
[137] Brooking (1996), pp. 13.

## 4.5 Methods for measuring intellectual capital

A relatively simple possibility to evaluate the intangible values of a firm - especially from an external perspective - has already been mentioned: Afterwards, intellectual capital can be easily expressed in numbers when one subtracts the book value of a company from its market value. The difference between these two factors then represents the intangibles of a company. This form of computing intellectual capital is simple and easily reproducible, assuming that everything that remains after the removal of the book value is intangible. The problem with this method of evaluation is obvious. The stock market is subject to many macro-economic factors. Constant changes on the entire stock market and their effect on the stock prices of individual firms would have to be considered when computing intellectual capital. This is clearly very difficult.[138]

### 4.5.1 Tobin's Q and CIV

In the meantime there is a wealth of other computing methods with which the entire intellectual capital of a firm can be registered and expressed in numbers. These methods avoid problems with the evaluation of market and book values.

An example is the, Tobin`s Q, a method developed by the Nobel Prize winner and economist James Tobin.[139] It is a quotient that compares the market value of an intangible with the cost of its reproduction. If q is less than 1, the market value of a product is less that the cost of its reproduction. Although Tobin's Q was not used as a procedure for computing intellectual capital, it can be used in this context. Alan Greenspan, the head of the Federal Reserve, had already noticed that a high q and the relationship between market and book value reflect the value of investment in technology and human capital. When the quotient q is high, the firm pulls in the highest income. According to Tobin, q measures when a company enjoys unusually high profit with something that other companies don't have. It is therefore an appropriate definition of the potential that is manifest in intellectual capital. This kind of firm probably has tangibles similar to other firms but clearly has a competitive advantage in those factors that determine intellectual capital such as workers, systems, or customers. It is possible to apply Tobin's Q to the entire company as well as to individual assets: the market value divided by the cost of the reproduction of tangible assets.

Another example is the calculated intangible value (CIV) that was developed by the firm NCI Research in Evanston, Illinois. Here intellectual capital is calculated as a relationship to the achievements of the average competitor, that is, to the

---

[138]    Stewart (1998), p. 219.
[139]    Stewart (1998), p. 220.

average of the entire branch.[140] This means that the entire value of the respective intangibles can be derived using the CIV, regardless of the capitalization of the firm on the stock market.[141] A requirement is that the entire capital profit of the firm is higher than average for the branch. If this is the case, the CIV is calculated as follows:

1. Computation of the average income before taxes in the last 3 years.

2. Computation of the average tangible assets in the last 3 years.

3. The result for tangible assets is calculated by multiplying the average assets by the profit of the branch.

4. The difference between the actual results before taxes and the results for tangible assets describes the results of knowledge capital.

5. Taxes paid for results from knowledge capital indicate the extra costs of immaterial activities.

6. By dividing the extra costs of intangible activities by an appropriate percentage (for example, capital costs), it is possible to arrive at the CIV, that is, the up-to-date net value of the intangible activities used.[142]

### 4.5.2 Measuring intellectual capital with non-financial indicators

The examples mentioned above serve primarily to determine and calculate intellectual capital and do not provide any kind of detailed information about the various immaterial assets. If a company wants to initiate the management of intellectual capital, the methods for calculation we've mentioned are of little use. Another means of assessing the intellectual capital of a company takes into account the previous classification of aspects of intellectual capital, as described in the examples above. The essence of this approach is that is based on far more detailed information and that it uses non-financial indicators. It is important to consider all the various conditions, functions, and purposes involved in an assessment of intellectual capital. For example, one has to decide whether the system for the determination of intellectual capital is intended for internal management or is to be communicated to external entities such as analysts, banks, and customers in order to improve investor relations.

Apart from the issue of for whom the analysis is designed, the aspect of which purpose it is to serve also has to be considered. There are basically two main

---

[140] A requirement is that the numbers for the entire capital profit in the respective branch are available. In this context, NCI used numbers from Robert Morris Associates' Annual Statement Studies for firms with the same branch code. Stewart (1998), p. 222.

[141] See Stewart (1998), p. 223.

[142] Cf. Edvinsson and Brünig (2000), p. 154.

purposes. Either the immaterial assets at a particular point in time can be assessed, or the emphasis can be placed on the assessment of changes and trends. These two purposes are often related to the issue of for whom the system is designed: external groups are certainly more interested in the situation as it currently exists, whereas internal groups tend to pay more attention to trends and changes.[143]

It is also essential that the classification and subsequent assessment of intellectual capital be aligned with the aims and strategies of the company. Just as a company may either be more interested in value extraction or value creation in terms of categorizing intellectual capital, the key success factors to be considered for a company must be identified so they can be provided with the appropriate indicators. Key success factors are, for example, new products and/or new internal/external customers and increased market penetration. They are provided with the relevant indicators, such as the number of new products, number of new customers, or percentage of customer business.[144] Of course, a method of assessment must also provide for comparisons. An assessment is meaningless if it cannot be compared to other data, such as that of another company, the previous year, or the budget. At least three time frames are necessary to assess immaterial assets.[145]

### 4.5.3    The measurement of intellectual capital by Sveiby

The methods for calculation currently used by many companies such as Celemi (see the Celemi case study in chapter 10), WM-data or PLS Consult were influenced by Sveiby. His suggestions about the assessment of intangibles therefore deserve discussion. As displayed below, his assessment indicators are based on his classification model, which has been described above:

| Competence | Internal Structure | External Structure |
| --- | --- | --- |
|  | Characteristic figures for |  |
| Growth/Innovation | Growth/Innovation | Growth/Innovation |
| Efficiency | Efficiency | Efficiency |
| Stability | Stability | Stability |

Fig. 4.4:    Scores of Intangible Assets According to Sveiby[146]

---

[143]   Sveiby (1998), p. 224.
[144]   Roos et al. (1997), pp. 65.
[145]   Sveiby (1998), p. 224.; the EFQM also requires three compartive time frames for candidates for an EQ-Award.
[146]   Sveiby (1998), p. 225.

To gain insight into specific methods for measurement, the use of the characteristic figures growth/innovation, efficiency, and stability are demonstrated using the example of employee competence. The growth and innovation factor is illustrated by the following indicators: number of years in the profession (seniority), by which the skills and experience of the individual employees can be assessed; level of education, by which the average level of education can be determined; the age of the employee; the costs for training and advanced training; and variations in competence. The variations in competence are calculated by measuring the average number of years or rather the change in the average number of years of work experience, as is displayed below.

| Variations in Competence in 1995 | Years | % of the total |
|---|---|---|
| Years of work experience gained by new recruitment | 150 | 1% |
| Years of work experience lost by employees leaving | -132 | -1% |
| Years of work experience gained by replacing employees that have left | 330 | 2% |
| Net increase in competence | 348 | 2% |
| Note: the percentages were calculated by dividing the numbers by 15000, the entire sum of years of work experience. | | |

Fig. 4.5:  Variations in Competence According to Sveiby[147]

Characteristic figures are calculated for other categories in a similar way.

---

[147]  Sveiby (1998), p. 232.

### 4.5.4    Indicators for measurement at Skandia

An intellectual capital report published by Skandia provides an example of a
concrete display of the intellectual capital measured:

| | 1996 (6) | 1995 | 1995 (6) | 1994 |
|---|---|---|---|---|
| **Financial Focus** | | | | |
| Premium income (MSEK) | 475 | 880 | 462 | 667 |
| Premium income/employee /SEK 000s) | 1,955 | 3,592 | 2,011 | 3,586 |
| **Customer Focus** | | | | |
| Telephone accessibility (%) | 96 | 93 | 93 | 90 |
| Number of individual policies | 296,206 | 275,231 | 256,766 | 234,741 |
| Satisfied customer index | 4,36 | 4,32 | 4,33 | 4,15 |
| Sweden's customer barometer | n.a | 69 | n.a | n.a |
| **Human Focus** | | | | |
| Average age | 40 | 40 | 40 | 37 |
| Number of employees | 243 | 245 | 230 | 186 |
| Time in training (days/year) | 7 | 6 | 5 | 3,5 |
| **Proccess Focus** | | | | |
| IT-employees/ total number of employees (%) | 7,4 | 7,3 | 7,4 | 8,1 |
| **Renewal & Development Focus** | | | | |
| Increase in premium income (%) | 2,7 | 31,9 | 47,8 | 28,5 |
| Share of direct payments in claims assessment system | 18,5 | 9 | n.a | n.a |
| Number of ideas filed with Idea Group | 90 | n.a | n.a | n.a |

Fig. 4.6:    Measurement Indicators at Skandia 1994 – 1996(6)[148]

### 4.5.5    Stewart's Intellectual Capital Navigator

Thomas Stewart, who - like Sveiby - has been working on the measurement of
intellectual capital for a long time, developed the following matrix in his model for
the determination and visualization of intellectual capital (Fig. 4.7).

Stewart uses the radar chart above as a navigator for the intellectual capital of a
fictitious company. It displays three indicators for human capital, structural
capital, and customer capital. Target or orientation values can be entered at the
markings of the individual axes. Where the axes intersect the circle, a company
goal can be entered, for example. If characteristic numbers that were previously
calculated are then assigned to the single indicators, an irregular polygon results.
What the company owns is displayed inside the polygon, and what the company
wants to acquire or attain is displayed outside it.[149]

---

[148]    Intellectual Capital, supplement to Skandias 1996 Interim Report, p. 10.
[149]    Stewart (1998), pp. 237.

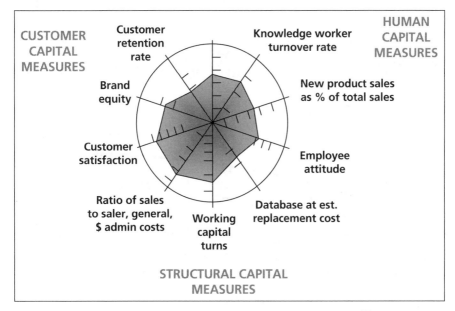

**Fig. 4.7:** The Navigator of Intellectual Capital according to Stewart[150]

### 4.5.6    The IC-Index of Roos et al.

Roos et al. try to go one step further. They consider the measurement indicators, each of which is listed and some which are very numerous, to be confusing and thus not very meaningful. Using the example of Skandia, Roos et al. found 24 different indicators in the system for measuring intellectual capital.[151]

For this reason, they suggest an index for intellectual capital (IC-Index) in which all of the calculated indicators are grouped together. The individual indicators for categories of intellectual capital and associated indicators thus become one single index, a relationship capital index, which is calculated using the following indicators: growth in number of relationships, growth in trust, customer retention, and the productivity and quality of distribution channels. The other categories of intellectual capital are dealt with in the same way, thus resulting in the infrastructure capital index and the innovation capital index. These indices can then be combined into an overall IC–index, an example of which is illustrated in the following diagram.

---

150    Stewart (1998), p. 238.
151    Roos et al. (1997), p. 71.

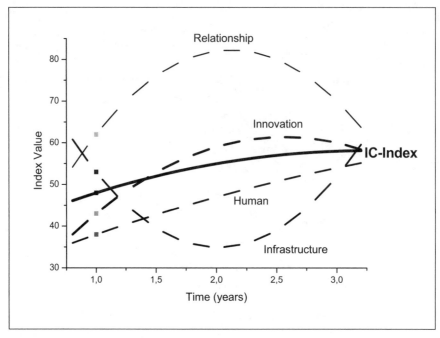

**Fig. 4.8:** IC-Index from Roos et al.[152]

According to Roos et al., the main benefit of such an IC-Index is that it makes uncertain and subjective feelings about what is happening in a company more visible. This forces management to discuss the issues and come up with a solution.[153] Roos et al. also list other advantages of the IC index, such as comparisons in intellectual capital and especially in intellectual capital performance. Thus, benchmarks can be established both in absolute terms and in the percentage of increases. Finally, an IC-Index provides external shareholders with a visualization of a greater part of the company.[154] Skandia used the IC index for the first time in its 1997 IC Supplement to the Annual Report.[155] In its intangible asset monitor from 1997, Celemi also grouped the individual indicators into one overall index (cf. Celemi case study in chapter 10).

[152] Roos et al. (1997), p. 89.
[153] Roos et al. (1997), p. 91.
[154] Roos et al. (1997), p. 91.
[155] Roos et al. (1997), p. 93.

## 4.6 Outlook

These are just a few examples of the perception, measurement, and visualization of intellectual capital. There are many others that are more or less similar. Many companies contribute greatly to the further development of new methods for the assessment and measurement of intangibles in this area especially with their active application of intellectual capital management. These companies increasingly find more and better ways to define the activities of intellectual capital they wish to influence, to manage those activities, and to find ways of measuring their inputs, processes, and results. These measures are gaining credibility as firms practice and improve their use.[156] The ability of many companies to create reliable reports on their intellectual capital activities will also advance. Such firms view external reporting as an opportunity to conduct critical reviews of company activities.[157]

In the future, the management and control of intellectual capital will be developed even more intensely and become an element of everyday business praxis. Frameworks such as the balanced scorecard, the Skandia navigator, or the Celemi intangible assets monitor all provide a suitable basis for further progress in this area. Even the increasing interest on the part of governments, professional associations, and financial institutions will support this development. However, there is still a wide number of questions for further research to improve our understanding, develop comprehensible methods, and practical tools for intellectual capital management.

---

[156] Sullivan (1998), p. 333.
[157] Sullivan (1998), p. 333.

# 5  Knowledge Management Tools

*Ingo Hoffmann*

Today, the support of daily work with software tools is normal. The use of software is expected just as much for simple work, such as writing a letter, as for the introduction of new methods for the organization of work. Even knowledge management is assumed to be able to offer more than a theoretical approach: it must also be practicable.

As a universal tool, the computer is used to handle the diverse tasks of many employees in a firm. However, work and the exchange of knowledge still take place in discussions, meetings, and so forth, as well as on the computer. Not all knowledge has to be or can be saved explicitly and directly in the system.

On the one hand, software that supports knowledge management should intelligently use as many existing electronic sources of knowledge as possible. On the other hand, such solutions should provide a means for the user to include knowledge that is not already explicitly available. All this should be acquired with the least possible user effort.

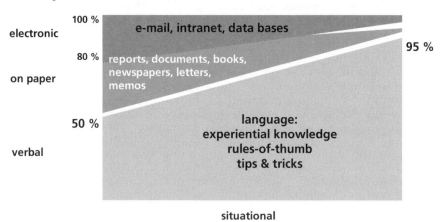

**Fig. 5.1:**   **Verbal Communication Dominates**[158]

The transfer of information and knowledge occurs primarily through verbal communication. Figure 5.1 shows that between 50% and 95% of all exchange is verbal, depending upon the situation. While the preparation of a project report is

---

[158]   Bair (1998), p. 2.

situated more to the left of the graphic, meetings and conferences are situated more to the right.

Computer-based tools for knowledge management only improve a small part of the exchange of knowledge in a company. The richness and effectiveness of face-to-face communication should not be underestimated.

Computer tools promote knowledge management. The access to knowledge they enable is not subject to time or place. A report can be read in another office one second or a week later.

In the following chapter, the reader is provided with a general classification of knowledge management tools that is oriented on the basic functions of knowledge management (core activities are: create, store, distribute and apply).[159] This makes it possible to independently classify tools according to one's own needs with the functions of knowledge management in mind. In addition, examples of market leaders and innovative products are included in our classification. This is very helpful for investment purposes.

First, we need a definition of which knowledge is targeted with knowledge management tools and what tools mean in this context. In order to specify the demands for tools we need a common understanding about the content, i.e. what does knowledge mean? The term 'tool' also needs to be specified in order to demonstrate the support for knowledge handling.

## 5.1   Definition of knowledge

Data, information, and knowledge are inter-related: the transition from one to the other is not always clear-cut. These three concepts form a continuum. In our opinion, a philosophical discussion about the use of knowledge management in firms cannot achieve goals. We will therefore formulate a pragmatic definition in this chapter.[160]

Data means the individual facts that are found everywhere in a company. These facts can be easily processed electronically and the gathering of large amounts of data is not problematic today. However, this process alone does not lead to appropriate, precise, and objective decisions. Data alone is meaningless. It only becomes information when it is relevant and fulfils a goal. Relevant information is extracted as a response to a flood of data.

However, which knowledge is sensible and useful is a subjective matter. The receiver of information decides whether it is really information or just noise. In order to give data meaning and thus change it into information, one condenses,

---

[159]   see Introduction.

[160]   Tiwana (2000), pp. 56.

contextualizes, calculates, categorizes, and corrects.[161] When data is shared in a company, its value is increased by different people contributing to its meaning.

As opposed to data, knowledge has a value that can be anywhere between true and false. Knowledge can be based on assumption, preconception, or belief. Knowledge management tools must be able to deal with such imprecision (e.g. documentation of experiences).

"Knowledge is simply actionable information. Actionable refers to the notion of *relevant, and nothing but the relevant* information being available in the right place at the right time, in the right context, and in the right way so anyone (not just the producer) can bring it to bear on decisions being made every minute. Knowledge is the key resource in intelligent decision-making, forecasting, design, planning, diagnosis, analysis, evaluation, and intuitive judgment making. It is formed in and shared between individual and collective minds. It does *not* grow out of databases but evolves with experience, successes, failures, and learning over time."[162]

Taking all these aspects into consideration, knowledge is the result of the interaction between information and personal experience. Furthermore we differentiate between tacit and explicit knowledge. Tacit knowledge is stored in the minds of employees and is difficult to formalize. Explicit knowledge is the kind that can be codified and transferred. Tacit knowledge becomes explicit by means of externalization.[163]

## 5.2　Definition of tool and IPK approach

Which kind of tools should we focus on? A broad definition of a knowledge management tool would include paper, pencils, and techniques such as brainstorming. In this chapter, we will examine only computer-based tools. The methods and techniques that are implemented by successful firms to support knowledge management are not limited to computer solutions only. Such successful solutions are represented in the case studies in this book.

E-mail and computer-videoconference systems can also be understood as tools for knowledge management. However, we consider this kind of software to be the basic technology, i.e., the building blocks for a knowledge management system. Groupware or an Intranet are initially systems for the management of information. This technology only becomes knowledge management tools when a structure, defined processes and technical additions are included, such as a means of evaluation by users.

---

[161]　Tiwana (2000), p. 62.
[162]　Tiwana (2000), p. 57.
[163]　Polanyi (1962); Nonaka, Takeuchi (1995).

This is not the place for a discussion about whether software can generate, codify, and transfer knowledge alone or whether software can only aid humans in these activities. For the success of knowledge management, the social aspects of its practical use are very important. For example a sophisticated search engine alone did not guarantee success as long as the user is not able to search effectively. It is not important for this study whether employees are supported in their knowledge management or whether the tool generates knowledge automatically on its own. This is an important point in the artificial intelligence discussion, but we would not like to go into detail here.

"Knowledge management tools are technologies, which automate, enhance and enable knowledge generation, codification and transfer. We do not look at the question if tools are augmenting or automating the knowledge work."[164]

According to our model of knowledge management, information technology is only one of six fields (see Fig. 5.2). Knowledge management tools that offer computer-based methods and techniques to companies come from this field. These tools are solutions that can handle the complexity of knowledge and cover the entire range of the core processes of knowledge management.

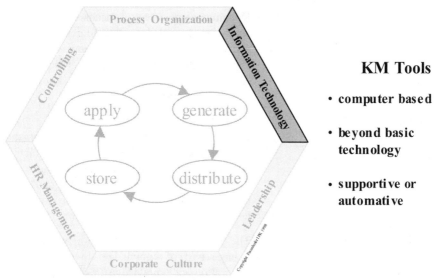

**KM Tools**

- **computer based**

- **beyond basic technology**

- **supportive or automative**

**Fig. 5.2:    IPKs Approach of KM Tools**

We will now introduce various possibilities for the classification of these tools.

---

[164]    Ruggles (1997), p. 3.

## 5.3   Main technologies

The following is an overview of the basic technologies used in every knowledge management solution. The following explanation of the basic technologies helps to examine and classify tools more precisely. These are the technologies that we find today in knowledge management.[165]

| | |
|---|---|
| Intranet technology | Intranets and Extranets are technologies that can be used to build a knowledge management system. The unified surface and access to various sources of information make this technology perfect for the distribution of knowledge throughout a company. |
| Groupware | Groupware is a further substantial technology that is used for knowledge management systems.[166] Groupware offers a platform for communication within a firm and for cooperation between employees. |
| Electronic document management | Documents are a central means of storing and spreading knowledge. Procedures for using and maintaining such documents, such as a check whether an update is overdue can be easily implemented for knowledge management systems. |
| Information retrieval tools | Information retrieval offers a solution to tasks from text searches to the automatic categorization and summation of documents. Advanced search algorithms use thesauri and text mining to discover contexts that could not be found with simple queries. Semantically text analyses can also be implemented. |
| Workflow management system | The business processes of a company contains a large part of knowledge. In addition, the integration of knowledge management into business processes is an important factor for success. |

---

[165]   see also Durlacher 1998, pp. 41-115.
[166]   Tiwana (2000), pp.80.

| | |
|---|---|
| Data analysis | Pattern recognition and classification and forecasting are the techniques used for data analysis. Data analysis is a possible method for generating new knowledge. |
| Data warehousing | A modern database is where data and information is stored. Connections that are not readily apparent can be uncovered with the use of data mining and OLAP. These techniques are part of data analysis. |
| Agent technology | Software agents based on the essentials of artificial intelligence enable the user to independently search for information according to a personal profile and to use various sources and other agents. |
| Help desks | Help desks are an important application area for case-based reasoning technology based on individual cases. Case knowledge can be quickly put into use in this way. |
| Machine learning | This technology from the field of artificial intelligence allows new knowledge to be generated automatically. In addition, processes can be automatically optimized with time with little necessity for human intervention. |
| Computer based training | This technology is used to pass on knowledge to colleagues. The spread of implicit knowledge is possible with multi-media applications. |

Different tasks of knowledge management can be processed using these basic technologies. In the following we would like to describe important functional aspects used in the presented technologies.

**Visualization** provides users with an opportunity to see connections among seemingly disparate items. Users can make inferences, interpretations, and decisions enhanced by this view.[167] An information visualization tool applies computing power in ways that supplement our natural abilities to recognize visual and spatial clues and patterns.[168] Visualization helps to retrieve knowledge by

---

[167] Bair, O'Connor (1998), p. 23.
[168] Rao, Sprague (1998), p. 70.

- helping the user to easily navigate through large quantities of information,

- presenting knowledge in a way that helps users see similarities and connections between information objects,

- presenting knowledge in an interactively accessible way.

This is done with computer graphics (2D and 3D), animation, and metaphors for navigational views for the representation of information.[169]

**Semantic functionality** helps the user to:

- recognize different concepts with similar meanings or similar concepts with different meanings in different contexts,

- quickly see similarities among concepts and to

- make sense of vast quantities of information objects based on their content.

This is done by means of clustering, automatic categorization, semantic networks, company dictionaries and thesauri, linguistic analysis and data extraction, rule-based systems and pattern identification.

**Collaborative functionality** helps to retrieve knowledge by

- focusing on the meaning and value given to information through collaborative use.

Collaborative filters track the popularity of concepts by paying close attention to evaluations by experts and communities of practice. These filters define what is likely to interest a user, based on what other users find significant or reliable and based on user profiles. They can alert the user whenever a new document is added or changes are made to existing ones.

## 5.4 Various classifications of knowledge management tools

We will now introduce various means of classifying knowledge management tools. We start with a short historical overview and refer to some approaches for classification. Historical classification often explains the special use of a certain product or how the manufacturer understands its use. The following historical roots are relevant:

- tools that are further developments of classical information archives or the retrieval of information,

---

[169]   Bair, O'Connor (1998), pp. 25.

- solutions from the field of communication and re-activated concepts from the field of artificial intelligence come into play in the analysis of documents and in automated searches,

- approaches to saving and visualizing knowledge also come from classical information archives,

- tools for modeling business processes and finally

- software that attempts to combine several techniques and to support different tasks in knowledge management equally.

The first approach is an example of a well-structured architectural model. The classification of tools beyond an abstract model of system development can help to classify existent technology. Tools that are on the market can be compared with each other and their strengths and weaknesses can be evaluated on different levels of the architectural model. In addition, this kind of model can help specify new, individually adjusted solutions. Even more than for individual solutions, this model displays how knowledge management can be formed beyond the limitations of one tool or of one company.

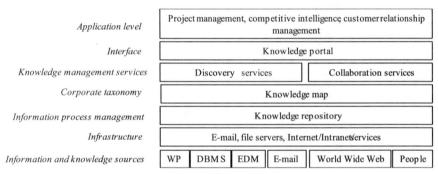

Fig. 5.3:    Ovum KM Tools Architectural Model[170]

Individual systems build these levels with differing degrees of intensity. Sometimes not all elements are at hand. The initial level of the model consists of information and knowledge sources (Fig. 5.3). These are delivered to the upper levels through the infrastructure. Next comes the administration level for the knowledge base where the access control is handled, for example. The corporate taxonomy defines important knowledge categories within the company. The next layer makes services available for the application of knowledge, e.g. through visualizing tools, and for collaboration, e.g. through collaborative filtering. The user interface is described as a portal through which the user can access the knowledge to use it in an application.

---

[170]    Woods, Sheina (1998), p. 8.

82

The next approach is characterized by the setting up of a continuum. This allows the technologies to be categorized multi-dimensionally, thus depicting inter-related areas. The selected continuum is directed towards the primary issues involved in the user's task. Classification along the axes *complexity / sophistication* and *intensity along the human / machine continuum* indicates whether certain tools can handle the complexity of the knowledge in question and what kind of work load this means for the user (see Fig. 5.4).

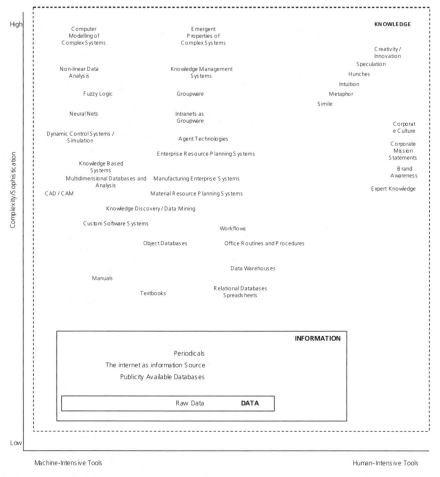

**Fig. 5.4:** **Complexity of KM Tools and the Human / Machine Continuum[171]**

"The goal of knowledge management is to make the use of these techniques, tools and technologies less human-intensive, and to develop products and services that

---

[171]     Syed (1998), p. 65.

incorporate complexity and sophistication, which is appropriate for specific knowledge work and is hidden so far as possible from users."[172]

A further possibility is categorization according to the basic technology from which knowledge management systems are constructed.

Most knowledge management tools use existing technologies to provide a collaborative framework for knowledge sharing and dissemination. They are implemented using e-mail and groupware, intranets, information retrieval and document management systems. Applications from data warehousing to help desks can be used to improve the quality of knowledge management.[173]

Finally, classification according to the core tasks of knowledge management makes sense. Tools can be examined for their support of the fields *create* knowledge, *store* knowledge, *distribute* knowledge, and *use* knowledge.

We want to suggest a categorization that implements aspects of the possibilities we've introduced. Individual products, i.e. kinds of products, can be graphically placed in a spectrum between the dimensions workload for the user and the core tasks of knowledge management.

When knowledge can be captured while knowledge workers communicate, the implementation of a knowledge management tool requires little extra effort on the part of the user. The work of the user is shifted from capturing to utilizing what is captured.[174]

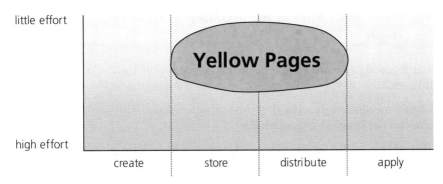

**Fig. 5.5:   IPK Categorization with Example**

Tools that aid the user relatively little are nearer the bottom while more complex tools that aid the user more are nearer the top (see Fig. 5.5). Yellow pages help to store and distribute knowledge about employee skills. Therefore this tool would be

---

[172]   Syed (1998), p. 63.
[173]   Woods, Sheina (1998), p. 36.
[174]   Bair, O'Connor (1998), p. 23.

placed in the figure as shown. Little effort is required of the user because the maintenance of the skill data only takes a short time.

Vertical categorization into the four main tasks is not as continuous as horizontal categorization. The assignment of a tool to a task is not always simple. For a further description of the vertical sections, we have provided a detailed description of the basic technologies involved.

The advantage of our model is that it connects the tools to the core activities of knowledge management. It also provides a means of analyzing strengths and weaknesses. It illustrates that the storage process is supported by several tools, whereas the distribution function is neglected. This analysis identifies shortcomings at an early stage, thus providing a valuable basis for decisions as to the selection of other tools. Our model provides a means of comparing and categorizing tools at an abstract level. The Ovum architectural model can then be used to assist with the actual implementation.

Integrated in our all-round knowledge management approach, the results supplied by the model also become relevant for other areas. For example, if there is no suitable tool for storing knowledge, employees cannot be expected to be able to exchange relevant project information systematically and to retain it for future reference. If the exchange is not supported technically, the analysis of the employees' behavior may provide a tool to support these activities.

## 5.5 IPK approach to categorization of knowledge management tools

The following is a description of the categorization of tools into the Fraunhofer IPK model.

The following classification (Fig. 5.6) of technologies is in accordance with the core tasks of knowledge management.

This table is an aid for the exact assignment of knowledge management-relevant technologies to the core processes. It was designed with a view to information technology. Activities strongly relating to IT applications are described, whereas the Fraunhofer IPK approach concentrates on four activities, integrating the points of view of the six different fields.

Before we deal with classification, we shall briefly discuss the problems involved in working with implicit and explicit knowledge. Processing explicit knowledge with a software tool requires the existence of information in an electronically retrievable form that the user can use to generate knowledge. Implicit knowledge is not easy to process or handle with a software tool because it is not yet written down. For example, one way to work with implicit knowledge is to use a camera to record a discussion between experts. This recording can later be digitalized and transcribed to make it retrievable with a computer. Another example could be a group of experts brainstorming, supported by the use of a program. It is always a question of how the implicit knowledge can be made explicit. Previously implicit knowledge is made explicit by using a software tool to store or use it. The question of how well the tool supports the use of implicit knowledge is more a question of how well it supports a means of making knowledge explicit.

| Knowledge Objective | Technolgy Enablers |
| --- | --- |
| Find knowledge | Knowledge-bases in consulting firms; search and retrieval tools that scan both formal and informal sources of knowledge; employee skills yellow pages. |
| Create new knowledge | Collaborative decision-making processes; DSS tools; rationale capture tools; Notes databases; decision repositories; externalization tools. |
| Package and assemble knowledge | Customized puplishing tools; information refinery tools; push technology; customized discussion groups. |
| Apply knowledge | Search, retrieval, and storage tools to help organize and classify both formal and informal knowledge. |
| Reuse and revalidate knowledge | Customer support knowledge bases; consulting firm discussion databases; past project record databases and communities of practice. |

**Fig. 5.6:   Knowledge Processes and Technology Enablers**[175]

We put tools into the *create knowledge* category if they help to generate new documents and files or if they teach the user something new. In the latter case, knowledge is stored in the mind of the user.

*Storing knowledge* involves marking it with the appropriate key words. The existence of taxonomy would be helpful here. One way to save knowledge is to add meta-data to extant information.

---

[175]   Tiwana (2000), p. 201.

Part of the *distribution of knowledge* is finding the right addresses. How does the tool support the delivery of the right knowledge to the right people? User profiles with a description of the knowledge needed or sought are used here. With respect to software tools, storing and distributing are very similar, so the use of taxonomy for profiles is common.

The *application of knowledge* is supported when the tool helps the user to find the right documents and files and then to easily apply that knowledge to the actual work to be done.

## 5.6    Lists of tools and market leaders

We have not categorized every single product. Instead, we grouped products with similar features together, according to the four aspects of knowledge management we've mentioned.

The following knowledge management tools were selected due to their leading market position, their innovative approach, and their wide use. The tools we have included were listed and investigated in the relevant professional literature. Our evaluation is based on information from those professional sources, from information that was otherwise accessible, and from our own research. The references include the following studies; the numbers in brackets are used in the last columns of the following tables: FhG Study[176] (1), Durlacher Report[177] (2), IT Research Report[178] (3), Ovum Report[179] (4), St. Gallen Study[180] (5), HMD Book[181] (6), KM Toolkit Book[182] (7), KM Magazin 3/2000[183] (8), KM Magazin 2/2000[184] (9) and Journal of KM[185] (10). The Web addresses are as of August 2000.

These tables can provide a template for the categorization of other tools and for their comparison with the tools we have included. Extant tools can now be categorized with the basic technologies in mind.

---

[176]    Bullinger et al. (2000), pp. 47.
[177]    Bottomley (1998), pp. 121.
[178]    Mühlbauer et al. (2000), pp. 100.
[179]    Woods et al. (1998), pp. 135.
[180]    Seifried et al. (2000), pp. 47.
[181]    Warschat et al. (1999), pp. 53.
[182]    Tiwana (2000), pp. 508.
[183]    Beltrametti (2000), pp. 16.
[184]    McKenna (2000), pp. 24.
[185]    Bair et al. (1998), pp. 20.

The groups of knowledge management tools we found are:

1. Search engines / categorization tools / intelligent agents
2. Portals
3. Visualizing tools
4. Skill management
5. Complete KM suites
6. Toolkits for developing individual solutions
7. Learn and teach
8. Virtual teams / collaboration

These groups are represented in the figures we have already introduced.

Every tool belongs to one group. Although some tools could be included in more than one group, the main emphasis of the product was decisive.

## 1. Search engines, categorization tools, and intelligent agents

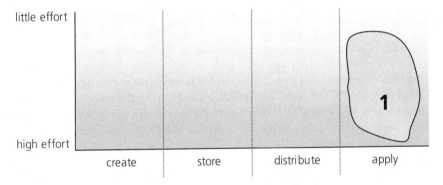

Fig. 5.7: Search Engines, Categorization Tools, and Intelligent Agents

These tools help to find the knowledge a user is looking for. This involves less user effort if the tool also categorizes knowledge or if knowledge is made individually accessible according to a profile given to an agent.

| Company | Product | Web | Ref. |
|---|---|---|---|
| Alexa Internet | Alexa | http://www.alexa.com/ | |
| CompassWare Development | InfoMagnet | http://www.compassware.com/ | 5, 10 |
| Inmagic | Inmagic | http://www.inmagic.com/ | |
| Magnifi | Magnifi | http://www.magnifi.com/ | 10 |

| Company | Product | Web | Ref. |
|---|---|---|---|
| NQL Solutions | StockVue | http://www.alphaconnect.com/ | 7 |
| Plumtree Software | Plumtree | http://www.plumtreesoft.com/ | 10 |
| SageWare | SageWare | http://www.sageware.com/ | 10 |
| Schema GmbH | SchemaText | http://www.schema.de/ | 3 |
| Semio | Semio | http://www.semio.com/ | 7 |
| USU AG | Knowledge Miner | http://www.usu.de/ | 1, 6 |

## 2. Portals

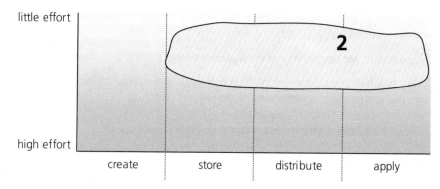

Fig. 5.8: Portals

The idea of a portal that makes all knowledge available at one time and place is found in many of the tools we investigated. Most of the complete knowledge management suites were implemented as portals. In this group, tools focus on a user interface that grants access to a multitude of different sources. A search engine is also included.

| Company | Product | Web | Ref. |
|---|---|---|---|
| Excalibur Technologies | RetrievalWare | http://www.excalib.com/ | 1, 2, 3, 4, 5, 6, 7, 8 |
| Xerox | AskOnce / DocuShare | http://www.xerox.com/ | 5 |
| zap AG | ucONE | http://www.zapnet.com/ | 3 |

## 3. Visualization tools

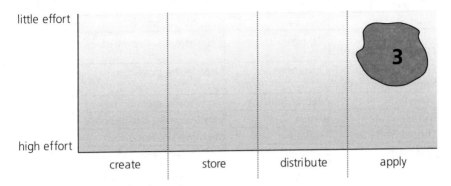

Fig. 5.9: **Visualization Tools**

These tools can be used as a supplement to existing knowledge management solutions or they emphasize the presentation of knowledge.

| Company | Product | Web | Ref. |
|---|---|---|---|
| Cartia | ThemeScape | Http://www.cartia.com/ | 10 |
| IBM | KnowledgeX | Http://www.ibm.com/ | 5, 6, 10 |
| InXight Software | Eureka | Http://www.inxight.com/ | 5, 10 |
| MindJET | MindManager | Http://www.mindman.com/ | 7 |
| Think Tools AG | Think Tool | Http://www.thinktools.com/ | 3 |

## 4. Skill management

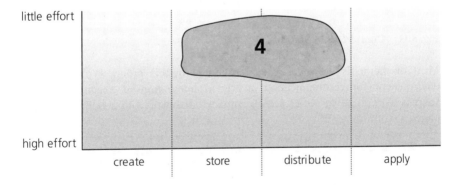

Fig. 5.10: **Skill Management**

To know where the skills of the company's staff lie is the point here. Yellow pages are a common way to distribute this knowledge.

| Company | Product | Web | Ref. |
|---|---|---|---|
| Arial Systems | ArialView | http://www.arialsystems.com/ | |
| GFT Systems GmbH | METAskill | http://www.gft-systems.de/ | |
| Group Decision Support Systems | QuestMap | http://www.gdss.com/ | |
| Meta4 | Meta4Mind-Set | http://www.meta4.com/ | |
| Mirus | arsitus | http://www.mirus-hrd.com/ | |
| Orbital Software | Organik | http://www.orbital-tech.com/ | 8 |
| SkillScape | Competence Manager | http://www.skillscape.com/ | |
| SkillView Technologies | SkillView Enterprise | http://www.skillview.com/ | |

## 5. Complete KM suites

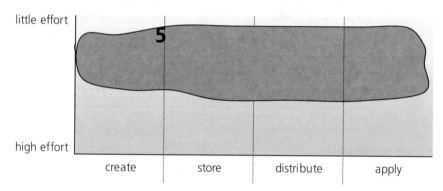

Fig. 5.11:   Complete KM Suites

Most of the tools we investigated are found in this group. We found a rich environment for communication and good integration of existing knowledge sources as well as powerful search engines combined with a portal and yellow pages.

| Company | Product | Web | Ref. |
|---|---|---|---|
| Autonomy | KM Suite | http://www.autonomy.com/ | 1, 3, 4, 5, 6, 10 |
| Blue Angel Technologies | MetaStar Enterprise | http://www.blueangeltech.com/ | 3 |
| Comma Soft AG | Infonea | http://www.comma-soft.com/ | 1 |
| Dataware Technologies | KM Suite | http://www.dataware.com/ | 3, 4, 5, 7, 10 |

| Company | Product | Web | Ref. |
|---|---|---|---|
| Documentum | Documentum 4i | http://www.documentum.com/ | 5, 9, 10 |
| Gauss Interprise AG | VIP' | http://www.gauss-interprise.de/ | 1, 3, 6 |
| grapeVINE Technologies | GrapeVINE | http://www.gvt.com/ | 2, 3, 5, 6, 10 |
| Hummingbird | Fulcrum Knowledge Server | http://www.hummingbird.com/ | 1, 4, 5, 6, 9, 10 |
| Hyperwave | Hyperwave Information Server | http://www.hyperwave.com/ | 1, 6, 7 |
| IDS Scheer AG | Business Knowledge Manager | http://www.ids-scheer.de/ | 3 |
| Lotus | Raven / Notes/Domino | http://www.lotus.com/ | 1, 5, 6, 8 |
| OpenText | Livelink | http://www.opentext.com/ | 1, 3, 4, 5, 6, 7, 10 |
| Pironet AG | Pirobase | http://www.piro.net/ | 3 |
| Practicity | Practicity | http://www.integrationware.com/ | |
| SAP | Knowledge Warehouse | http://www.sap.com/ | 1, 3 |
| Verity | Portal One | http://www.verity.com/ | 1, 2, 3, 4, 5, 6, 10 |
| Wincite Systems | Wincite | http://www.wincite.com/ | 2, 4, 5, 10 |

## 6. Toolkits for developing individual solutions

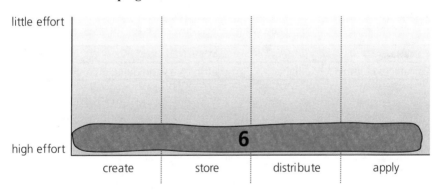

Fig. 5.12:   Toolkits for Developing Individual Solutions

92

These are development environments for implementing individual knowledge management solutions. Although every knowledge management tool has to be adapted to individual company needs, the tools in this group need more work to become a knowledge management solution.

| Company | Product | Web | Ref. |
|---------|---------|-----|------|
| arcplan | DynaSight | http://www.arcplan.com/ | 3 |
| BackWeb | BackWeb | http://www.backweb.com/ | |
| Microsoft | Digital Dashboard | http://www.microsoft.com/ | |
| Vignette | StoryServer | http://www.vignette.com/ | 5 |

## 7. Learn and teach

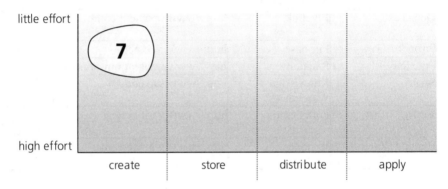

Fig. 5.13: Learn and Teach

In this group ,tools help to create new knowledge with enriched presentations. Users can learn from others and create new knowledge for themselves.

| Company | Product | Web | Ref. |
|---------|---------|-----|------|
| Chromedia GmbH | MediaNaut | http://www.medianaut.com/ | |

## 8. Virtual teams / collaboration

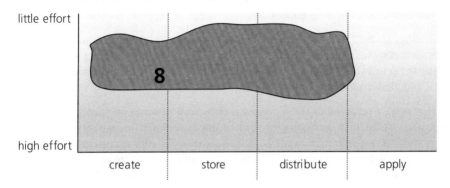

**Fig. 5.14: Virtual Teams / Collaboration**

These tools strongly emphasize the communication aspect of knowledge management. Discussion groups and virtual team rooms are examples here.

| Company | Product | Web | Ref. |
|---|---|---|---|
| eRoom Technology | Eroom | http://www.eroom.com/ | |
| HyperKnowledge | HyperKnowledge | http://www.hyperknowledge.com/ | 7 |
| Intraspect | c-business | http://www.intraspect.com/ | 4, 5, 10 |

## 5.7   Outlook

Our model demonstrates very clearly that it is not the basic technology that is essential: it is the involvement of the employee. The employee is to be supported in the central aspects of knowledge management, create, store, distribute and apply. We thus recommend that the selection of knowledge management IT solutions be guided by theory. This enables them to be better suited to the specific requirements. In the future, the basic technologies will be standard and increasingly integrated. This will require the integration of knowledge management in everyday business as well as a sense of responsibility from each individual.

This will result in the subject of knowledge management becoming less apparent. It will be taken more and more for granted.

For the exchange of knowledge to continue improving, meta-knowledge will become increasingly important. Meta-knowledge helps to describe knowledge and to specify it's meaning. This form of description will have to be standardized due to the growing need for a global exchange of knowledge. This is made apparent by the increased importance of Internet markets, which require a globally accepted description of products and thus knowledge.

94

In the IT industry, the dominant trend is towards takeovers of small, innovative companies. The market leader can then integrate new technologies into his standard product and advance it.

Another future trend is towards knowledge management being practiced not only within companies, but also between them. Moreover, the Internet will reinforce the trend towards small companies being able to benefit more from the exchange of knowledge with other companies.

However, a sense of disillusionment is occurring in some companies with regard to the use of new technologies. For example, Intranet technology is taken for granted as a medium nowadays, although there is still uncertainty about what kinds of information it should transfer to yield the maximum benefit. Despite continuing technological improvements in the future, man will still remain the definitive force.

Part II


**Survey**

# 6  Benchmarking Survey Results

*Peter Heisig, Jens Vorbeck*

Knowledge management is an emerging field for research and business. Therefore we decided to base our research on a comprehensive survey of the German TOP 1000 and European TOP 200 companies, because large companies could usually affort the investments and effort required to develop and introduce new management methods.

The survey questions were organized in three sections: general understanding and status of knowledge management activities in the whole company; status of knowledge management activities in the business process the company considers as their best practice; and demographic data about the company.

We have structured the survey results according to the business processes (chapter 6.1), the design fields for knowledge management (chapter 6.2) and the specific operational methods which are used by the companies to carry out knowledge management (chapter 6.3). After a brief description of the survey sample (chapter 6.4), the chapter concludes with the description of the selection process of the best practice companies (chapter 6.5).

## 6.1  Knowledge management and business processes

### 6.1.1  Understanding of knowledge management: people and processes

Nowadays, the use of the term "knowledge management" is increasing. However, the understanding of the term varies greatly. Our analysis of publications prior to May 1998 revealed that technological conceptions of knowledge management were then predominant. But even these early reports emphasized the importance of human factors in the successful application of knowledge management. It was therefore one of our most important goals to ascertain what the decision-makers in industrial and service companies understood knowledge management to be.

The results of our study show that knowledge management is understood neither as a technological term nor as an intangible asset. It is understood as a part of corporate culture and as a corporate approach. It is the sum of the procedures that determine the generation, storage, distribution, and application of knowledge to achieve organizational goals (Fig. 6.1).

Again, a clear difference was appearent in the responses of service and industrial firms. In the service companies, knowledge management was understood primarily (65%) as corporate culture. On the other hand, the majority of the industrial firms we interviewed (50%) considered it to be a corporate approach.

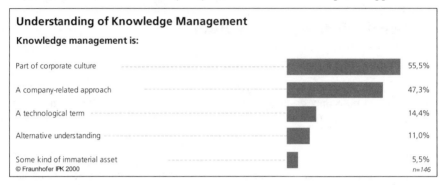

**Fig. 6.1: Understanding of Knowledge Management**

Many companies also stressed the process orientation and methodology of knowledge management in their conception:

- Knowledge management is "a generic term for all activities that are carried out to optimize the creation, utilization, distribution, and storage of knowledge" (consulting company).

- "For us, knowledge management is a collection of techniques to obtain an in-depth, dynamic perception of our business and its boundary conditions. Perception / knowledge / sensibility about our business is obtained not only by means of formal collection" (engineering company).

- "Controlling these four dimensions: Content: Which knowledge is relevant for whom? Culture: How can one promote the exchange of knowledge? Process: With which processes can one manage knowledge? Infrastructure: Which medium of communication is suitable?" (consulting company).

- "A set of procedures, corporate rules and a cultural framework, a mindset about human resources, attitudes and aptitudes, and IT resources that let all of us share knowledge in order to improve each core capability to better serve our customers and our competitive capabilities" (EDP company).

- "The sum of procedures that serves to create, evaluate, distribute, and apply knowledge in order to attain predefined goals" (metal processing company).

- "All corporate measures that help to convert individual information and knowledge into universal know-how, and are thus made available for the success of the company" (consulting company).

## 6.1.2 Importance of knowledge management for business processes: increase in value

Knowledge management enables a company to improve its organizational goals and is therefore closely connected with corporate business processes. In this context, the importance of knowledge management for distinct business processes is great.

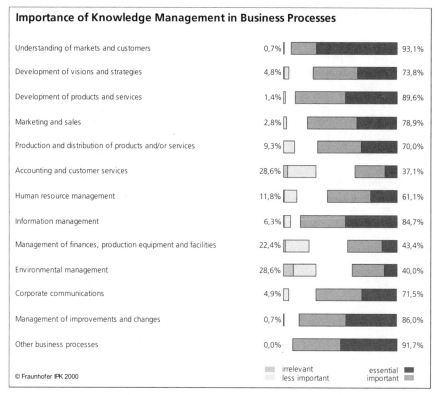

Fig. 6.2: Importance of Knowledge Management in Business Processes [186]

The results of our survey (Fig. 6.2) showed that the participants thought knowledge management to be most important for the following business processes: understanding markets and customers, development of products and services, management of improvements and changes, and information management. Due to increasing customer orientation and fiercer competition,

---

[186] The percentages in figure Fig. 6.2 summarize the two answering options of each extreme, thus "not relevant" and "less important" on the one hand, and "essential" and "important" on the other. The percentage of the answers "medium" is represented by the colorless bar in between.

100

knowledge about customers and competition is of utmost importance. The great importance of the business process "development of products and services" is due to its close relationship to the core activities "apply knowledge" and "create new knowledge". The value of the supporting business process "management of improvements and changes" reflects the increasing importance of identifying and distributing tacit and explicit knowledge such as best practices, ideas, and suggestions. The business process "information management" represents the technical infrastructure for the transportation and storage of data and information, i.e., the raw material of knowledge.

### 6.1.3 Core capabilities and the start of knowledge management: a close relationship

A central question for the introduction of knowledge management is where to begin with the systematic management of the knowledge resources of a company. Should the company focus on its core capabilities in order to strengthen them, or should it concentrate on those points where it can expect quick success?

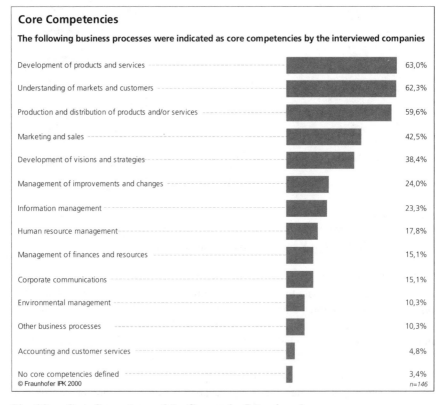

**Core Competencies**

The following business processes were indicated as core competencies by the interviewed companies

| | |
|---|---|
| Development of products and services | 63,0% |
| Understanding of markets and customers | 62,3% |
| Production and distribution of products and/or services | 59,6% |
| Marketing and sales | 42,5% |
| Development of visions and strategies | 38,4% |
| Management of improvements and changes | 24,0% |
| Information management | 23,3% |
| Human resource management | 17,8% |
| Management of finances and resources | 15,1% |
| Corporate communications | 15,1% |
| Environmental management | 10,3% |
| Other business processes | 10,3% |
| Accounting and customer services | 4,8% |
| No core competencies defined | 3,4% |

© Fraunhofer IPK 2000                                                                 n=146

**Fig. 6.3:    Core Competence of the Companies Interviewed**

According to our results, more than two thirds of the companies described between two and five business processes as their core capabilities (Fig. 6.3). Only 3.4% of the companies did not define any core capability

The results of our question about where knowledge management was started paint a similar picture. About half of the companies began their knowledge management activities in two or three business processes. The study shows that about 20% of the companies concentrated on one business process, and only one company in eight included four business processes. The business process that received the most attention was developing products and services (Fig. 6.4.).

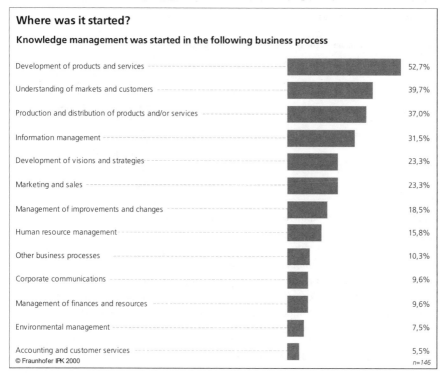

**Fig. 6.4:  Where Was Knowledge Management Started**

Clearly the companies began with knowledge management in those fields where they saw their core abilities. Once again, large deviations were apparent between service and industial firms. About 40% of the service companies started knowledge management with information management, while this was the case with only a quarter of the industrial companies. In the industrial sector, the greatest focus of knowledge management was initially the development of products and services. This was the case with only a third of the service companies. The large number of companies that mentioned the business process information management signifies the importance the companies ascribe to this

102

area when applying knowledge management. There is a clear correlation between the core capabilities of a company and those business processes to which knowledge management is first applied.

### 6.1.4 Duration and status of knowledge management: pilot projects predominate

About a third of the companies interviewed have carried out knowledge management activities since 1993-1995. Another third started between 1996 and 1997. One out of six companies commenced activities less than a year ago. About 25% have been working with knowledge management for over six years (Fig. 6.5).

**Fig. 6.5:** **Duration of Knowledge Management Activities**

However, our question about the status of knowledge management revealed that 57% of the companies interviewed primarily carry out pilot projects. About 20% of the companies are currently planning a project. One third of the companies are currently incorporating knowledge management into their daily business activities. About one sixth of the companies are currently applying knowledge management to all of their business processes (Fig. 6.6).

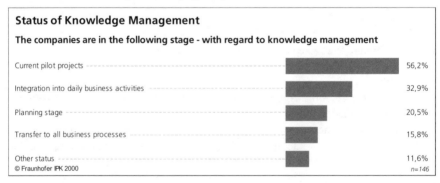

**Fig. 6.6:** **Status of Knowledge Management**

### 6.1.5 Level of the development of knowledge management: potential not yet realized

It is very important for benchmarking to examine how the level of development of relevant methods and procedures in a selected area - in this case knowledge management - is rated by companies.

The average assessment of the level of development showed obvious potential for improving the systematic management of the resource "knowledge" in all business processes. Very few companies found the level of development of their knowledge management activities to be excellent (Fig. 6.7).

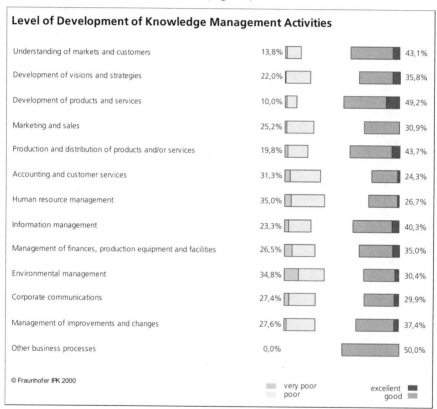

**Fig. 6.7: Level of Development of Knowledge Management Activities**

### 6.1.6 Corporate goals: major contribution of knowledge management

Corporate knowledge management helps to achieve the primary goals of a company. Our results revealed that the managers interviewed believe that knowledge management can best be used to increase innovative ability and to improve customer satisfaction. Although companies see the core activity "distribution of knowledge" as something necessary, users of knowledge management believe that it contributes little to the achievement of time-related goals (reducing the time of implementation and increasing the effectiveness of schedules). The distribution of knowledge therefore contributes more to an increase in productivity than it helps reach a goal faster. With an average of 60%, knowledge management contributes "strongly" or "very strongly" to the realization of central corporate goals (Fig. 6.8).

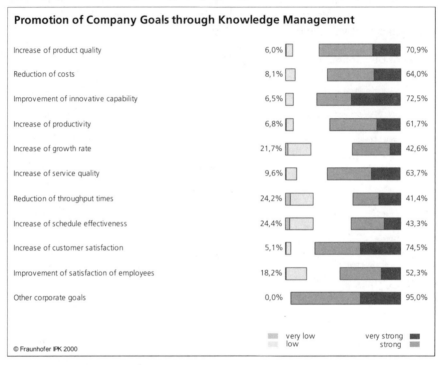

Fig. 6.8:    Promotion of Company Goals through Knowledge Management

### 6.1.7    Central aspects of knowledge: procedures, products, and customers

For knowledge to be useful to the organization, it has to relate to relevant aspects of business. The knowledge of people and organizations always has a specific content.

The results of our open question regarding this topic revealed that four out of five companies describe "procedures" as their central aspect of knowledge. Every second company mentioned "products", 40% checked "customers", and around one third of the companies noted "markets" and "competitors." Most users who deal with knowledge management therefore seem to focus on the question "How is it best/most inexpensively made?", i.e., what are the most efficient procedures or what are the best practices. The knowledge of products and procedures refers primarily, but not exclusively, to knowledge that is already part of the organization. But, the knowledge of customers, markets, and competitors also concerns the corporate environment. For the companies, access to this knowledge is critical. Only about 7% of the companies described employees as relevant "knowledge objects" (Fig. 6.9). Clear differences were again evident between service and industrial sectors. Naturally the service firms saw their customers as the most important object of knowledge (55.7%). For the majority of the industrial firms, this was products (62.9%).

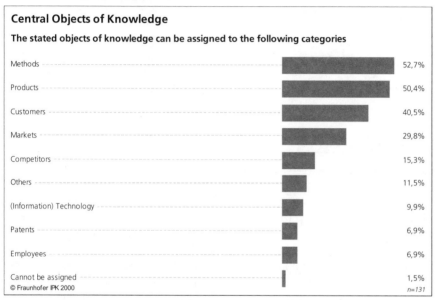

**Fig. 6.9:   Central Objects of Knowledge**

## 6.2   The design fields of knowledge management

The conceptualized design of integrated knowledge management is decisive for the quality of a core process. Aside from various operative instruments, methods, and concepts, it is particularly important to create a suitable environment for the design of knowledge management. This is done on a normative and strategic level. To design knowledge management, users have to describe associated fields. The selection and relative worth of these fields were conclusively confirmed by this study. Answers to the following question were classified and categorized: "What are the essential factors of success for efficient knowledge management in this business process (as evaluated by the company)?" (Fig. 6.10).

106

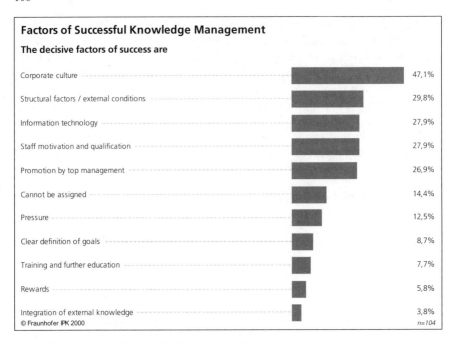

**Fig. 6.10: Factors of Successful Knowledge Management**

The distribution of answers reflects the importance that the companies place on different design fields. Corporate culture contributes the most to the success of knowledge management (47%). Once again, considerable differences were evident between service and industrial sectors. Half of the service companies we interviewed named corporate culture as a decisive factor, as opposed to only 12.7% of the industrial firms. In the industrial sector, staff motivation and qualification were in the highest positions (22.5%). The relatively high contribution of human resource management is not that obvious at first glance. However, the categories staff motivation and qualification, training and further education, and rewards taken together account for about 35%. This is the second most important factor for this design field. The field leadership amounts to 25%. It includes promotion by top management and clear definition of goals. Information technology, an independent category, amounts to 28%. The category structural factors/external conditions, i.e. process organization claims almost 30%. Companies that have been involved with knowledge management activities for more than three years, i.e., about half of the companies we interviewed, placed slightly more importance on all success factors mentioned above. In actual numbers, this means that all categories increased by about 3 to 5%. Only the category "information technology" did not increase.

### 6.2.1 Process organization: flow of knowledge through chains of processes with few interfaces

The alignment and optimization of business processes is necessary for the creation of a knowledge-oriented company. The coordination of tasks and the reduction of interfaces along the chain that creates value - even beyond the boundaries of the company – leads to measurable success.

The management of knowledge-oriented business processes requires the creation of integral process chains without many interfaces. These chains can then improve the flow of knowledge throughout the corporate organization. To concentrate on those core capabilities that are necessary for corporate success and to structure the organization according to core capabilities or decentralized business units results both in flexibility about market requirements and in favourable conditions for the usage and spread of successful knowledge.

This is why our study does not stick to the organizational structure of the company. An orientation towards operative and supporting business processes is essential for all stages of the introduction of knowledge management. The diagnosis, implementation, and maintenance of corporate knowledge management includes dealing with functional (departments) and physical (location, factory, buildings) barriers.

### 6.2.2 Human resource management: financial rewards are not everything

Personnel management and the functional areas of personnel development and corporate training and education have been traditionally established to equip corporate areas with certain qualifications. Holistic knowledge management integrates human resource management. This means that personnel policies are aligned with the predefined corporate strategy, including knowledge strategy.

Fig. 6.11 illustrates the attempts of companies to motivate their employees to conduct effective knowledge management activities. Almost 41,5% of the companies have tried to improve staff motivation by handing out financial rewards. The relationship between wages and motivation or job satisfaction has been confirmed by previous studies at Fraunhofer IPK.[187] However, the significance of this traditional "motivator" should not be overestimated. A financially induced increase in motivation cannot be compared to intrinsic motivators that have much greater and sustained effects. These intrinsic motivators include feedback or an expansion of the scope of activity or responsibility. Correspondingly, the answers to Fig. 6.11 reveal that these latter motivators are mentioned much more often than so-called incentives.

---

[187] Fraunhofer IPK conducted surveys with around 20,000 employees in more than 10 companies between 1996 and 1999.

108

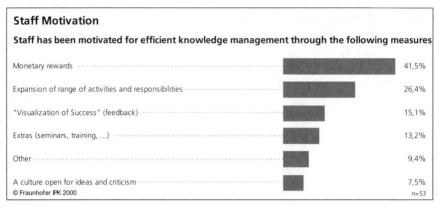

**Fig. 6.11: Staff Motivation**

15% prefer the "visualization" of success, for example through awards and public recognition. More than 10% of the companies try to enhance their employees' commitment to knowledge management through non-financial rewards like training sessions and seminars.

### 6.2.3 Management systems: active management is required

Management is of pivotal importance in any concept of knowledge management. It determines the path of strategies and indicates with its behavior whether these targets have actually been achieved. Only management is able to pave the way for a knowledge-oriented corporate culture. In this way, management can be defined as the formulation of a central corporate vision that can be used to develop strategies and to plan and convert corresponding operative concepts. These strategies are then aligned with the know-how and thinking of the organization's members. Management has to communicate tasks and create a motivating environment based on trust and credibility. By making demands and offering support, managers enable individual staff members to coordinate their own work and to develop a learning organization through their teamwork.

Fig. 6.12 illustrates the answers to the question about the management of the companies we interviewed. It is striking that the answers reflect a characteristic sign of management that has already been established in many previous studies. Most companies stated that their managers "create conditions for autonomous actions", i.e., that they create an atmosphere of passive management. First, passive management is a neutral fact. This distinguishes passive management from active management, something that employees expect of their superiors and that managers often do not recognize. Coaching, mentioned by about 46% of the companies, often signifies just supervision, not the support of employees. However, the following four aspects of active management can be understood in their entirety as a sensible supplement to the aspects of passive management mentioned above: "promote the acceptance of external knowledge", "acknowledge employees", "promotion of learning through experience", and "examples of knowledge behavior".

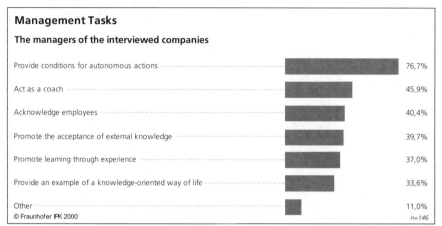

**Fig. 6.12: Management Tasks**

In Fig. 6.13, answers to the question about managerial aspects that facilitate knowledge management in business processes indicated two new categories that had not been considered before. One category is that of "open communication". As we will see later on, this is an aspect that describes corporate culture and that reveals how closely management, corporate culture, and personnel management are interconnected. A second category is that of "personal support". This shows that the persons we interviewed realized that knowledge management requires managers who possess great knowledge of their respective line of business and a good command of interpersonal skills.

Finally, we must say that the active components of management mentioned above are often underestimated. Personal support (11.4%), the model function of managers (12.3%), and the promotion of learning from experience (14.9%) obviously all lag behind.

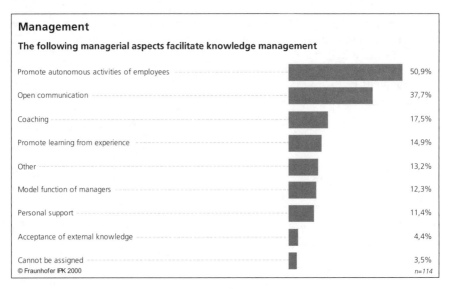

**Fig. 6.13: Managerial Aspects that Facilitate Knowledge Management**

### 6.2.4 Corporate culture: various design opportunities

The design of a knowledge-oriented organization is closely connected to the development of a corporate culture that is influenced by all other fields of knowledge management. The concept of corporate culture provides useful insights into important organizational relationships that have often been neglected in business research. The organizational culture of a company is reflected in its philosophy and vision, management style, and in its physical organizational structures, such as the architecture of buildings and the layout and design of rooms. Users have to analyze their corporate culture in order to change it purposefully. They use instruments and methods that allow them to decode fundamental assumptions.

Corporate cultures are unique. Imitation can lead to completely different results. Corporate cultures establish whether subcultures can be incorporated without high frictional losses or whether there will be many strong individual cultures. The contribution of corporate culture to high corporate efficiency is determined by the combination of individual, yet coordinated cultural elements. Therefore, we cannot ascertain whether a "soft" or "strong" corporate culture is more suitable to support the goals of a company. Instead, the efficiency of a system is determined by the alignment of corporate culture with available corporate, information, and communication structures, and with the prevailing idea of human beings.

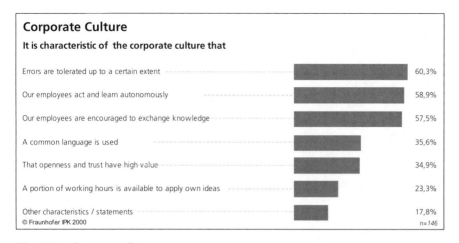

**Fig. 6.14: Corporate Culture**

Fig. 6.14 illustrates the fact that corporate culture is essentially characterized by three aspects: 60% of the companies mentioned that "errors – up to a certain extent – are tolerated", "the exchange of knowledge is encouraged", and "autonomous actions and learning are encouraged". "Development of a common language" and "openness and trust" are mentioned by every third company.

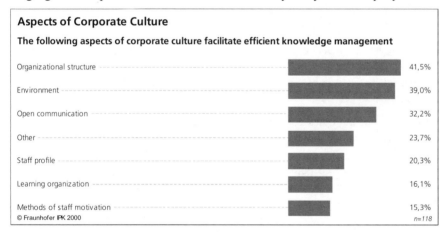

**Fig. 6.15: Aspects of Corporate Culture**

According to 41.5% of the companies, knowledge management activities are facilitated by organizational structure (Fig. 6.15). 39% of the companies mentioned environment and 32% open communication as aspects that positively effect the activities of knowledge management. As mentioned in the section on human resource management, the answers to this question again reflect the close relationship between culture and the two design fields mentioned above. The persons responsible also state that corporate culture is not static. It can be influenced positively both by open communication initiated by managers and by suitable methods of staff motivation initiated by personnel management.

### 6.2.5  Information technology: intranet and databases are the standard

Information technologies support communication, cooperation and coordination, and the timely access of information and the sources of knowledge. The simple installation of a modern information infrastructure does not change the way one deals with the resource "knowledge." However, it is a necessary requirement to accelerate the core process of knowledge management. Partial solutions and solutions that are best for a certain area allow users to store explicit knowledge in databases or to distribute knowledge through group support systems. The technology that nowadays is most often used to support knowledge management in companies can be divided into three groups:

- Data warehouses collect and condense data from productive systems that are used in production, accounting, and other similar departments, and thus establish a uniform data interface. Systems that support decision making help to interpret this data.

- Groupware, Intranet and Internet allow users throughout the entire company to communicate and cooperate informally. These systems thus support the core activity of distributing knowledge. In addition, they represent the basic infrastructure for knowledge databases and workflow applications.

- Through knowledge databases and workflow applications, codified knowledge that has been authorized by experts and that, therefore, can be regarded as reliable can be made available to the members of the organization.

Information technologies can support the measures mentioned above only if the users accept new technologies. This requires that barriers against learning and sharing knowledge, departmental egotism, and fixed power structures must be reduced. As part of corporate culture, the information and learning culture of a company influences decisively the conditions under which information systems and software tools are used.

The following figure (Fig. 6.16) illustrates the self-assessment of companies we interviewed regarding the methods of knowledge management that are supported by information technology. More than 60% of the companies think that their utilization of databases with information on aspects of knowledge and of intranets is "good" or "excellent." "Intelligent agent technologies" and "expert systems" are handled "poorly" or "very poorly" by an absolute majority of the companies. It reflects a lack of familiarity with the available applications of agent technologies.

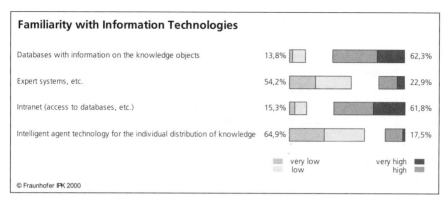

Fig. 6.16: Familiarity with Information Technologies

## 6.2.6 Control: extensive need for further development

Controlling knowledge in organizations is one of the biggest obstacles. To examine predefined targets, we need measuring systems that allow us to evaluate organizational knowledge. Without suitable instruments to evaluate knowledge, we cannot detect aberrations in the conversion of knowledge management at an early stage. We are also unable to introduce correction actions.

Only about 3% of the companies believe that the evaluation of success is not a matter of urgent necessity (Fig. 6.17). Thus they assume that those who do not evaluate their success will soon follow the majority. Most companies prefer a combination of "hard" and "soft" indicators.

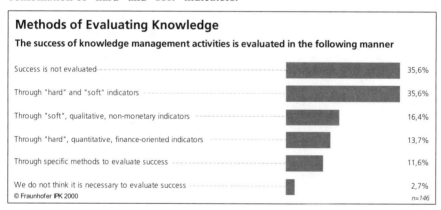

Fig. 6.17: Methods of Evaluating Knowledge

## 6.3   The core process of knowledge management

The concept of knowledge management recognizes six core process activities. The stages "identify knowledge" and "define knowledge goals" trigger the process and control its dynamics. The other core activities "create knowledge", "store knowledge", "distribute knowledge", and "apply knowledge" can be understood as a cycle that is continuously reproduced.

Prior to our study, we summarized and classified the relevant methods of knowledge management for each core process. This is currently the most advanced summary available. Due to rapid innovations in knowledge management, we focused on the identification of new developments as well as the evaluation of current methods. The participants of the study were therefore able to indicate their own methods that support each respective subprocess within the relevant core process.

### 6.3.1   Evaluation of core process activities: confirmation of the approach

The participating companies confirmed the relevance of our approach in their assessment of the individual core activities. More than 65% of the companies confirmed that almost all core activities were "very important" or "essential" (Fig. 6.18).

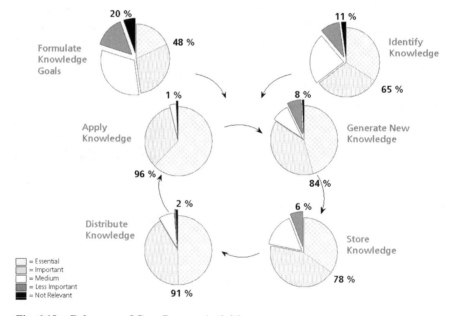

**Fig. 6.18:   Relevance of Core Process Activities**

The only exception was the activity "formulate knowledge goals." Only 48% of the companies said that this activity was either "very important" or "essential." The reduced importance of this activity indicates that the companies may not use appropriate instruments. The greatest significance was ascribed to the activities "apply knowledge" and "distribute knowledge". More than 90% of all companies think that these activities are either "very important" or "essential."

## 6.3.2    Identify knowledge: complex methods are in need of further development

The identification of knowledge is the indispensable basis for every knowledge management project. The aim is to find out which corporate knowledge is available, who the carriers of knowledge are, and where this knowledge is stored. The source of knowledge can be found internally and externally, i.e., with suppliers, customers, or in research institutions.

More than half of the companies said that they have "good" or "excellent" command of "internal and external benchmarking" and the "creation of manuals" (Fig. 6.19). This statement clearly indicates that the benchmarking approach is widely used and accepted. However, most companies use "visualization with knowledge maps" and the "creation of knowledge portfolios of internal vs. external knowledge" "poorly" or "very poorly." Both methods require the companies to simplify complex facts and to exert considerable effort in their further development.

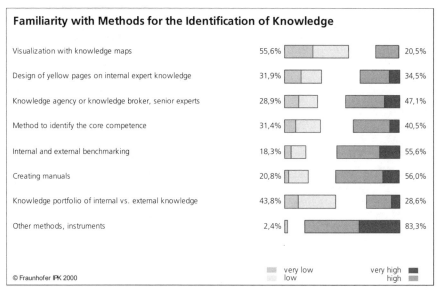

Fig. 6.19:   Familiarity with Methods for the Identification of Knowledge

### 6.3.3 Goals of knowledge: clarity, improvement of processes, and competitiveness

Sensible knowledge management starts initially with the development of clear goals. This is vital for the selection of suitable methods and for the subsequent control and evaluation of performance. In the questionnaire, companies were asked to name three typical goals of knowledge for the business process at hand.

Due to the open nature of this question, a multitude of goals were mentioned by the participants. We therefore categorized the answers in order to interpret the results. We divided the goals into short-term (clarity), medium-term (process improvement, easier decisions and predictions), and long-term goals (success and market leadership, customer orientation and satisfaction). The most important goal is the clarity of potentials, problems and/or processes (Fig. 6.20).

Altogether, almost 50% of the companies stated these targets. Long-term goals, such as success, market leadership, customer orientation or customer satisfaction were mentioned by 20% of the companies. The category "facilitate innovation" was selected by only 4% of the participants. This was surprising, as especially the Anglo-Saxon countries have often emphasized the close connection between the management of innovations and the management of knowledge.

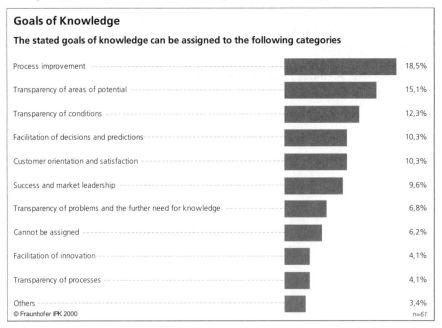

**Goals of Knowledge**

The stated goals of knowledge can be assigned to the following categories

| | |
|---|---|
| Process improvement | 18,5% |
| Transparency of areas of potential | 15,1% |
| Transparency of conditions | 12,3% |
| Facilitation of decisions and predictions | 10,3% |
| Customer orientation and satisfaction | 10,3% |
| Success and market leadership | 9,6% |
| Transparency of problems and the further need for knowledge | 6,8% |
| Cannot be assigned | 6,2% |
| Facilitation of innovation | 4,1% |
| Transparency of processes | 4,1% |
| Others | 3,4% |

© Fraunhofer IPK 2000   n=61

**Fig. 6.20: Goals of Knowledge**

## 6.3.4 Create knowledge: primarily through teamwork

The basic discussion about the basis for organizational knowledge demonstrates that such knowledge depends primarily on people. It is usually stored in routines, documents, and corporate culture, and thus in the behavior of the organization. But, the creation of new knowledge cannot take place without the participation of the individual members of the organization. This is because organizational knowledge originates from organizational processes of learning, which for their part rely on individual processes. The process of the creation of knowledge requires the identification both of available knowledge and of knowledge that is necessary for the success of the company.

Most companies rely on "project teams" whose work is considered to be successful. The work of "internal experts" (67%) is used more often than the work of "external experts" (53,6%) (Fig. 6.21). The "acquisition of external knowledge" was rated relatively positively. Methods that are expensive and organizationally demanding, such as the "simulation of future worlds" and the development of "learning labs" are at a rather low level of development. Most companies consider their ability to work with these methods as "poor" or "very poor." The companies' assessment of their ability to "uncover tacit knowledge" is equally poor. The application of this method is fairly demanding.

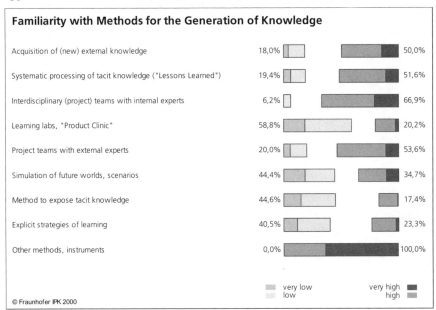

**Fig. 6.21: Familiarity with Methods for the Generation of Knowledge**

118

## 6.3.5   Store knowledge: potential of expert systems

The influence of the organizational memory has previously been neglected by many companies. Therefore, outsourcing measures or a high rate of staff turnover usually led to a loss of organizational knowledge. However, to be able to access important information in the future, the information has to be stored on the different data carriers of the organization. This requires that the users identify that knowledge that is to be preserved. Stored knowledge has to be continuously updated. It must also be studied whether the information is still up-to-date to the company.

Methods for storing knowledge are used successfully by most of the companies interviewed (Fig. 6.22). More than 60% of them indicated that they have "excellent" or "good" command of "databases with information on knowledge objects" and "manuals of standards and established methods". Half of the companies also have "excellent" or "good" command of "case studies, progress reports, and success stories." The predominantly negative self-assessment of the companies regarding their command of "expert systems and systems of case-based reasoning" reflects the high preparatory expenses of these methods. Their full potential has yet to be utilized.

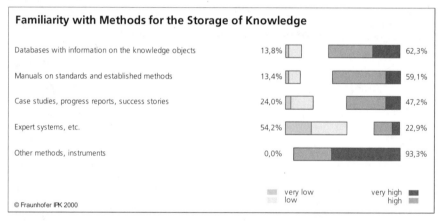

**Fig. 6.22:   Familiarity with Methods for the Storage of Knowledge**

## 6.3.6   Distribute knowledge: teams and technology

Stored organizational knowledge can only be applied if it is transferred into relevant areas. It is necessary to transfer knowledge to those members of the organization that do not participate in the development process. Users should take into consideration the fact that knowledge is not always needed in all organizational areas. The usefulness of knowledge is based on its availability at specific times and for specific purposes.

Like the methods of storing knowledge, the companies also judged their ability to handle methods of distributing knowledge to be predominantly positive (Fig. 6.23). The only exception is the utilization of "intelligent agent technologies" for which there are hardly any suitable applications available. In this area lies great potential. 65% of the companies judged their ability to handle this method to be "poor" or "very poor." However, another technological development of the recent past, the Intranet, is used widely throughout the companies. Almost 62% of the companies claim to be able to have good command of this method. The direct exchange of "interdisciplinary project teams" is also seen positively.

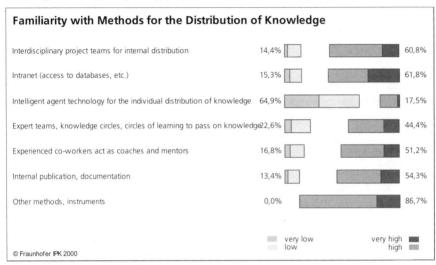

Fig. 6.23:  Familiarity with Methods for the Distribution of Knowledge

### 6.3.7    Apply knowledge: self-management, interdisciplinarity and the carriers of know-how

The goal of knowledge management is the application of the relevant knowledge that is available after it has been distributed. Only the application of knowledge allows new individual and collective processes of learning. As a result, new knowledge is created. The core process of knowledge thus may be considered a closed cycle.

In this core activity of knowledge management, the companies assessed their "autonomous interdisciplinary teams" and their ability to "coach teams through experienced experts" to be predominantly positive (Fig. 6.24). "Initiatives against the not-invented-here syndrome", however, are judged to be "poor" or "very poor" by 44% of the companies we interviewed. Even worse was the assessment of the companies' own activities regarding "measures for controlling knowledge". 48% of the participants said they had "poor" or "very poor" command of this method.

120

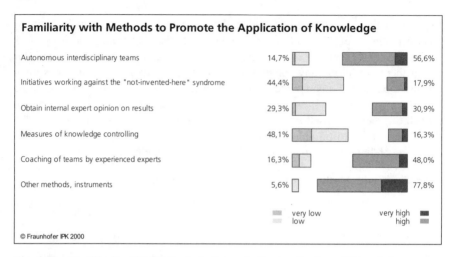

**Fig. 6.24: Familiarity with Methods to Promote the Application of Knowledge**

## 6.4 The sample

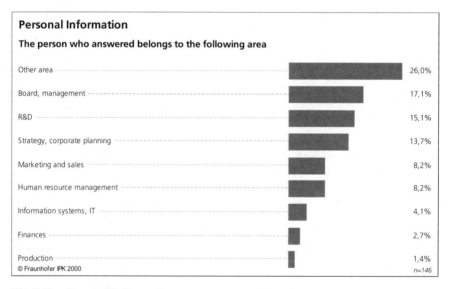

**Fig. 6.25: Personal Information**

148 questionnaires (12.3%) were returned. In view of the extent and complexity of our survey, we believe this to be an above-average response rate. It is important that our study was titled "Benchmarking Knowledge Management." This obviously led to greater participation by companies that have already had some experience with knowledge management. In many conversations with interested

companies, we also found that some did not participate because they felt their knowledge management activities had not yet matured.

As expected, the persons who replied were from different functional areas (Fig. 6.25). Most were attached to the board and management, strategy and corporate planning departments, or research and development. It was surprising that only 1.4 % of the participants were from production.

We found that knowledge management is used in all industries. However, the leading industries are chemicals and pharmaceuticals, computers and telecommunications, media, consulting, and automotive and aircraft (Fig. 6.26).

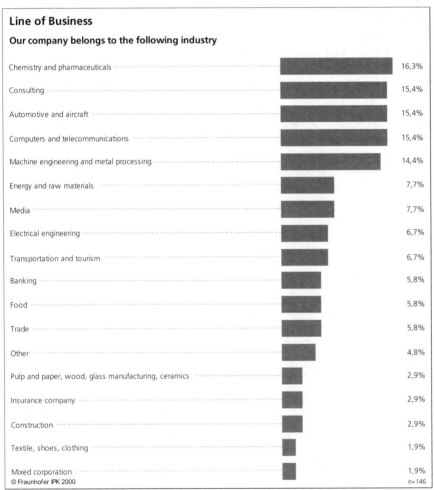

Fig. 6.26: Line of Business

## 6.5    Selection of best practice companies and case studies

The identification of best practices in knowledge management requires comprehensive research and many discussions with actual users and scientists. One difficulty arises from the fact that many of the methods and procedures of knowledge management are currently being developed – as can be seen by the many pilot projects.

To select best practice companies, we – in addition to interviewing the German TOP 1000 and the European TOP 200 companies – evaluated extensive secondary data from international scientific reviews and journals, business and management publications, and conference proceedings. In Germany, Europe and the United States, we talked to more than 100 executives and project managers, both scientists and businessmen, and visited national and international conferences on knowledge management. The information we gained was used to interpret the results of our questionnaire, and to prepare the best practice case studies.

We designed this study as a benchmarking study. Therefore, we were careful to select the best practice companies in a comprehensible manner. All participants were allowed to learn from the best, and, therefore, to improve their methods and processes purposefully. The participating companies suggested 119 business processes as best practice candidates in knowledge management (Fig. 6.27). The selection was based on a combination of applied knowledge management methods and the quality of application in that business process that had been named by the respective company as a best practice candidate. We were therefore able to identify a sample of 26 best practice companies. We then contacted the companies to describe the best methods of knowledge management in in-depth case studies.

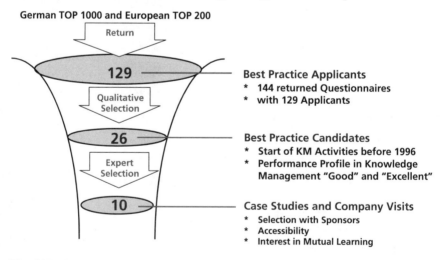

**Fig. 6.27:   Selection of Best Practice Candidates in Knowledge Management**

The distribution of the given answers reveals that most case studies concerned the business processes "development of products and services" and "understanding of markets and customers" (Fig. 6.28). The case studies will be described in the second part of our benchmarking study. The relevant data and information for the case studies were collected by the members of the IPK benchmarking team in one- to two-day visits in July and August of 1998. We paid particular attention to discussions with the respective project managers and the operative staff that mainly or in part is responsible for knowledge management tasks. The benchmarking team also used the opportunity to examine the software applications of benchmarking partners on the spot.

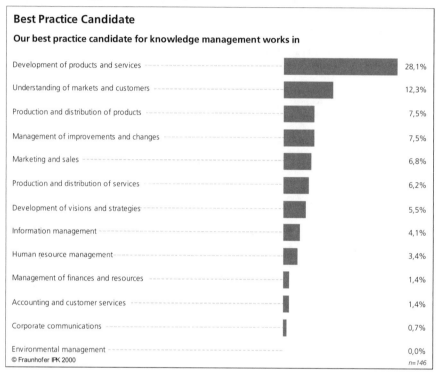

**Best Practice Candidate**

Our best practice candidate for knowledge management works in

| | |
|---|---|
| Development of products and services | 28,1% |
| Understanding of markets and customers | 12,3% |
| Production and distribution of products | 7,5% |
| Management of improvements and changes | 7,5% |
| Marketing and sales | 6,8% |
| Production and distribution of services | 6,2% |
| Development of visions and strategies | 5,5% |
| Information management | 4,1% |
| Human resource management | 3,4% |
| Management of finances and resources | 1,4% |
| Accounting and customer services | 1,4% |
| Corporate communications | 0,7% |
| Environmental management | 0,0% |

© Fraunhofer IPK 2000                                                                 n=146

**Fig. 6.28: Best Practice Candidates**

Part III

**Case Studies**

# 7 Knowledge Management: The "One Company Platform" - Arthur D. Little, Inc.

*Peter Heisig, Frank Spellerberg*

In 1886, Arthur Dehon Little, a chemistry professor at the Massachusetts Institute of Technology, founded the company with the same name. His goal was to advise companies on how to develop more efficient production processes and organizational forms. Today, the company is one of the world's five premier consulting firms, with 3400 staff members based in 51 offices and laboratories around the globe. In 1999, Arthur D. Little Inc. had an income of € 670 million.

**Arthur D Little**

http://www.adl.com

| | |
|---|---|
| *Industry:* | **Consulting** |
| *Business Process:* | **Development and Delivering of Services** |
| *Employees:* | **3.400** |
| *Sales:* | **€ 670 Mio. (1999)** |
| *KM Best Practice:* | **Case Debriefing** **ADL-Link** |

**Fig. 7.1: Company Overview - Arthur D. Little**

In Germany there are offices in Wiesbaden, Berlin, Düsseldorf, and Munich with approximately 200 consultants in various "practices." These "practices" are organized according to the industry they serve: chemistry and pharmaceuticals, consumer goods, automobile manufacturers and suppliers, mechanical and plant engineering, electronics, information technology and telecommunications, banks and insurance companies, energy, resources and utilities, and public administration and services. The "practices" are further divided according to the services offered: safety and risk, strategy, design and development, EHS management, operations management, program management, technology and innovation management, information management, organization, and environmental science and technology. Product and process development is handled by staff members of Cambridge Consultants Ltd., a subsidiary of Arthur D. Little. ADL helps organizations create innovation in the full spectrum of their activities, from creating strategies and shaping organizational culture to developing cutting-edge products and technologies.

The responsibilities of global practice leaders at ADL include combining information with knowledge about its practices.

## 7.1 Distributed teams as the starting point

Arthur D. Little has offices in many parts of the world. This worldwide distribution and the focus of individual staff members on certain industries led in the early nineties to the question: "Are we one company? What are the common features of telecommunications and administrative experts?" A pilot project with Lotus Notes in 1995/96 quickly led to the realization "that the computer system was but one element in a broad initiative to maximize the potential of our knowledge resources. In addition to the hardware/software, we had to concern ourselves with issues of content, culture, and process. In fact, technology provided only about 20 percent of our overall solution."[188]

As a result of these early results, ADL set up two task forces with directors of different practices and providers of internal information. The goal was two-fold. First, ADL wanted to analyze current developments in management technology, particularly in consulting in order to come to a common understanding of knowledge management. Second, it wanted to test and determine the strategic importance and direction of knowledge management for its own development. The members of the task forces had to have very good knowledge of the corporate philosophy and the strategic goals of the firm. The first important result of the discussion – and the first important step in the introduction of knowledge management – was the regular involvement of top management in talks and joint meetings. The goal was to make sure that managers supported the initiative in the long-term. Staff members were acquainted with management's views and visions on knowledge management through presentations in an internal communications program and through articles in the company journal.

According to Arthur D. Little, the vision of knowledge management is combined with the idea of a "one company platform":

- From individual to institutional knowledge – simply, quickly, and globally.

- All staff members make an effort to contribute to the knowledge base for the benefit of the company and the customers.

- To be able to respond to the needs of customers faster and better than our competitors.

---

[188] Chait (1998), p. 84.

## 7.2 Content and culture are in the process of being assessed

According to the approach of ADL, "managing knowledge is a multidimensional process. It requires the effective concurrent management of four design fields: content, culture, process, and infrastructure."[189]

"Content" includes the task of identifying all elements of knowledge and of understanding the relative importance of each element to individuals, groups and corporate objectives. It is also important to analyze the context of different elements of knowledge and their actual or possible applications. These estimates are very important for setting priorities and creating plans. Both task forces handled this job company-wide.

The results were used as a basis to monitor the application of the explicit elements of knowledge that are accessible to all staff members world-wide through the IT application ADL Link. For this purpose, ADL introduced a system to track individuals' usage of and experiences with knowledge. So far, analyses of the behavior of usage have been carried out only by the knowledge management team in the USA. The results have not yet been published.

Arthur D. Little has recognized the importance of a cultural dimension for successful knowledge management.

The traditional culture of "industries" in the consulting business that focuses on generating billed days of consulting work dominates the cultural orientation of each consulting firm. For ADL, this meant the following: "For example, in our case, we are driven by what we call 'business impact' toward selling our services and keeping our people billable. In the end, that focus does not leave much time for knowledge management."[190]

At ADL offices in Germany, this focus leads to a comparatively bad image of learning, of internal service jobs, and of appearances at symposiums. Getting ahead in a consulting firm is based totally on work with customers alone.

The general corporate culture has been termed "network-oriented". This is illustrated by the fact that 90-95% of all co-workers quite willingly offer support and information during telephone calls, even though they have never met the caller in person. The philosophy of the German branch that was developed by the founder of ADL Germany, Tom Sommerlatte, is in accordance with the central motivation factors of the staff: team spirit, levels of freedom, great interest in jobs and responsibilities (handling challenging problems), high innovation, and a lower degree of career-focused ambitions. In this context, "you need knowledge management to avoid being too innovative: `Oh, a lot has been done already in this area`" is often an enlightening experience.

---

[189] Chait (1998).
[190] Chait (1998), pp. 86.

130

So far, an analysis of the company's corporate culture using a method developed by the ADL employee Peter Scott-Morgan called "Unwritten Rules of the Game" has been carried out only in the USA.

ADL attempts to indirectly influence cultural realities that function as barriers by taking steps in the areas of organizing knowledge management (process), rating performance, allocating earnings, and project budgeting.

## 7.3    ADL-Link: A straightforward intranet approach

ADL describes its activities to develop and make accessible the hardware and software basis of knowledge management as the design field "infrastructure". In this respect, ADL does not differ from other global companies that operate an Intranet through which they provide search possibilities and information. ADL Link is a Lotus Notes application hosted by a series of Domino servers and available to staff members globally via Netscape browsers.

**Fig. 7.2:    Homepage of ADL Intranet**

ADL's Global Director of Knowledge Management, Laurence P. Chait, realistically rates the importance of the technical infrastructure of knowledge management: "The bottom line here is that while technology is critical for effective knowledge management, it is only about 20 percent of the challenge."

Due to the current high rate of innovation in web applications, ADL follows a fast modular development strategy that allows developments or new applications to be incorporated on a monthly basis.

The ADL Link serves as a portal to knowledge repositories, information bulletins, collaboration tools and resource guides. The main aspects of knowledge accessible to all staff members can be divided into the following main categories: staff members, projects, tools and products, i.e., the firm's functional expertise.

The category "staff members" includes a global telephone directory with basic information on each person (title, department, etc.), detailed staff profiles with information on casework and additional qualifications, and staff resumés as text documents.

Casework is described in different categories. A "case summary" includes general management information, customer data, and brief job descriptions. The database also contains information on finances, participating staff members, and case abstracts as a case history. The case abstracts include detailed information on work and keywords encripted in ADL's industry code. In addition, there is information on the location of case documents and their accessibility, and on staff persons to contact for further information. Finally, users can download reference descriptions and regulations for their use.

In the products and tools section, users have access to the description of methods, training materials, analyses, reports, benchmarking data, and customer presentations. The user is also provided with templates, tools, and case proposals that are internally understood as a best practice.

This infrastructure ensures fast and simple global access to elements of knowledge. Frequent hyperlinks allow to quickly access relevant information in related areas. The usage of the ADL Link depends on the quality of its content. Staff members have to enter knowledge in a pre-defined process. This brings us to the fourth design field of knowledge management at ADL, the "process."

## 7.4 Elaborated knowledge roles complement the knowledge management process

The core concept of knowledge management at ADL comprises two essential domains: (1) The definition of the individual steps necessary to develop and maintain the knowledge base. (2) The description of roles required to be filled by the participants of knowledge management.

### 7.4.1 The process

The process steps defined by ADL describe the general management of different knowledge elements that have been identified as being relevant (consulting cases,

132

offers, etc.), summaries of staff members, customer information and presentation documents. Subprocesses, such as updating biographies or writing project abstracts, are considered routine processes.

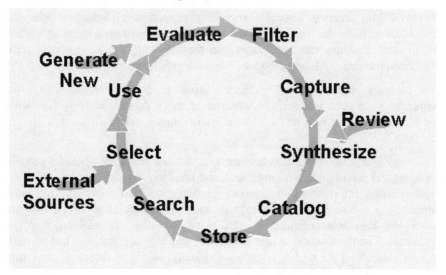

Fig. 7.3:    Process Steps of Knowledge Management at Arthur D. Little

## 7.4.2    The roles

To apply knowledge management, ADL defined the roles of "Knowledge Advocates", "Knowledge Stewards", and "Knowledge Coordinators". The central tasks of these roles are to ensure the lasting support of knowledge management by all members of the organisation, and to implement knowledge management in each practice/group. The original idea to fill the role of the „Knowledge Steward" without additional personnel had to be given up. However, due to more efficient processes in the long run, ADL hopes to manage with fewer consultants. Each practice/group finances the expenses for its "Knowledge Steward(s)" and, therefore, autonomously manages the tasks. In Germany, there are currently ten "Knowledge Stewards". A "Knowledge Steward" has to have professional know-how (industry, practice), communicative capabilities (interview skills), and capabilities to prepare and condense data and information. He has to be curious and persistent ("There must be something interesting."). Working exclusively as a "Knowledge Steward" is hard to reconcile with full dedication to the daily consulting business. This has been identified as a major problem, since so far, the prevailing corporate culture and career criteria have not promoted the fulfilment of this role by consultants. ADL has devised a new set of carreer stages for knowledge professionals to attract and retain high caliber personnel in these roles.

| Role | Description | Task | Effort |
|------|-------------|------|--------|
| Knowledge Coordinator | Strategic role to define, communicate, and coordinate knowledge management activities | Defines knowledge management roles, processes, and technological requirements<br><br>Informs knowledge stewards of knowledge management updates<br><br>Coordinates knowledge management development and input of content for a continent | 1-2 full-time staff members per continent |
| Knowledge Advocate (KA) | Top manager and expert | Represents practice/group when communicating the knowledge management requirements<br><br>Provides support when handling knowledge management activities and global coordination<br><br>Gives orientation in knowledge management | 1 KA per group of 50<br><br>5 % working time |
| Knowledge Steward | Operative role carry out knowledge management activities | Carries out the knowledge management process for practice/group<br><br>Informs practice/group of knowledge management procedures<br><br>Makes the connection between practice/group and the global knowledge management team<br><br>Ensures global coordination | 1 staff member per group of 50<br><br>50 % working time |

Fig. 7.4: Knowledge Management Roles

## 7.5 The Knowledge Steward

Due to the essential importance of the role of the "Knowledge Steward" the following section describes the main responsibilities:

- plan and carry out so-called "case debriefing" meetings in which the project is analysed critically, and experiences are collected (Fig. 7.5);
- initiate and ensure the creation of knowledge assets;
- initiate and ensure expenses to close knowledge gaps;
- study knowledge assets regarding quality and consistency;
- examine knowledge assets periodically, including updates, corrections, and discards;

- assess the benefits if including items in the knowledge database;

- inform co-workers of new knowledge assets;

- ensure global consistency;

- sanitize sensitive customer data from case studies;

- define and introduce the local roles, processes, and standards of knowledge management;

- hand in requirements to expand the system ADL Link;

- categorize and store knowledge assets (library card);

- extract erroneously placed items;

- share best practices.

**Case Debriefing :**
Systematic treatment of
project experiences .

Case debriefing" can be divided into three stages: At the beginning of a project data are continuously collected and analyzed. During the project knowledge assets are identified and captured. Debriefing sessions in the end serve the purpose to document all relevant contacts, lessons learned and dos and don'ts. The aim is to reflect project work for more efficient future project management.

**Fig. 7.5:    Case Debriefing**

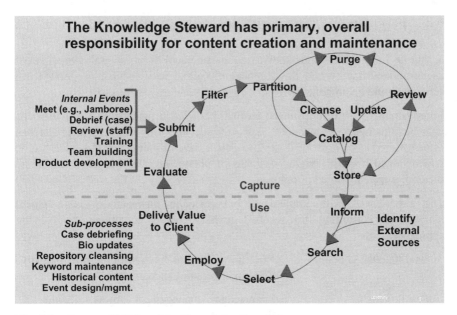

Fig. 7.6:    Responsibilities of the Knowledge Steward

The newly created roles at ADL were furnished with evaluation grids. These allow the firm to evaluate the performance in relation to the individual activities. The following table is an example of evaluation criteria for the role of "Knowledge Steward":

| Activity in Knowledge Management | Fulfills Requirements | Highly Exceeds Requirements |
| --- | --- | --- |
| Acquisition/Capture | Carries out the case debriefing process for the practice or department | Identifies and collects proactively relevant information on industries and practices during the case debriefing process |
| Dissemination | Informs the practice or department regularly of new content | Contributes continuously to improving productivity and/or quality |

Fig. 7.7: Evaluation Criteria for the Knowledge Steward

## 7.6 Principles and qualitative success stories

Arthur D. Little understands knowledge management as an integral component of its corporate strategy and development: "Without knowledge management our services would be unthinkable."

Improvements that were achieved through knowledge management activities can only be illustrated by anecdotes. For example, the time required to prepare an offer was reduced from 1.5-2 days to half a day. In particular, this acceleration was obtained because lengthy searches or phone inquiries became either more focused, were eliminated or reduced.

The experiences with implementing knowledge management in a global management consulting firm resulted in the following guidelines of successful approaches:

| | |
|---|---|
| Global, Global, Global | Priorities and plans have to be defined globally. The implementation occurs on a local level. |
| Roles, no jobs | Knowledge management roles should be distributed; one person should handle knowledge management and non-knowledge management. |
| Roles to be taken seriously | Knowledge workers are rated according to their performance regarding knowledge management activities. |
| No "One Size Fits All" | Each practice/group must decide globally how it implements knowledge management roles and processes. |
| "In the sweat of one's brow" | Knowledge management is hard work. |
| All roads lead to the link | All knowledge elements are managed through ADL Link. |
| Community | We have to be an active community of interests. |
| Security | The "Network Security Agreement" is our law. |
| Ownership | We have to protect the rights of ownership. |

Consulting firms generally require a systematic management of the central corporate resource "knowledge." Arthur D. Little has begun to implement a strategy that is applicable to the entire firm. The strengths of the approach clearly include the definition of the relevant knowledge elements, and the establishment of clear process steps with appropriate roles.

The original idea to have the consultants fill these roles was not carried out. This is where we have identified a potential area for improvement: To secure important experiences, project work should be connected better to knowledge management activities. ADL should not only apply the evaluation criteria of knowledge management to all staff members, but should also design the so-called "soft" aspects of the corporate culture actively. In addition, the application of the desired collaboration tool to support teamwork and the utilisation of knowledge suitable for knowledge management activities are supplied at the same time.

Strengths were seen in the definition of relevant knowledge elements, the establishment of process steps of knowledge management, the definition of required roles of knowledge management, the establishment of a catalog of criteria to evaluate performance and simple and comfortable IT platform "ADL Link".

On the other hand side potentials were identified: Better integration into daily business operations and project work, increase in routine processes and better incorporation into the corporate culture.

# 8 Cultural Change Triggers Best Practice Sharing - British Aerospace plc.

*Peter Heisig, Jens Vorbeck*

In 1997, British Aerospace plc had global sales of 25.6 billion DM (£ 8.6 billion). With its 47,900 employees, it is the fourth largest manufacturer of aerospace and defence systems in the world. In November 1999, British Aerospace merged with Marconi Electronic Systems to form BAE SYSTEMS; with sales £ 12 billion and an order book of £ 36 billion. With 100,000 people in nine home markets (UK, USA, Canada, Germany, France, Italy, Australia, Saudi-Arabia, Sweden) across the globe, BAE SYSTEMS is the world's second largest defence company.

In 1998 at the time of data collection for this case study, British Aerospace was divided into two sections: the commercial sector that includes the business unit "British Aerospace Airbus" and the defence sector. Only the defence sector achieved a balanced operating revenue. The commercial sector was able to reduce losses from almost £ 400 mill. in 1992 to £ 20 mill. in 1997. As it is typical of the aerospace and defence systems industry's development of products in long-term international and national projects, British Aerospace plc participates in 29 larger international partnerships or joint ventures and, additionally, in 50 larger global programs.[191]

| | |
|---|---|
| **BRITISH AEROSPACE** | |
| | *Industry:* Aerospace and Defence Systems |
| | *Business Process:* Management of Improvement and Change |
| | *Employees:* 47.900 (1998) |
| Since 1999: | *Turnover:* £ 8.6 billion (1998) |
| **BAE SYSTEMS** http://www.baesystems.com | *KM Best Practice:* Cultural Change Program Virtual University Best Practice Centre |

**Fig. 8.1:    Company Overview - British Aerospace plc., since 1999 BAE SYSTEMS**

Changing market conditions - characterised on the demand side by vigorous cuts in national defence budgets since the beginning of the nineties and on the supply side by the merger of the large US aircraft corporations Boeing and McDonnell Douglas - have forced British Aerospace to make internal changes. In addition, the company was operating at a very low margin of profit in the early nineties. British Aerospace's stock price at that time thus stood at about £ 1 per share. In the

---

[191]    British Aerospace Annual Report (1997).

meantime, the price per share has risen to £17 (1998). In 1999 a share splitting took place on a one to four ratio. In the early 90's, British Aerospace was still characterised at the management level and in its organisational structures and processes by the holding structure created in the late eighties. "It is the problem of runaway divisional and staff 'fiefdoms'. Lacking sufficient unity and internal coherence, these firms pay too heavy a price for decentralisation. (...) BAe's fiercely independent fiefdoms spring from its historical origins in the late eighties as a holding company formed by the merger of disparate pieces of the British aircraft industry."[192]

## 8.1   The cultural change program: Benchmark BAe

The former CEO and chairman of British Aerospace plc, Sir Richard Evans, was convinced that the individual divisions of British Aerospace would only be competitive as a synergistic unit, not as excellent but solitary production units. After intense and controversial discussion, the board of British Aerospace turned the initial idea of sharing capabilities into a vision of the "Benchmark BAe Program." The goal of "Benchmark BAe" was to develop the company into a model for the entire industry: "British Aerospace was 'dedicated to working together and with our partners, and to becoming the benchmark for our industry, setting the standard for customer satisfaction, technology, financial performance, and quality in all that we do."[193]

Today in 2000, within BAE SYSTEMS the cultural change programme is under review taking into account the British Aerospace cultural change programme and the equivalent initiatives at Marconi Electronic Systems. The following paragraph will focus on the status in 1998 of the cultural change program in British Aerospace only.

### 8.1.1   From values to operational goals

The next step of the cultural change program in British Aerospace involved discussions with the two or three top managers in each business unit. The managers were to explain which characteristics could be promoted and shared to define the conditions that would contribute to achieving the goals of "Benchmark BAe." These discussions with a total of 130 managers resulted in the following five basic values:

1. people are our greatest strength,

2. customers are our highest priority,

---

[192]   Evans (1998).
[193]   Evans (1998).

3. partnerships are our future,

4. innovation and technology is our competitive edge, and

5. performance is the key to winning.

In the third step, the 130 top-level managers discussed these values with each other. Then, middle-level management was included in this process.

But, the simplicity of the statements conceals the far more important process of the top managers of the various divisions of British Aerospace, who, with their "cherished histories and strong identities"[194], had just jointly come to a homogenous understanding of their tasks. The goals of the discussion that was carried out on all levels of the company were to break up traditional ways of thinking and to promote questions that eventually led to a new sense of identity and purpose.

New values also require new behaviour characterised by openness and personal candour. These are traits that had previously not widely been seen in the upper management levels because "the fiefdom mentality went so deep that many of them had never met before or even spoken on the phone."[195]

Rather than discussing "values", the lower management levels discussed specific examples of behaviour, specific methods, and specific practices. This led to the establishment of five teams that were each staffed by twelve of the 130 top-level managers. Each team worked on one of the five corporate values. The goal was to develop a company-wide plan of values that would then be disseminated to the different business units. This plan is understood as an ongoing business plan named 'value plan' that contains specific goals for each of the five corporate values. This plan is reviewed continually against the actual performance and adjusted. So the value plan has become an extremely effective tool for managing the business.

For example, an action from the "people" value is to make benefits, which had previously been restricted to the managerial level available to all employees of British Aerospace (personal development plans, car leasing programs, and health insurance). The company produced a video biannually for all the employees that portrays the actual status of their efforts and the respective targets. The personal development plan (PDP) consists of two parts: (1) objectives linked to the business unit value plan and agreed upon with the particular manager, and (2) an individual career plan.

---

[194] Evans (1998).

[195] Evans (1998).

### 8.1.2 Monitoring and coaching

British Aerospace developed and applied an evaluation tool that is based on the predefined corporate values to verify the 130 top managers' pattern of management. The tool is used by the managers themselves to judge whether their behaviour corresponds to and thus promotes the values. The tool was introduced as an Intranet application. A video portrays the self-evaluation of CEO Evans. The result of the evaluation reveals a specific ranking to the respective manager, the CEO, and the project manager. The PDP includes specific coaching measures to improve the individual pattern of management. In a further step, the next lower level of the company's hierarchy with approximately 1,500 managers will be included. For a later stage, British Aerospace aims at 360° feedback.

The BEST program was developed for the Change Management Program "Benchmark BAe" to service the learning and training requirements of the senior management. The program reaches out to all 1,500 managers, and includes the following aspects in five units (length: 1 x 4 days and 4 x 3 days):

- Understand the requirements of the business, the team, and the individual to eventually become a model for the industry;

- Apply efficient managerial abilities in order to manage change;

- Complete a 360° feedback (peer, manager, staff member) before and after the training;

- Show the necessary understanding and the required abilities to coach and support "Team Value Planning";

- Realise the importance of behaviour guided by values and learn the required techniques and tools to support exemplary (benchmark) behaviour;

- Conduct a self-assessment and 360° feedback and receive an EFQM evaluation to improve performance;

- Understand "value planning" and apply the lessons learned in BEST in daily business.

An international program for British Aerospace employees who worked outside the UK was developed and run in 1999. The experience gained in BEST is to be incorporated into management development programs.

The commitment of the top management was ensured with the following measures:

- Active role model of the board members.

- Monitoring of the change by top management itself.

- Integration of the expectations of the 1,500 middle managers by intensive discussions.

## 8.2 British Aerospace Virtual University

In creating the Virtual University (VU) in May 1997, British Aerospace positioned people, knowledge and know-how at the core of the company's growth, in support of the business strategy to become the Benchmark Company in a highly competitive and consolidating global aerospace sector. Knowledge and innovation embedded in products and customer services are valuable company assets in sustaining business activities, attracting investment, and winning new international business. Today the VU is fully operating as an extended enterprise, twinning academic and business excellence, to build the capability and skills of the workforce through lifelong learning, research and technology and best practice.[196]

Strategic partnerships are crucial as no one has a monopoly on knowledge. Collaboration between the world's best in academia and enterprise on clearly articulated business needs, brings leading edge knowledge to the VU programmes, through jointly developed content, best practice and internationally recognised accreditation. The Virtual University includes the Faculty of Learning, the Faculty of Engineering and Manufacturing Technology, the International Business School, Research and Technology Centres, and the Best Practice Centre at Farnborough. British Aerospace has appointed experienced managers from the business units as deans and directors of the university.

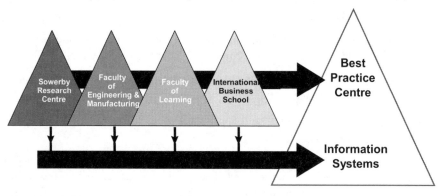

Fig. 8.2:     Virtual University in 1998

In May 2000, the BAE SYSTEMS Virtual University has won the U.S.A. Corporate University Xchange Excellence Award, co-sponsored by Financial Times, for its innovative utilisation of technology to create a continuous learning

---

[196]     Kenney-Wallace (1999).

environment for all 100,000 employees. The Virtual University has developed intelligent research and retrieval techniques, such as Autonomy, to bring any user a 'one stop shop' of pertinent, timely information needed, saving hours of unnecessary surfing – critical for a large geographically dispersed company. "Creating, sharing and leveraging knowledge is fundamental to competitiveness for any organisation in this era of globalisation. I am delighted that this Award fully recognises BAE SYSTEMS' commitment to lifelong learning and the development of talents of all our people and applying technology to accelerate innovation and share business benefit across the Company. These vital components of BAE SYSTEMS drive towards competitiveness and becoming the industry benchmark."[197]

The Virtual University is essentially the organisational umbrella for learning, research and development and best practice and ensures synergy across all areas of the company. In 1998, the Virtual University was staffed with twenty employees; four of whom co-ordinate the best practice centre. Today the Virtual University continues within BAE SYSTEMS endorsing the crucial importance attached to developing, sharing and applying knowledge throughout the new global company.

## 8.3    Best Practice Sharing at British Aerospace

The understanding of knowledge management at British Aerospace can be described as a best practice approach: "To capture and share best or good practices throughout the company". We understand this concept of best practice in the following way: "If you have a practice or process that has worked (i.e., has created something successful) then everybody should be able to use it as well." "Best Practice Sharing" is derived from the values "partnership" and "performance." As mentioned above, business planning at British Aerospace is based on five specific corporate values. The corporate goals are thus based on internal and external benchmarks. The focus on "partnership" helps to create an atmosphere of trust and support. This atmosphere promotes the exchange of information and knowledge among staff members, departments, business units, and external partners, such as customers and suppliers. It also helps eliminate the "not-invented-here" syndrome. The adherence to the values and the achievement of goals are monitored by the peer evaluation at the managerial levels and with the 360° feedback in the future.

## 8.4    Best Practice Sharing in 1998

Organisationally, knowledge management is incorporated into the BAE SYSTEMS Virtual University. Knowledge management at BAE SYSTEMS is defined through virtual centres of excellence that are the focal points. A virtual

---

[197]    John Weston, CEO BAE SYSTEMS

centre of excellence is characterised by the physical or virtual combination of internal and external "elements". This virtual centre combines two main dimensions of knowledge. The tacit and implicit dimension as well as internal and external dimension.

Internal elements are the community of experts and best practices. Best practices include the users (staff members of British Aerospace), the processes, knowledge bases (e.g., databases), and other facilities of British Aerospace. External elements or partners are seen in the areas of research and development, in other industrial companies, in external best practices, and in learning from others. The experts with their knowledge represent the tacit dimension. The explicit knowledge is documented in the Best Practice Database, which is accessible via the Intranet (Fig. 8.3).

Virtual centres of excellence are a response to the need to create focal points for learning; the transfer and sharing of best practices are to be channelled internally and externally. In addition, the centres are to function as knowledge centres. The overall goal is to develop and maintain the company's core capabilities at a world-class level.

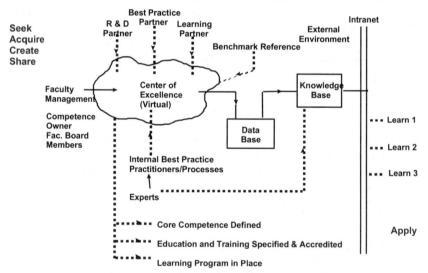

Fig. 8.3:    Knowledge Management at British Aerospace in 1998

### 8.4.1 The benchmarking & best practice centre acts as knowledge broker

In accordance with the understanding of knowledge management, the best practice centre acts as a broker of knowledge that identifies and documents best practices both internally and externally. It makes this information accessible through the Intranet and workshops. The application of these best practices is assured by the integration of these benchmarks into the definition of the value plan and the personal development plan (PDP). This process design assures an integrated knowledge management process.

The Benchmarking & Best Practice Centre has the following goals:

- maintains an enabling framework to support benchmarking and best practice sharing;

- provides an electronic Benchmarking & Best Practice Library service;

- supports the establishment of special interest groups and communities of practice;

- supports best practice links with National and International organisations (e.g. CBI, SBAC, American Productivity and Quality Centre);

- supports National benchmarking and best practice campaigns (e.g. CBI's Fit for the Future programme);

- maintains a central web-based repository of internal and external benchmarking and best practice data;

- maintains a Company best practice web-site;

- supports the establishment and management of external benchmarking partnerships;

- maintains corporate membership of relevant external benchmarking organisations;

- carries out research into Knowledge Management and supporting web-based technology;

- sponsors and co-ordinates Business Excellence and Best Practice Learning events.

To facilitate the use of the best practice web site, simple electronic forms (best practice templates) and aids (search engines, agents) are offered. In addition, staff members facilitate the exchange of knowledge in workshops where simple questions are asked ("What are you willing to share? What do you need or like to learn?"). The results are published in the intranet to stimulate mutual exchange. Explicit knowledge is shared via the intranet while tacit knowledge will be shared during the workshops.

146

### 8.4.2    How to structure knowledge and best practices

To guarantee easy retrieval of information, knowledge and best practices a business-oriented structure has been put in place in 1998. To structure the knowledge of internal and external best practices, the centre uses acknowledged management-oriented models, e.g., those of the European Foundation for Quality Management (EFQM), Probe of CBI, and "Investors in People" (IiP). The results of EFQM self-assessments are published on the web site to make good practice methods accessible to everyone. British Aerospace supplements this structured information with general contextual data (e.g., what?, how?, why?) in order to promote the transfer of knowledge (Fig. 8.4).

## Knowledge Management

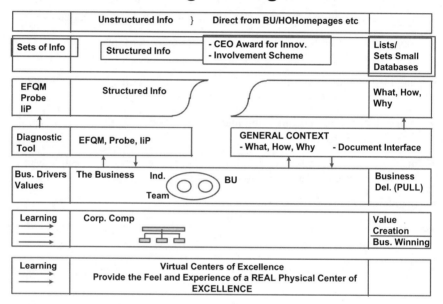

Fig. 8.4:    Aspects of Knowledge at British Aerospace in 1998

## 8.5    Moving forward to 2000

The commitment of BAE SYSTEMS to best practice sharing has been underlined by John Weston, the Chief Executive of BAE SYSTEMS: "Adoption of best practice is no longer optional for business. In fact we believe that a key discriminator for companies is now based on the speed at which they acquire, implement and realise the benefits from best practice in order to support the necessary change demanded by an ever increasingly competitive market place."

BAE SYSTEMS current approach in 2000 to best practice exploitation is a balanced one recognising that sharing ideas and creating new knowledge is as much about behaviours and culture as it is about process and databases. The approach is based on four key elements (Fig. 8.5): Involvement (Internal/External Networks), External Reference Models, Communication & Recognition, and Tools, Processes & Measures. A six-step process is used to help guide the selection, sharing and implementation of best practices, which have the greatest potential benefit for the company.

By the end of 1999 the best practice database contained over 300 best practice cases and a wide range of activities to support best practice sharing are undertaken. The latest business excellence learning day on April 13, 2000 was attended not only by 140 physical visitors but around 1400 attendees on the virtual forum worldwide.

**Fig. 8.5:    BAE SYSTEMS Benchmarking and Best Practice Framework in 2000**

# 9 Sophisticated Information Technology to Promote Knowledge Sharing and Communication - Booz Allen & Hamilton

*Jens Vorbeck, Dr.Rolf Habbel*

Booz Allen & Hamilton (BA&H) is one of the leading international management and technology consulting firms that was founded in 1914. In 1999, it had sales of $1.8 billion.

| BOOZ·ALLEN & HAMILTON | Industry: | Consulting |
|---|---|---|
| | Business Process: | Development and Delivering of Services |
| | Employees: | 9,800 |
| | Sales: | $ 1.8 Bill (1999) |
| http:// www .bah. com | KM Best Practice: | KOL – Knowledge On-Line<br>Knowledge Sharing Barriers<br>Corporate Culture and Management |

**Fig. 9.1:    Company Overview - Booz, Allen & Hamilton**

Booz Allen & Hamilton is a private company that internationally employs more than 9,800 people in 100 offices. Its consulting services are divided into two key business areas: worldwide commercial business and worldwide technology business.

## 9.1    Chief Knowledge Officers in each practice

Consulting firms, such as BA&H, live both by spreading their knowledge and experience and reincorporating their experience with customers back into the company. The body of knowledge BA&H offers customers is immense. However, there are many staff members, particularly those who are new to the firm, whose knowledge gained through personal experience is comparatively small. Only the consistent use of the knowledge of all staff members creates the basis for a competitive organization.

During its strategic realignment "Vision 2000", BA&H initiated a program of knowledge management in 1993/94 that included the development of an online knowledge database (KOL). Furthermore, "Vision 2000" focused on positioning BA&H on the market, doubling its growth rate, estabiilising multidimensional or interdisciplinary emphases, and directing the company towards larger international corporations. The clear focus on target clients resulted in a situation in which 85% of all sales are made through former or present clients' follow-up orders.

To strengthen the knowledge management program organizationally, BA&H created the position of "Chief Knowledge Officer" (CKO). In each of its eight practices, BA&H set up an internationally responsible team of roughly four persons (one part-time project manager and two to three full-time staff persons) who were to enter existing knowledge (not older than two years) into the KOL database. In addition, BA&H set up so-called "Innovation Teams" or "Intellectual Capital Teams" for each practice. Their task was to develop new consulting products and methodologies. To gain the support of BA&H's roughly 240 Partners, i.e., the owners, the company organized an "IC Fair" that enabled the Partners to learn about selected topics. The topics had been selected by the CKO and the managers of the various practices. In summary, the implementation of the knowledge management program depended heavily upon the personal commitment of the responsible partners.

## 9.2 Knowledge sharing barriers guide the way to new solutions

As part of knowledge management, BA&H identified five so-called "unnatural acts" that occur as barriers between the idea and the implementation of knowledge management.

1. Collaboration: Build on the ideas of others.
2. Application: Admit that the thoughts of someone else might be better than one's own thoughts.
3. Share: Share one's best thoughts – often representing a personal competitive advantage – with others.
4. Invest: Provide the infrastructure that allows knowledge management to occur in the first place.
5. Improve: Continuously develop new ideas and pursue yesterday's ideas.

Although the culture of consulting firms makes it comparatively easy to establish a system of knowledge management. these five "unnatural acts" not only identify barriers, but also point to solutions[198]:

**1. Collaboration:**
- Hire new staff members selectively
- Assemble the project team according to skills and developmental objectives and wishes

---

[198]  Rüter (1998).

| | |
|---|---|
| **2. Application:** | • Program for cultural change |
| | • Develop and demonstrate specific advantages in daily business |
| **3. Share:** | • Plan home office days to exchange knowledge with co-workers and Partners |
| | • Organize Intellectual Capital Days with lectures and discussions on selected topics of the future, the results of which are then entered into the KOL database |
| **4. Invest:** | • Introduce the intranet-based knowledge online database |
| | • Expand database fo expert skills |
| **5. Improve:** | • Introduce teams for innovation and intellectual capital |
| | • Initiate Innovation Program to identify important topics of the future |

## 9.3    The BA&H approach to knowledge management

BA&H has an explicit understanding of knowledge management. This is expressed in the company's definition of knowledge and the core process of knowledge.

BA&H understands knowledge as "an ability that reflects the understanding of how something works [and] what the future will be like". This view pragmatically combines procedural and content-related aspects of knowledge with each other (Fig. 9.2).

Knowledge management is an "institutionalized iterative process that creates knowledge, shares and spreads knowledge, uses and applies knowledge, and improves and develops knowledge." This concept of knowledge management reflects the corresponding concepts of many other consulting firms.

According to BA&H, knowledge management is the "conditio sine qua non." This condition is characterized by the collection of the intellectual ability of an organization that makes decisions either about specific competitive advantages or the daily business routine. In this context BA&H describes four areas: best practices, lessons learned, products and services, and history and success stories. Furthermore, knowledge management includes the development of processes that standardize intellectual capability (structure, presentation, availability, and accessibility). Finally, the company provides knowledge via technological platforms.

From a user-oriented point of view, it also seems important to refer to the organization, "the knowledge enterprise, ... an organization that uses knowledge for lasting competitive advantages, and ... that has identified knowledge as a strategic resource." BA&H points out that it is necessary to combine conceptual approaches with the targeted implementation of knowledge management. It is clear to BA&H that knowledge management needs a clear objective to be implemented successfully.

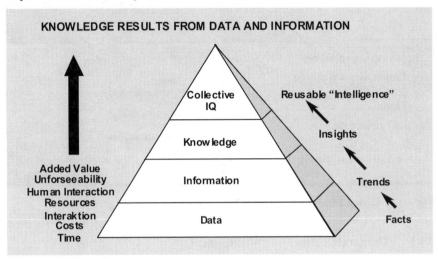

Fig. 9.2:    Definition of Knowledge at BA&H

## 9.4    A "Consultant's Culture" facilitates cooperative knowledge exchange

The successful implementation of knowledge management at BA&H is due in part to the identification of design fields: "The regular creation of knowledge requires organizational and human networks, particularly in four areas".

152

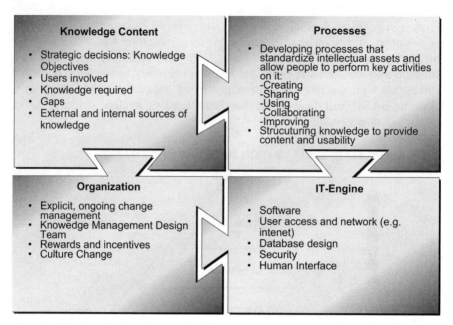

**Fig. 9.3:** Design Fields of Knowledge Management at BA&H

## 9.4.1 Corporate culture and management

When asked to describe the company's culture, our contacts mentioned the following attributes and characteristics:

- competitive and achievement oriented,

- up or on careers paths,

- idea of networking,

- open (first name basis in the entire company, the open door),

- ability to handle conflicts,

- everything is handled by teams – practical arguments count.

Communication between the (at most) six hierarchical levels takes place directly, without barriers, and in a project-oriented way. This requires a co-operative style of management that is characterized by a transfer of responsibility to lower levels. This is to ensure that staff members actively express their opinions and assume responsibility as early as possible.

## 9.4.2 Career plans, incentive systems, 360° evaluation

BA&H has realized that the staff members' careers are the site where the company has the best leverage. Therefore, the development of the organization and thus the development of intellectual capital significantly influences professional careers.

Among other things, BA&H applies an appraisal system. This includes self-assessment and an assessment by an objective appraisor whether a particular staff member has contributed to corporate knowledge. The appraisor talks to approximately fifteen people about each consultant: secretaries, assistants, co-workers, and Partners. This evaluation takes place annually and helps decide upon career future, development initiatives and bonus payments. The appraisee, the consultant, and her or his mentor discuss the results in detail.

## 9.5 Knowledge On-Line – BA&H's intranet solution

In parallel to the strategy "Vision 2000" that was initiated in 1993/94, BA&H introduced in the summer of 1994 the program "Knowledge Online". In the spring of 1995, the roll-out was combined with a communications campaign, and in the summer of 1996 the program was presented to the public.

As in the roll-out of the first version in 1995, the roll-out of KOL 2 was accompanied by a comprehensive framework. This was done to support usage and personal identification with this tool. Staff members received two installation disks that enabled everyone to access the system and that explained the benefits of the application in an interactive multimedia show. A KOL newsletter, a roadshow, a KOL hotline and extensive internal marketing programs were organized to continuously promote KOL.

Knowledge Online is an intranet-based database …

- … to store and share knowledge globally,
- … to create access to the employees' thinking,
- … to exchange and spread knowledge and new ideas,
- … that represents a communication instrument … which

… is accessible by each staff member of Booz Allen & Hamilton.

The content of KOL is typical for consulting firms: bids, reports on industries and functions, profiles of experts and resumés of consultants, products and methods, discussion forums, telephone and office directories, and a market of ideas.

Contributions to KOL are entered by partners, principals and project managers of the firm. The Partners both pay attention to the quality of documents and the content, and check whether confidentiality agreements are observed. Each practice additionally set up editorial teams that check the keywords (some are given, some can be selected freely) and indices.

**Knowledge Management Marketing Program** :
A campaign to internally promote the introduction of knowledge management.

Well thought out marketing campaigns will improve tolerance and acceptance for KM introductions.
Respective components could be: Early information, user participation (if possible in the design of the system), easy installation of IT solutions, an appealing design of the user interface, especially motivated pilot team members, success stories and interactive tutorial systems, etc.

**Fig. 9.4:  Best Practice - Knowledge Management Marketing Program**

The consultants create KOL documents in their free time, simply because it helps their career. However, the development of KOL documents is also partly recognized as an aspect of marketing, as abstracts of reports are sometimes published as articles.

The Intellectual Capital Teams, of which there is one per practice, are responsible for identifying and creating new and state of the art know-how. At the end of each year, they present their results, and can suggest publication in respected journals (e.g., Strategy & Business or HBR).

To assess the use of the system, BA&H evaluates access according to topics ("Which topic was accessed?"), the age and kind of document, and the position (Consultant, Project Manager, Partner) of the user. The rate of usage illustrates the success of BA&H's efforts: 96% of 3.500 potential users in the business unit Worldwide Commercial Services use the system annually, 55% use it monthly. The users are equally divided among all levels.

During the annual evaluation of each staff member, BA&H also evaluates the authorship of KOL documents ("Who did what?").

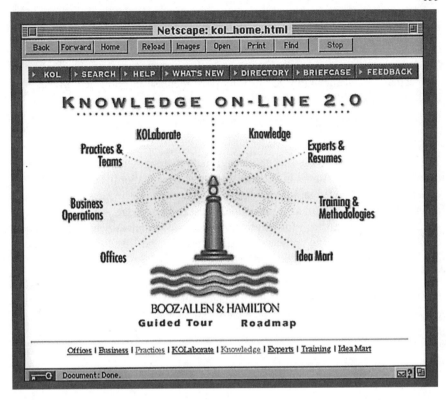

Fig. 9.5:  Knowledge On-line

## 9.6  Experiences with the system

Five years of experience with KOL has revealed that a continuous feedback of success is highly important to ensure a high rate of usage. It is equally important to secure the support of the partners (owners) as "power brokers" or "knowledge champions."

In practice, KOL is often used to identify and localize internal experts. As experience has shown, the users less often access the "yellow pages" to retrieve relevant information, but rather look for documents which clearly demonstrate the author's competence: "Reading is often not enough. You have to talk to people. The documents bridge the gap between experts and novices." According to BA&H, "such a system cannot ever replace personal contact."

At BA&H, cultural barriers that other global companies have quite often encountered when dealing with knowledge management have not turned out to be barriers. BA&H attributed this to its selective hiring process that focuses on applicants with similar high-level education (e.g. PhDs, business schools), international experience, language skills, social competence, and – in part – professional experience in industry.

The strong connection between careers ("up or on") and the contribution to intellectual capital inevitably led to a massive increase in published articles and books (increase of 90%), and quotes from BA&H documents (increase of 50 %).

Personally, the users of the KOL database benefit by saving time and learning faster.

The implementation of knowledge management at Booz Allen & Hamilton had a decisive advantage: The main product and its documentation (KOL) are also the core aspects of knowledge. Knowledge management therefore does not necessitate repetitive tasks when collecting and documenting knowledge – as is the case in manufacturing industries, for example. Adequate technological infrastructure combined with internal processes that preserve the results of knowledge production can be implemented fairly easily.

The barriers that may be typical for the corporate culture of consulting firms - and that might have impaired knowledge management - were removed in a way that is quite common in this industry. This pattern can be applied to other industries only with great care.

# 10 Measuring Intangible Assets for Sustainable Business Growth - Celemi AB, Medium-Sized and Fast Growing

*Peter Heisig, Janet Runeson*

Celemi International AB, "Celemi" is a medium-sized consulting company for change management with approximately 80 employees. Its headquarters are in Malmö and it has offices in Sweden (Stockholm), Belgium (Brugges), the UK (Guildford), the USA (Simsbury and Chicago), Australia (Melbourne), New Zealand (Auckland) and Finland (Espoo). In 1997, Celemi International AB had gross sales of about SKr 98 million. In that year, Celemi was recognized as one of the 500 fastest growing companies in Europe. Since 1993 the number of employees has increased eight-fold. During the same period, sales have almost quadrupled (from SKr 23 million in 1993 to SKr 98 million).

**CELEMI**
THE POWER OF LEARNING

http://www.celemi.se

| | |
|---|---|
| *Industry:* | **Consulting** |
| *Business Process:* | **Strategic Management and Management of Financial and Intangible Assests** |
| *Employees:* | **100 and 200 - 300 free agents worldwide** |
| *Sales:* | **98 Mio. SKr (1997)** |
| *KM Best Practice:* | **Intangible Asset Monitor** |

**Fig. 10.1: Company Overview - Celemi AB**

Celemi's learning concept design focuses on improving the understanding of the business that impacts on the effectiveness of organizations. The center of active learning methods is the promotion of communication between people, departments, and divisions of an organization. The pedagogical principles are described by the chief developer Klas Mellander in "The Power of Learning"[199]. Celemi's most well-known learning tools are: Decision Base, Apples & Oranges, Livon, Celesta and Tango. These tools are used to help create "big picture" understanding in a wide range of companies. Price-Waterhouse Coopers, Daimler Chrysler, Siemens, and 3M are just some of Celemi's customers.

The main emphasis of our case study on Celemi International AB was placed on experience with the Intangible Asset Monitor. This monitor is used by the company to measure financial and intangible assets and to compare these figures

---

[199]   Mellander (1993).

with strategic target values. Celemi has used this evaluation tool since 1995. For the first time the annual report of 1997 included an evaluation of business trends that was related to the strategic business plan. The CEO, Mrs. Barchan, emphasised that applying knowledge is one of the central aspects of the daily business routine.

## 10.1  Open corporate culture

Corporate culture at Celemi has been described as open and lacking in hierarchies. There are no titles or positions, only responsibilities and assignments. This openness also applies to the exchange of information. For example, there are weekly meetings at each office open to every staff person. The results of these Monday morning meetings are published by each location in the intranet the same day. All information is accessible except for the minutes of board meetings and personnel data.

Another aspect we noticed during our visit in Malmö was the highly simplified office layout. The open atmosphere is created by high narrow windows looking out onto the hallway.

The focus of this case study is also influenced by the fact that the Swedish Council of Service Industries advised its members in 1994 to use the concepts and methods to measure intangible assets developed under the direction of Sveiby in their annual reports. In addition, Celemi is an excellent example of the many small and medium-sized service companies that contribute greatly to employment in Europe's developed economies.

## 10.2  Introduction of the Intangible Assets Monitor

The introduction of the Intangible Assets Monitor at Celemi resulted from meetings in the early 1990's with Dr. Karl Erik Sveiby (then a doctoral student in Stockholm, nowadays a professor and consultant residing in Australia), who was looking for a business tool that fit his way of evaluating intangible assets. He contacted Celemi for this reason.

During the joint development of the management simulation TANGO, the board of Celemi decided to apply Sveiby's method to internal evaluation and strategy planning tasks. Dr. Sveiby has conducted annual audits at Celemi since 1995.

The development of the Intangible Assets Monitor was based on the realization that traditional financial statements do not reflect the essential assets of Celemi:

- "Where was it reflected that we were a team of highly skilled professionals who provided effective services to our clients?

- Where would a stakeholder be able to assess the value of the unique learning processes that we were creating for our clients?

- Where did we account the value of our loyal and growing customer base?"[200]

It is important to emphasize that Celemi searches for and tries new methods to improve the monitoring of corporate performance.

In the first step, the company identified the following three core areas which – according to the board – would result in competitive advantages and which the company should measure or monitor in the future:

- "Our Customers: based on the value provided by the growth, strength and loyalty of our customer base;

- Our Organisation: based on the value derived from our systems, processes, creation of new products and even management style;

- Our People: based on the value to the company provided by the growth and development of employee capabilities, and how well these capabilities match customer needs."[201]

## 10.3 The Intangible Assets Monitor at Celemi AB

The Intangible Assets Monitor[202] reflects visible capital resources ("our financial capital") in the first column and intangible assets in the next three columns. Intangible assets are categorized into external structure, i.e., "our customers", internal structure, i.e., "our organisation", and competence, i.e., "our people" (Fig. 10.2).

The following indicators are assigned to three main categories: growth/renewal, efficiency, and stability. Since 1997, the values of these primary categories have been graded on a scale from 0 to 1000 and have then been aggregated into a performance indicator. These evaluation scales were derived from the strategic business plan. The basic idea of this assessment stems from the consideration that a performance indicator of each index number between 500 and 600 represents a performance level that corresponds to the corporate strategy. A value of 1000 means that the result outclasses the plan by far. A value of 100 reflects very poor performance. For example, an annual increase in revenue of 100% would be valued at 1000, while a 10% increase would be represented by the value 100. A turnover rate of 20% in experts diametrically opposes the stability of the company, and thus results in the value 100. A turnover rate of 6% would be much more

---

[200]    Barchan (1998).
[201]    Barchan (1998 ).
[202]    Celimi (1998).

favourable, and would therefore be represented by the value 1000. Fig. 10.4 shows the evaluation of the indicators during the period 1995 to 1997.

Celemi Intangible Asset Monitor

| **Tangible Assets** | | | **Intangible Assets** | | | | | | | | |
|---|---|---|---|---|---|---|---|---|---|---|---|
| **Our Financial Capital** | | | **Our Customers** (External Structure) | | | **Our Organization** (Internal Structure) | | | **Our People** (Competence) | | |
| | 1997 | 1996 | | 1997 | 1996 | | 1997 | 1996 | | 1997 | 1996 |
| **Growth/Renewal** | | | **Growth/Renewal** | | | **Growth/Renewal** | | | **Growth/Renewal** | | |
| Equity growth | **26 %** | 30 % | Revenue Growth | **22 %** | 50 % | Organization-Enhancing Customers (17) | **49 %** | 44 % | Average Professional Competence (3,8), Years | **8.0** | 7.0 |
| Net Investment Ratio (12,14) | **55 %** | 63 % | Image-Enhancing Customers (11) | **70 %** | 46 % | Revenues from New Products (23) | **71 %** | 70 % | Competence-Enhancing Customers (4) | **65 %** | 46 % |
| | | | | | | Intangible Investments % Value Added (12,29) | **27 %** | 27 % | Growth in Professional Competence (10) | **47 %** | 61 % |
| | | | | | | | | | Experts with Post-Secondary Degree (5,7) | **68 %** | 66 % |
| **Efficiency** | | | **Efficiency** | | | **Efficiency** | | | **Efficiency** | | |
| Profit Margin (18) | **4.2 %** | 5.5 % | Revenues per Customer (25), TSEK | **269** | 245 | Proportion of Administrative Staff (2,20) | **21 %** | 16 % | Value Added per Expert (8.16.29), TSK | **753** | 728 |
| Net Return on Equity (15) | **26 %** | 36 % | | | | Revenues per Administrative Staff (2,16,24), TSEK | **8,478** | 12,246 | Value Added per Employee (16,29), TSEK | **620** | 629 |
| Profit/Value Added (19,21,29) | **13 %** | 22 % | | | | | | | | | |
| **Stability** | | | **Stability** | | | **Stability** | | | **Stability** | | |
| Liquid Reserves (13) | **41 %** | 19 % | Repeat Orders (22) | **54 %** | 46 % | Administrative Staff Turnover (1,2) | **0 %** | 0 % | Expert Turnover (6,8) | **6 %** | 19 % |

**Fig. 10.2: Celemi Intangible Asset Monitor**

1) *Administrative staff turnover:* Number of administrative staff leaving divided by numer of administrative staff at beginning of year.

2) *Administrative staff:* Employees other than experts.

3) *Average professional experience:* Experts' average professional experience in number of years.

4) *Competence-enhancing customers:* Share of revenues from customers with projects that Celemi's expert learn from.

5) *Education level:* Employees at year end with primary education calculated as = 1, secondary education =2 and post-secondary education =3.

6) *Expert turnover:* Number of experts leaving divided by number of experts at beginning of year.

7) *Experts with post-secondary degree:* Number of experts with a post-secondary degree divided by total number of experts.

8) *Experts:* Employees working directly with customer projects. Top management are regarded as experts.

9) *Five largest customers:* Share of revenues from five largest customers.

10) *Growth in professional competence:* Growth over last year in total number of years of professional competence.

11) *Image-enhancing customers:* Share of revenues from renowned clients that speak of their use of Celemi solutions.

12) *Intangible investments percent value added:* Investments in R&D, Marketing and IT charged as cost in normal P&L, divided by Value Added.

13) *Liquid reserves:* Cash reserves in number of days, assuming normal business.

14) *Net investment ratio:* Investment in tangible fixed assets as percent of fixed assets.

15) *Net return on equity:* Profit after 28% tax divided by average equity.

16) *Number of employees:* Two definitions are used: Average number employed during year for efficiency indicators, year-end numbers for growth/renewal and stability indicators.

17) *Organization-enhancing customers:* Share of revenues from customers that improves Celemi's organization, brings R&D or projects that can be leveraged.

18) *Profit margin:* Profit before tax divided by total revenues.

19) *Profit/Values added:* „Real" Profit divided by Value Added.

20) *Proportion of administrative staff:* Number of administrative staff divided by number of total staff at year end.

21) *„Real" profit:* Profit adjusted for R&D charged as cost in normal P&L.

22) *Repeat orders:* Share of revenues from customers buying also in 1996.

23) *Revenues from new products:* Share of revenues from products and concepts launched less than five years ago.

24) *Revenues per administrative staff:* Total revenues divided by average number of administrative staff.

25) *Revenues per customer:* Total revenues divided by total number of customers.

26) *Rookie ratio:* Number of employees with less than two years' seniority.

27) *Seniority:* Number of years as Celemi employee.

28) *Solidity:* Equity divided by Total Assets.

29) *Value added:* The value produced by Celemi's employees after payment to all outside vendors.

**Fig. 10.3: Celemi Intangible Assets Monitor, Description**

The implementation of the Intangible Assets Monitor supports two important management tasks. Managers can focus their marketing strategy not only on attaining sales targets, but also on evaluating customers and potential orders with regard to the remaining three target fields. This enables them to assess whether a certain customer order improves Celemi's image, strengthens organizational procedures, or develops the competence of the staff. In the words of the CEO of Celemi: "Choose the right clients, who bring in money and know-how."

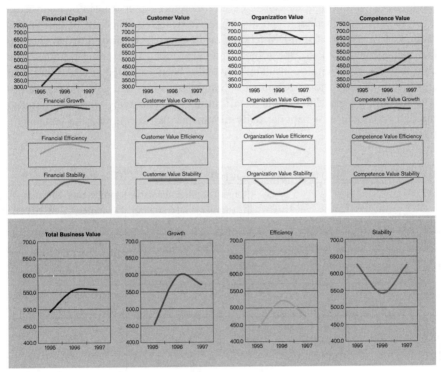

**Fig. 10.4: Assets at Celemi 1995 - 1997**

## 10.4 How to calculate the intangible assets

After concluding a project or a customer order, the managers discuss benefits and evaluate each work package as to whether its value has contributed to strengthening the internal and/or external structure, or staff competence. The respective contract value is then entered into the calculation of the performance indicator. A project with a contract volume of DM 100,000 divided into five work packages worth DM 20,000 each could therefore be evaluated in the following manner.

Work package 1 (WP 1) included the development of a brand new learning process which in later projects may be used as a model. For this task, the project staff had to move into a new field of application. WP 2 consisted of conducting internal interviews. The method and procedure of this task did not differ from previous data gathering interviews. Therefore, the project staff could rely on existing routines. The same applies to the evaluation (WP 3). The development of appropriate measures (WP 4) mainly involved the ability to conduct a workshop to work out the appropriate measures. Celemi therefore set up a team that consisted of an experienced facilitator and a younger staff person. The cost of the "junior facilitator" was estimated at DM 5,000. For the purposes of project documentation and management (WP 5), the project staff also relied on existing routines. The contributions of a "junior consultant" have also been estimated at DM 5,000. The satisfaction of the customer who ranks among the country's largest 100 companies was not only conveyed to Celemi's staff during the concluding workshop but also through an article in a national daily newspaper that mentioned the company's name positively.

| Work Package | Our Customer | Our Organization | Our People |
|---|---|---|---|
| WP 1 | | Organization-Enhancing Customer = DM 20,000 | Competence-Enhancing Customer = DM 20,000 |
| WP 2 | | | |
| WP 3 | | | |
| WP 4 | | | Competence-Enhancing Customer = DM 5,000 |
| WP 5 | | | Competence-Enhancing Customer = DM 5,000 |
| Total | Image-Enhancing Customer = DM 100,000 | | |
| Growth/ Renewal | Image-Enhancing Customer = 100 % | Organization-Enhancing Customer = 20 % | Competence-Enhancing Customer = 30 % |

Fig. 10.5: Example of the Allocation of Work Packages

The internal structure, i.e., the organization, was enhanced only by work package WP 1 because the questionnaire and project documentation can later be used for further projects even if staff persons leave the company in the meantime. The other work packages (WP 2-5) relied on existing processes. Therefore, only one fifth of the project budget can be assigned to the performance indicator "Organisation-Enhancing Customer." Because work package 1 resulted in opportunities for learning, and work packages 4 and 5 included "junior consultants" who received additional qualification through "training-on-the-job",

Celemi can assign DM 30,000 to the performance indicator "Competence-Enhancing Customer."

This fictitious example results in the following allocation to the respective basic data of each performance indicator. Altogether, this project greatly improved the external structure because the customer publicly mentioned his satisfaction with the work done by Celemi.

## 10.5 Results

According to the CEO, the benefits of using the Intangible Asset Monitor result essentially from improvements in long-term competitiveness. A corporate strategy entirely focused on maximizing profits would probably have resulted in even higher profit margins. But, the company would then have had to abstain from investments that ensure future development. "We would have a better bottom line, if I didn't invest in the future." The importance of the Intangible Assets Monitor is therefore primarily its function as a "lead indicator", as opposed to the "lag indicator" of a traditional financial statement.

## 10.6 Lessons learned

Business development of subsidiaries located in other countries and parts of the world can be supported very effectively with the Intangible Assets Monitor. For example, when considering the growth/renewal of their internal structure, Celemi Inc. in the US decided to invest in a local design corner to increase revenues, diversify their client base and develop the competence of their people.

In addition, the process of developing and regularly evaluating intangible assets has helped all staff members to clearly understand the factors for corporate success. "Additionally, Celemi found the process of measuring in itself illuminating, bringing forth value adding information on, for example, the types of client they were attracting, and should be aiming to attract."[203] The evaluation of indicators that grade internal structure triggers internal processes. For example, the importance of meticulously documenting and maintaining template libraries for all products is now understood much better. Documentation enables the organization to function independently from its experts and allows it to react more flexibly to the needs of the customers.

The Intangible Assets Monitor is a simple and proven example of the benefits for strategic and operative management that result from the application of relatively few performance indicators (22 for intangible assets).

---

[203] Barchan (1998), p. 13.

The Intangible Assets Monitor is a particularly good basis for developing and expressing knowledge goals. Today, there are neither fully developed methods nor documented examples of this kind of target definition.

When attempting to skillfully apply the tool to management action, it is important to "accept" qualitative evaluations and to learn how to operate with fuzzy numbers. The ethics of an entire group of professionals may therefore stand in the way of successful application.

# 11 Knowledge Management and Customer Orientation
## Hewlett Packard Austria

*Jens Vorbeck, Peter Heisig*

Hewlett-Packard Ltd. Austria in Vienna (HP Austria) was founded in 1970. The company is responsible for markets in Austria, Switzerland, Central and Eastern Europe, the Near East, and Africa. In 1997, 444 employees handled a contract volume of € 1.07 billion, mainly in the telecommunications, banking, and gas and oil industries.

| HEWLETT® PACKARD | | |
|---|---|---|
| *Industry:* | **Electronics** | |
| *Business Process:* | **Sales & Customer Service** | |
| *Employees:* | **420 (HP Austria)** | |
| *Turnover:* | **223 Mio ECU (1998)** | |
| *KM Best Practice:* | **Culture of Couriousness** **Customer Voice** **Internal Knowledge Assessments** | |

www.hp.com/austria

**Fig. 11.1: Company Overview - Hewlett Packard Austria**

HP Austria is a purely marketing company that is divided into eight sections: enterprise account (computers for large customers), computers for HP partners, consumer market (computers for chain stores), medical engineering, measuring and testing equipment, chemical analysis, consulting, and operating business, i.e., managing computer centers – including servicing, repairing, financing, and leasing – as an outsourcing partner.

## 11.1 Customer knowledge and customer orientation as the main motivation for knowledge management

HP was developed from a company that originally produced industrial measuring systems. Corporate culture is therefore strongly influenced by measuring. For example, there is a long tradition of measuring many aspects of customer satisfaction. The responsible managers were indeed proud of the traditionally positive comments the company had received from its customers. Then, HP began to notice that competing companies were catching up, and some had even been left

HP behind. Research revealed that customer expectations had grown faster than HP itself had developed.

A so-called "10X Program" was initiated to improve product quality 10-fold. Employees noticed that one division had not achieved all the technological improvements planned, but that it still received the best grades by customers. In a worldwide "Reengineering Quality Conference" in 1995, the company reached the logical conclusion from this analysis: The focus on production was replaced by a focus on customers. As one result, the company introduced the program "Quality One On One".

The core of this program is represented by the knowledge of customers. This is made up of three central aspects: a) a deeper understanding of customer requirements, b) the organizational adjustment towards customers, and c) a "passion for customers".

Hewlett-Packard Austria tried to apply this program as profitably as possible. In 1995, the company reached its goal: It was awarded with the HP President's Award for Quality.

The initial situation was characterized by the conviction that a high degree of internal customer orientation was the basis for successfully applying external customer orientation. In internal workshops, individual departments studied neighboring departments as if they were external companies. They analyzed, discussed, and defined customer segments to be observed, products to be offered, and the respective usage of customers. In these programs for quality maturity, departments were allowed to 'hire' an expert from another department who provided his or her knowledge. In regular review meetings the company evaluated the "maturity" of quality. The long-term effect of this approach can be verified by the following anecdote. There was one project that discussed outsourcing hardware repairs. An internal department – against external suppliers, won the public bid for these services. HP Austria attributed the outcome to knowledge management activities and the quality maturity program.

At Hewlett-Packard, external customer feedback has existed for many years. In the beginning of the year 1996 the company put together a so-called "break team" that consisted of six members from six departments. Their job was to analyze existing customer feedback. This "Customer Voice System" will be described in a later chapter as an example of how HP Austria applies knowledge management.

A further example is the SPOC concept (Single Point of Contact), which has existed since 1995. The concept is based on the idea that there is only one entrance to HP. Everything else is then coordinated internally. This is an approach similar to concepts of "one-face-to-the-customer" that are found increasingly in companies worldwide.

Our contact at HP Austria indicated that this approach was very important because it was the basis for project teams that stepped over departmental boundaries to focus consciously on customer-oriented approaches. The responsibilities of these teams included cross-functional tasks, e.g., how to improve the telephone accessibility of staff members. In this case, the team found two solutions: first the system must indicate the presence, not the absence of staff, and secondly the company developed software that allows the central switchboard to connect the call to the correct staff member who signals his or her presence.

## 11.2 Challenges in the process of "understanding customers and markets"

The approach to knowledge management at HP Austria is different from the traditional approach. The business process that was analyzed in depth, "Understanding Customers and Markets", focuses on existing activities. Its purpose is to reveal and eliminate deficits in order to promote long-term, autonomous, and accelerated learning in an environment that constantly changes.

The goal is not only to encourage the internal learning of good or better solutions to problems, but to supplement the external product range with services that allow users to manage changes when introducing information technology systems. Customers have criticized the fact that HP supplies excellent soft- and hardware solutions that do not, however, reach their full potential. The reason for this was seen as a lack in attention paid to the so-called "soft factors", especially staff members at customer companies, i.e., the users of the new IT systems.

One barrier in the course of knowledge management was identified in the transfer of knowledge from experts to non-experts. It turned out that experts are not very interested in exchanging or transferring knowledge.

The customer voice system would soon be useless if the organization was not able to react to warning signals: "I've told you twenty times already, and nothing has happened." The organization has to maintain its curiosity.

## 11.3 Corporate culture: a traditional strength of HP

A lot has been written about the specific features of corporate culture at HP. It is, therefore, not astonishing to read the following statement: "There is no question that HP's corporate culture promotes the development of knowledge. It is quite difficult to implement knowledge management if employees are suddenly confronted with a more or less standardized way of dealing with knowledge. In any case, an open team spirit promotes the development of organizational knowledge, and supports motivation of the staff."[204]

---

[204] Schuller (1998).

The artifacts of HP Austria's culture, i.e., the aspects of corporate culture that are accessible to external analysts can be characterized as open, clear, participative, and communicative. The manager whose desk is located in an open-plan office and who joins all other employees for lunch at the cafeteria is as normal as the communicative atmosphere created in lounges for just this purpose.

These artifacts are obviously compatible to the publicized values of the company. However, HP does point to new ways for the future. For example, with regard to knowledge management, the company confidently assured us that "the pleasure of displaying something new is much greater than the fear of being copied". Such statements are partly due to the promotion of a culture that rewards the reusability of new ideas. This is particularly important if one realizes that the criterion "Innovation" represents a convincing incentive in the specific way the company thinks, and that reusability as such would not be regarded as particularly important if it were not be promoted.

In this context it is noteworthy to mention the so-called "School of Vienna." As the name indicates, this is a specific feature of the Austrian branch. This approach, established in 1997, is based on the question: "How can we develop new business opportunities with all employees"? To allow for "humane change management", HP Austria starts with the premise that people learn slowly, and that corporate activities must always be based on people within the company.

Two examples to examine how HP Austria tried to establish the homogenous culture it desired: 1) When hiring new personnel the recruiters pay particular attention to the integrative capabilities of the applicants. 2) HP developed a particularly exemplary way of treating new employees. To integrate them into the culture described above, they receive detailed information of the company's ideas, purposes, and goals. Among other things, HP shows videos that are prepared for this purpose to familiarize new staff with the processes of the new environment.

A cornerstone of the HP way is the spirit of cooperation that pervades the entire company. This spirit is characterized by a participative management style. This paraphrase of the words of founder David Packard also applies to HP Austria. Even in the stage of defining or strategically aligning the location Austria, management had realized that their ideas could only gain acceptance if they were supported by the employees. The company's hierarchy is correspondingly lean, and there are no barriers if staff persons wish to communicate across departmental or hierarchical levels.

Hewlett-Packard's evaluation system also takes contributions to the internal and external transfer of knowledge into consideration. According to our contact at HP Austria, the most important question is: "What has a staff person done to make his or her knowledge accessible", i.e., to what extent does this person contribute to the transfer of knowledge and information about a customer into the company. For this purpose, HP Austria includes three indicators: the self-assessment of the staff person, the comments of the customer about the staff person, and the evaluation of the superior.

HP does not ascribe specific value to these indicators, but "one of our most important improvements has been to include through this measure the staff's spread of knowledge when calculating incentive payments."

What is true for external customers is obviously also relevant to internal customer orientation. Another aspect of evaluation concerns internal transfer: What has staff recently done to make their knowledge accessible to their teams?"

Cooperation in HP's cross-functional teams is very popular because participation is highly beneficial to one's career. In an internal job search, any evidence of having cooperated in teams increases an individual's chances greatly. In the case of management positions, we might even say that there is a direct relationship between work in cross-functional teams and further career development.

## 11.4 Customer Voice: if you want to know the customer's needs - ask him and don't presume you allready know the answer

The term "Customer Voice" refers to an approach at HP Austria to create knowledge about customers. During management of customer responses, all information on the customer is collected systematically, analyzed according to patterns of customer expectations, and transferred into the company while appropriate measures are developed (Fig. 11.2).

This information can reach HP on different paths: as a short note written by a staff person, as a transcript of a telephone message from a customer or a telephone interview with a customer, or directly from the customer through the Internet.

Earlier procedures attempted to reduce customer feedback to central statements and categorize this information according to certain keywords. Today, the collection of information has been separated from its evaluation. The largest sources of information are handwritten and signed notes by staff persons of HP, telephone inquiries, and customer feedback through the Internet and e-mail. 5-7% of all information is collected through letters, 20% through telephone calls, and more than 60% through the handwritten notes mentioned above. Customer surveys through the Internet have the highest growth rates.

About 15-20 staff persons have been trained to analyze incoming comments as to their urgency and the patterns or frequency of certain (sub) processes and information requirements ("frequently asked questions"). Feedback analyzed as urgent is immediately forwarded to the responsible manager. "Customer voice analysts" act not only solely as carriers of knowledge, but also function as a hub of information, as navigators, multipliers, and transmitters of impulses. In contrast to earlier procedures that involved centralized input into customer databases, every department may nowadays add to the database, and may thus contribute to the storage of knowledge about the customer.

**Customer Voice :**
Identify customer knowledge systemically and holistically .

Customer requests and complaints are recorded in full text using plain paper sheets. All information is passed on to customer voice analysts. They categorize the given information and forward long term issues to product development and strategic departments. Short term issues are forwarded to customer support. The separation of information gathering and analysis guarantees unprejudiced judgment and excels most sophisticated pre -categorized schemes.

**Fig. 11.2: Best Practice - Customer Voice**

**JEDER KUNDENKONTAKT – EINE CHANCE**

Hast Du Feedback von einem Kunden zu Service & Support erhalten – positiv und/oder negativ –, dann nimm Dir kurz Zeit und teile es uns möglichst wortgetreu mit. Du hilfst uns damit, uns weiterzuentwickeln und zu verbessern!

**From: Christina Taborsky**

**To:** Support Feedback

Datum: _____

Bitte kreuze einen der folgenden Bereiche an, auf die sich das Kundenfeedback Deiner Meinung nach bezieht:

**Support Bereiche:**
☐ Anrufannahme
☐ Admin. Kundendienstverträge
☐ Hardware-Support
☐ Software-Support
☐ Reparaturzentrum (Bench)
☐ Other Services
☐ Support Sales & Marketing
☐ Other: _____
☐ _____

**Kundeninformation (optional):**
☐ Name: _____
☐ Kontakt: _____
☐ Tel.: _____

**Möglichst wortgetreuer Kundenfeedback:**

_____
_____
_____
_____
_____
_____
_____
_____
_____
_____

**HEWLETT PACKARD**

Date _____

To: _____

From: _____

☐ Please approve          ☐ Let us discuss
☐ Please handle           ☐ For your information
☐ Please comment          ☐ For your file
☐ Please call me          ☐ As requested
☐ and return              ☐ Are you interested?
☐ Please complete/attach: ☐ Please forward to:

Remarks:

**HEWLETT-PACKARD Ges. m. b. H.**
A-1222 Wien, Lieblgasse 1, Postfach 72, Telefon (0222) 25 000-0, Telex 134425

**Fig. 11.3: Customer Voice Sheet (Facsimile)**

It is very important to strictly separate the collection of data from its analysis. This guarantees that typical distortions and preconceptions are reduced or even eliminated, and that the exact context of the information remains intact. It was often clear that to leave out these two steps leads to distortion. This results in information that includes only data that fits the existing pattern, e.g., regarding customer wishes. This approach shows the importance of the context of data. The "customer voice analyst" retains the context and evaluates the complete information and transforms this info into valuable knowledge.

To spread and apply knowledge, the management teams of the departments meet monthly or quarterly to discuss and act upon internal and external feedback. The connection to medium-term business plans is verified during internal management audits that analyze whether the results of the customer voice program have been linked to the company's business plans.

"Those who listen to the voice of customers on a daily basis, for example, salespeople, but who are too tired at night to write a report, need incentives to document the information and to make it accessible." For this reason, HP Austria handed out simple personalized notepads and developed an Internet/Intranet solution that supports data entry and data retrieval.

**Further approaches to knowledge management**

In the key account business, HP also analyzed offers in special workshops. The analysis focuses on the twenty most and the twenty least successful offers. Workshops employ the so-called "scenario technique" ("what if ..."). Central aspects include a) the essential requirements of the customer that are hardly ever expressed anymore, b) the price-performance ratio, and c) the attractiveness of Hewlett-Packard. As one result, the company discovered that HP is successful if management techniques are addressed. A further result was the following: "The more integrated HP's approach to the customer is, the faster contract volume grows."

With regard to internal customer feedback, the latest worldwide staff survey revealed that there are deficits in the way internal and external resources are dealt with. A project team of eight pursued these deficits in approximately 40 interviews. The results revealed a lack in up-stream management. Instructions from the headquarters were adopted without critical reflection.

A very interesting approach is the combination of the processes "Understanding Markets and Customers" and human resource management. For example, customer engineering looked for typical clusters of virtues that make a staff person successful. The know-how on the "successful past" of a staff person is then used for personnel recruiting and development purposes.

In close connection to this approach is the attempt to refrain from training in personnel development, and in the return to a focus on "tapping into internal knowledge." For this purpose, HP Austria conducts assessments of internal knowledge to decide which staff person earmarked for development is to be brought into contact with which other staff.

## 11.5 New project management in the business field "Professional Services"

Because of its unsatisfactory profit, Hewlett-Packard's business field Professional Services was reorganized. The worldwide hierarchical organization with country-specific orientation was replaced by a committee-oriented structure with logical working teams. In this framework, the company established eight to nine "Fields of Interest" and developed a process for knowledge management called "Structured Intellectual Capital" (SIC).

While developing the SIC approach, an approach that was based to a large degree on the experiences of big consulting firms, HP identified three models suitable for the application of knowledge management: a) learning communities, b) expert communities and c) project snap shots.

- Learning Communities:

Learning communities have the goal to promote the transfer of know-how between "novices" and "experts."

- Expert Communities:

Regular meetings of experts have the goal to identify the "blind spots" of one's expertise, and to initiate the appropriate acquisition of knowledge.

- Project Snap Shots:

In cooperation with the Project Management Institute in the USA, Hewlett-Packard has developed a new project management method. All project managers were trained in this method. The new project management approach is based on the life cycle model. It is divided into six stages: (1) Initiation, (2) Planning & Proposal, (3) Selection, (4) Implementation, (5) Warranty, and (6) Support. It includes 70 to 80 tools. To promote the utilization of existing solutions it is, for example, necessary to check the database about existing offers or offer modules when developing new offers.

The Project Snap Shot is a structured meeting conducted by an external moderator to collect and evaluate all positive and negative experiences. An important responsibility of the moderator is to make sure that the meetings do not focus on typical searches for guilty parties or on mutually apportioning blame. The "lessons learned" are formally entered into the database in the Intranet. Currently, the staff person who enters the data may freely select individual keywords. The company is currently discussing whether to develop a catalog of keywords. The database is accessible to all HP employees.

Project snap shots are developed on the basis of two milestones. The first occurs after the third stage in which the customer concludes the selection of an offer. Here, criteria for success and failure are identified. The customer may be incorporated directly. A second meeting, which is connected to a project meeting, if possible, occurs after the stage of implementation.

In summary, the SIC approach focuses on the development of networks of experts and the availability of knowledge in databases that are accessible through the Intranet.

## 11.6 An "evolutionary" knowledge management approach

The case study Hewlett-Packard Austria impressively reveals how comprehensive knowledge management can be connected to customer orientation – how one concept is based on another, and how synergies are created by skillfully networking modern management tools.

Three aspects of this case study are particularly impressive:

The example of HP Austria emphasizes the supporting effects of the design fields, especially of the 'soft' areas of personnel management, management, and corporate culture. The company was able to find an evolutionary way to efficiently produce knowledge management that is appropriate to the characteristics of these design fields. This is evolutionary because the company based its approach on long experience and previous knowledge was systematically reused for further development. HP Austria learned from mistakes and, particularly concerning Customer Voice Analysis, has even taken one step back from complex procedures embedded in categories to simpler but more effective methods.

The example of HP Austria revealed clearly that knowledge management is neither simple nor fast. The costs, e.g., for evaluating the customer voice notes, are hardly insignificant. However, the results seem to justify the expenses.

The example of HP Austria reveals the importance of a unified core process for efficient knowledge management. Not a single activity – creating, storing, spreading, and applying knowledge – is neglected. If we remember how human resource management is incorporated into the business process mentioned above, it seems that HP has even moved one step ahead by connecting several business processes. Perhaps this efficiency can be traced back to the "culture of curiosity" that was quite often mentioned by our contacts.

# 12 Knowledge Management in a Global Company - IBM Global Services

*Jens Vorbeck, Peter Heisig, Andrea Martin, Dr. Peter Schütt*

IBM is one of the world's leading information technology companies. In 1999, IBM employed 307,000 persons and had revenue of $87,5 billion. IBM Global Services, IBM's business segment responsible for IT services, employs 150,000 persons and had sales of $32 billion. In 1999, it was the world's leading provider of information technology services.

| | |
|---|---|
| *Industry:* | EDP-Systems, Software and Consulting |
| *Business Process:* | Produce and deliver services |
| *Employees:* | 307.000 |
| *Sales:* | 87.5 Billion USD |
| *KM Best Practice:* | Intellectual Capital Management Tool ShareNet -Conferences Category Owner Intellectual Capital Seeker |

http://www. ibm.com

**Fig. 12.1: Company Overview - IBM Global Services**

The business segment Global Services is divided into three units: Business Innovation Services (business strategies and e-business solutions), Integrated Technology Services (design and implementation of infrastructure solutions), and Strategic Outsourcing Services (systems, network and data center outsourcing). The business unit Consulting is assigned to each of these three units. In Germany, the Consulting unit "IBM Unternehmensberatung GmbH" is an autonomous subsidiary of IBM.

This case study describes the experiences and achievements of the unit "Infrastructure & Systems Management" which employs 400 professionals in Germany and 4,000 professionals worldwide. Its responsibilities include carrying out international projects in the systems management and infrastructure area. Another example covers the unit "Automotive Services" which employs 300 professionals in Germany and 3,500 worldwide.

## 12.1 Introduction of knowledge management

"Competitiveness, profitability, and intellectual leadership" are the keywords to explain the introduction of knowledge management at IBM.

The focus IBM has placed on knowledge management stems from the growing requirements of the company's services. Based on the dynamics of the corporate environment and on the goal to secure and expand competitive advantages, IBM's Consulting Group began to develop a model for knowledge management in October 1994. Under the rubrics "personnel turnover", "mobility", "global customers", and "global competition", IBM raised the questions: "How can we acquire new knowledge? How can we turn local knowledge into globally available knowledge? How can we – in view of staff turnover – preserve knowledge, and utilize knowledge growth?". Because the ability to learn faster than the competition is today's only sustainable competitive advantage.

This was IBM's second such attempt after their first had revealed that it is not sufficient to develop databases to store information, experiences, and know-how. "From a technological point of view, the results were successful; however, they were economically disappointing." The assumption that users would come knocking at the door if only technology were made available proved to be wrong.

The development team consisted of up to fifteen professionals who successfully applied their idea of knowledge management to a Lotus Notes application to support communication. The idea was called "Intellectual Capital Management (ICM)." "Since 1994, the IBM Consulting Group has employed the ICM effort as part of the company's re-engineering project. The idea of ICM has been to institutionalize and make knowledge management more formal throughout IBM Global Services and Global Industries."[205] Knowledge management at IBM is not an isolated solution. Instead, it is an integral component in a program initiated to optimize customer relations under the title "Customer Relationship Management (CRM)."

From that point on, the development of further activities was based on an international strategy that was adapted to the specific requirements of the individual business segments.

## 12.2 The important dimensions of knowledge

IBM's knowledge management activities are based on the definition of two dimensions of knowledge. Knowledge may be either explicit or tacit, and it may be only available to an individual or to a certain group or even a whole community.

IBM defines explicit knowledge as documented and (ideally) structured knowledge that is fairly easily accessible, and that is available in different media. On the other hand, tacit knowledge exists in the heads of the company's professionals. It includes experiences, ideas, rules of thumb, and tips and tricks

---

[205] Kuan Tsae Huan (1998).

that have not yet received the attention from previous management models they deserve. Intellectual capital contains information, explicit and tacit knowledge, and experiences and ideas that are structured in such a way that they can be exchanged and reused to provide the best possible usage for clients (innovation, best practices) and the company (operational effectiveness).

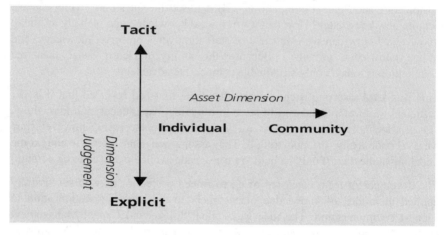

**Fig. 12.2: Dimensions of Knowledge**

This idea contains two decisive and remarkable aspects. The pragmatic understanding of tacit knowledge that contrasts with an otherwise understanding that refers to tacit knowledge in the sense of mental models and routines, which store knowledge in the human brain. IBM focuses on the management of this pragmatic tacit knowledge. Additionally the two-dimensionality includes possibilities for omni-directional exchanges. IBM's clearly expressed goal is not only the identification of explicit knowledge, but also the retransfer of tacit knowledge into the heads of the professionals through new methods of learning and topics that better relate to daily practice.

The second dimension focuses on "publicizing" individual knowledge – tacit and explicit – internally wherever it is relevant to operational performance making it available to a wider audience.

IBM communicates this idea in the following manner: "It is not necessary, realistic or sensible to devote time to defining knowledge. What is important is to achieve an understanding of what it means to use knowledge in contrast to Information. (...) The story I most frequently use to distinguish between knowledge and information is to use the metaphor of a map and a human guide. A map is a set of data organized into a coherent and reusable form - it is information. The guide, on the other hand, is knowledgeable. She does not need to consult a map, takes into account recent experience and has the ability to relate my ability to her knowledge of the terrain. The guide is the fastest way to achieve my objective, provided that I trust her. If I do not have the trust, and am not prepared to take the risk of experimentation, then I will fall back on information - the map. It should also be noted that someone with knowledge of the territory has created the map. If I share the same culture and background as the mapmaker then I am able to use the information. A different background may mean that the map is just data - useless stuff without context."[206]

## 12.3 IBM's approach: Intellectual Capital Management

Intellectual capital management (ICM) is a framework of values, processes, people, and technology set up to collect, make available, reuse and further develop knowledge, experiences, and information (Fig. 12.3).

By using the basis "Vision – Strategy – Values," IBM focuses on homogenizing and adjusting its interests to help customers. Processes fulfill their purpose through consistent standards and methods that support the reusability of knowledge worldwide, and that keep the core process of ICM running. This takes place in an organization that maintains an appropriate balance and relationship between informal and formal networks by using all-inclusive and uniform technology.

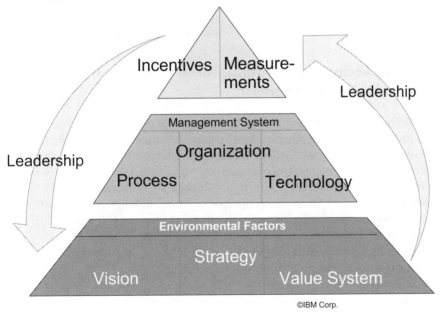

©IBM Corp.

**Fig. 12.3: Framework of Intellectual Capital Management**

---

[206] Snowden (1998), p. 7.

„motivator" may also replace the term „incentives". This aspect is to receive more emphasis. The goal at the top of the pyramid is to motivate staff to actively participate in knowledge management. In this context, the term "incentive", that connotes the allocation of financial assets, would lead in the wrong direction. Finally, it is the managers who have to visibly commit to and promote ICM by implementing active and professional leadership.

IBM's strategy of knowledge management focuses on the following metaphor by Peter Drucker: "In knowledge economy everyone is a volunteer, but we have trained our managers to manage conscripts. ... the real issue is that most of the volunteers still think like conscripts."

The following tasks are part of knowledge management at IBM:

- Making intellectual capital available (technologically and procedural; each staff person structures and stores knowledge while being supported by the respective core teams),

- Reusability of intellectual capital (each staff person),

- Maintaining intellectual capital (core teams),

- Structuring the respective knowledge domain (core team, sometimes special task forces – "solution boards"),

- Creating and/or further developing intellectual capital (each staff person).

## 12.4 Intellectual Capital Management at the unit Infrastructure & Systems Management

Within the knowledge area of systems management an informal people network has been established for over five years that mainly consists of professionals from the unit Infrastructure & Systems Management and the IBM Consulting Group. Actually, it's a cross-organizational network – a so-called Community of Practice – with over 4,000 members worldwide. A Community of Practice Leader together with a core team of about 25 people have form the Community of Practice for systems management. The core team members are working part time for the core team and most of the time as professionals in client engagements.

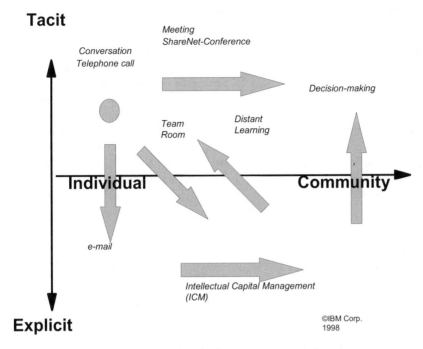

**Tacit**

*Conversation*
*Telephone call*

*Meeting*
*ShareNet-Conference*

*Decision-making*

*Team*
*Room*

*Distant*
*Learning*

**Individual**

**Community**

*e-mail*

*Intellectual Capital Management*
*(ICM)*

©IBM Corp.
1998

**Explicit**

**Fig. 12.4: Methods and Tools to Support the Exchange of Knowledge**

The manager of the core team is generally allowed to spend 60% of his or her working time on this project. The other core team members dedicate 10% of their time to this job. IBM has not officially regulated how these expenses are accounted for. The core team's job is to:

- Sense and respond to the community's requirements and needs,

- Structure, manage and maintain the knowledge of the community and make it available

- Develop methodologies and harvest knowledge and experiences where these are missing, and

- Communicate to the community about all topics of interest for the Community of Practice.

### 12.4.1   ShareNet

In order to get in contact with the community and to get the opportunity to identify the requirements of the community the members of the core team organize so-called "ShareNet meetings" where the participants get the chance to exchange and spread tacit knowledge, the core team can evaluate and structure contributions to the ICM database made by the over 4,000 co-workers of the network, and where the core team can organize the presentation of "best of beed" material and methodologies for the knowledge area.

Worldwide ShareNet meetings take place semi-annually in Europe and North America. The conferences last for three days. Up to 150 professionals from the systems management knowledge area participate. These meetings are open to all employees of IBM. Travel expenses and conference fees have to be paid by the participants themselves, which limits the number of participants considerably. The most important topics on the agenda are "ShareNet breaks", breaks between sessions to exchange experiences, ideas, etc. (tacit knowledge) freely. The organizers invite external speakers, clients or scientists to get fresh impetus and to shift the focus to an external view on certain topics. Participants who have actual experience in the field occupy the largest part of the discussion. They report on their latest projects, results, and methodologies. The organization of additional national or regional ShareNet meetings takes the cultural peculiarities of a global corporation into account.

A relatively new initiative is the organization of joint ShareNets with related Communities of Practice so that the participants can share and exchange experiences beyond the "borders" of their own Community of Practice with members from a different, but closely related knowledge area.

### 12.4.2   ICM tool to support knowledge exchange

The ICM-tool, which has received several GIGA Global Excellence awards for outstanding knowledge management and commitment to enhance client service supports the movement of the individual tacit knowledge of each of the numerous members of one network to explicit knowledge that is available to all members of the network.

The approach to this service segment – the systems management knowledge area - is described as a "solution life cycle" that defines the phases "assess, design, deploy and operate" that each product runs through. The ICM database is structured accordingly. It supplies the content of the methods of the "solution life cycle", i.e., specific applications. Specifically, the process can be described in the following way:

All members of the network are able to document knowledge (e.g., the description of a project) that they find to be relevant. A "router" is responsible for acknowledging each new entry. He or she must also initially evaluate the data and pass it on to the appropriate reviewer. A reviewer supervises a certain subject field and evaluates the contributions. A subject field may be a certain category in the ICM database associated to a phase in the solution life cycle or it may be a certain skill area associated with the knowledge area systems management (e.g. a particular method or process). Evaluation criteria include the following aspects:

- Completeness (Does it contain a summary in English?, Have contacts been identified? Have all relevant documents been attached?),

- Reusability and

- Determination whether the contribution is genuinely new or at least considerably better than any previous information on this topic.

This means that the reviewer has to remain in touch with the contributor to perfect the document and to achieve the best possible quality. The reviewer can also initiate translations of contributions to this one particular network that are in demand. For each language, the Community of Practice for systems management has identified a national language assistant who gets active when contributions are not in English.

In 1999, 160 out of about 200 contributions were accepted through this method for the knowledge area of systems management. In the meantime, IBM has clearly exceeded the critical minimum amount for such ICM databases. Therefore, it has become very important to remove contributions that are now irrelevant or have now been surpassed by newer and better documents.

Fig. 12.5: ICM AssetWeb

The ICM tool is a good example of how IBM – through experience – became conscious of some of the barriers to knowledge management and the reasons for them. Three main classes of barriers have been identified: culture, technology, and language.

"Not everyone has the right consciousness for knowledge management" is a cultural problem that can only be solved through the support of upper management, one-on-one talks, and information meetings. The measures taken include the regular publication of a journal that focuses on different aspects of ICM at IBM. Another cultural barrier rises from the fact that it is deeply humiliating in some societies if one's contribution to the ICM tool is rejected. This could be overcome by intensive communication and support by the Category owner or a IC seeker with the contributor.

The language problem comes from the company's international nature. It is suspected that some members of the network have not sent in contributions due to language barriers. The Community of Practice for systems management has, therefore, implemented the role of the national language assistants mentioned above.

A third barrier is due to the IT infrastructure that is still fluctuating. However, the performance enhancement of the worldwide implementation of Lotus Notes have solved this problem quickly as well as the fact that ICM is now also available through the intranet. However, the performance – especially when connecting to the tool via a phone line – could still be improved in some regions.

With the new release of the ICM tool local replication of the tool has been simplified so that you are now able to search, reuse and provide knowledge and experiences even if you are not online.

### 12.4.3 IC seekers

IC seekers volunteer for knowledge management programs. Their job is to find sources of knowledge and to tap into this potential. They are, so to speak, "scouts for knowledge."

Currently, forty to fifty staff members do this job worldwide for the knowledge area systems management. These IC seekers attempt to promote the idea of "give and take" when individually talking to participants. They act as ambassadors for intellectual capital management at IBM. Their achievements are also part of their annual performance evaluation.

This means that one of these IC seekers approaches an expert and motivates her or him to share her or his knowledge with colleagues by documenting a project in the ICM tool. Another way would be to tell participants that they could use a certain tool to handle projects more easily. The IC seekers also utilize the ShareNet meetings mentioned above to identify relevant knowledge and the persons connected to this knowledge.

### 12.4.4 Knowledge cafés

Work Room, Team Room, etc. are Lotus Notes applications that promote the cooperation of real and virtual (i.e., sometimes international) teams. In the framework of intellectual capital management, these applications facilitate the transfer of individual tacit knowledge into explicit public knowledge (Fig. 12.4). A new, even more comfortable application called the "knowledge café" is now available within the ICM framework.

### 12.4.5 Methodology databases

Within the phases of the solution life cycle for systems management several methodologies are in place. These methodologies are a fundamental part of most of the client engagements that IBM performs in the systems management area.

In order to provide the methodologies to all professionals trained in a certain methodology several databases – one for each methodology – have been established outside the ICM framework. The reason why these databases – an integral part of the knwoledge management for systems managemet – reside outside ICM is easy to explain: ICM is accessible by all IBM Global Services professionals after the initial registration with the tool. The methodology databases should only be accessed and applied by professionals who are trained in the methodologies in order to avoid sub-optimial use of the methodologies.

The contents of the methodologies and the respective databases take into account what the core team knows about the requirements and needs of the community. This is one aspect of the "sense and respond" task that the core team has. If the community requires a standardized approach for a certain phase of the solution life cycle this may lead to a development project for a new methodology. The development project is ideally performed with client involvement so that the new methodology may be developed and verified in a real world environment. The approach itself as well as sample client deliverables and an engagement profile (marketing approach, sample project plan, staffing of a project, etc.) are then documented in the respective methodology database.

### 12.4.6 Communications

Another very important aspect of knowledge management within IBM, which has been neglected for a long time, is the bi-directional communication between the core teams and their communities.

Within the knowledge area of systems management several communication means are in place:

- An intranet site for fast-aging news in the systems management area plus a download site with important whitepapers, presentations, etc.

- An internet site with information also accessible for clients and with a download area that holds documents that may be presented at clients.

- A quartely newsletter (hardcopy and available as download from the intranet) with changing focus areas in each edition that not only spans the systems management knowledge area but also the related knwoledge area of networking and connectivity.

- An Email service (every 4-6 weeks or when required) offering the latest news in the systems management area, recently publicized and valuable intellectual capital and other news in the ICM area, class and event announcements, successfully completed and referencable client engagements, etc.

- Conference calls with associated online presentations about the most recent developments in the systems management area where the listeners also have the chance for questions and discussions.

- Newsgroups within the ICM framework where a question and answer section provides the opportunity for the community to fill information gaps.

The benefits of these communication media are verified through the feedback of the community – either online or personally at events such as a ShareNet conference.

In this way all areas of knowledge management at IBM - the ICM tool, ShareNet conferences, methodologies, communication, etc. - are interconnected.

## 12.5 Intellectual Capital Management at the unit Automotive Services

The unit Automotive Services has experienced that "the wheel was reinvented several times" while developing software. Because software development requires a lot of preparatory work – due to the necessary compatibility with existing systems –, and because the team of developers is distributed all over the world, the unit has decided to give the introduction of knowledge management priority over the introduction of the re-use of software solutions.

The unit's approach to knowledge management is very similar to the approach taken by the unit Systems Management Services. For example, the Team Room is only one tool among many others. The ShareNet is called Solution Board, and is responsible for developing innovative topics and leadership in this field. When topics have been thought through sufficiently, they are published through the ICM tool.

A specialty is that the ICM tool is tracked with a tracking tool. This enables the administrators to track the number of accesses, the duration, and number of documents that were read. The tool may even call the attention of users who have not accessed the system for a long time to the possibilities of its use. Incorporating the council into the core team solved objections by members of the works council.

The motivation to participate in knowledge management is based on financial, cultural, and social grounds. IBM has initiated a program that awards active members with up to $5,000. The company has also tried to create a certain composure in its active staff persons that stimulates cooperation. Particularly the IC seekers are able to motivate their co-workers during one-on-one talks. The goal is to escape the necessity of "survival of the fittest", and to experience a colleague who manages knowledge as a friend.

## 12.6 Achievements

The unit Automotive Services estimated that careful evaluations revealed that each document stored in the ICM tool leads to a time reduction of 30 minutes in the preparation of a new project. An Austrian marketing manager spoke of the invaluable benefits of the ICM tool concerning quality: "I've felt much more competent after preparing a presentation with the Knowledge Network [ICM tool]".

In the knowledge area of systems management the development of the methodologies – especially when they provide templates that are ideal for reuse in any client engagement – has saved a lot of time in client engagements and therefore can create a lot of additional profit when appropriately priced. One methodology can claim that 80% of its contents and templates are ready for reuse in every client engagement and that only 20% have to be adapted to the specific client situation.

Additionally the ICM tool now allows the indication of the time saved through the reuse of a certain piece of intellectual capital. Thus you can document and report how much time has been saved – and the results are amazing: Several sample deliverables saved much more than a week when working on a client engagement. In fact, even the average time that is saved when re-using a piece of intellectual capital is 5 days.

However, it is probably even more important to bear in mind the costs that would occur if knowledge management would not be carried out than to calculate precisely the benefits of the program!

# 13 Open Minded Corporate Culture and Management Supports the Sharing of External and Internal Knowledge - Phonak

*Peter Heisig, Christian Berg, Peter Drtina*

Phonak, the world's fifth largest developer and manufacturer of hearing technology, was founded in 1964 by the engineer Beda Diethelm and the executive Andy Rihs. In its first years, the company copied hearing aids from other manufacturers, while improving the product's quality. However, Phonak soon realized that hearing problems must be treated interdisciplinarily. The cooperation of professionals in microelectronics, micromechanics, medicine, psychoacoustics, psychology, physics, and audiology enabled the company to set landmarks on the road to "optimal hearing solutions." Due to the lack of suitable manufacturing equipment, Phonak also developed the appropriate production technology while it produced hearing aids. Nowadays, this development is still reflected in the company's interdisciplinary mix of research, development, and production.

## PHONAK

http://www.phonak.ch

| Industry | Medical devices |
|---|---|
| BusinessProcess | Research& Development |
| Employees | 1270 (31.3.2000) |
| Sales | 314 Sfr (1.4.1999 – 31.3.2000) |
| KM Best Practice | External knowledge sharing Corporate Culture & Management |

Fig. 13.1: Company Overview - Phonak

Today, Phonak is a company with more than 1,200 employees and a global marketing network. Its main markets are the USA and Europe. The company's sales and profits have risen significantly during the past few years. In 1999, Phonak created an additional 164 jobs. The company's headquarters in Stäfa, Switzerland, were equipped with a new technology center that now allows the firm to triple previous output capacity.

Apart from the traditional area of hearing technology, Phonak's communication technology has also gained increasing market shares in security services (surveillance and protection of persons), sports (communication between athletes and coaches), and media (studio technology).

## 13.1  Knowledge as part of the corporate philosophy

It is hardly possible to speak of an explicit introduction of knowledge management at Phonak. The consciousness of the importance of knowledge and its management is part of its traditional corporate philosophy, and not due to an explicit decision to introduce and apply measures to maintain the intellectual capital of the company. A member of Phonak's management described knowledge as "the tool to deliberately make decisions". The acquisition of knowledge and the best possible communication and cooperation among staff members has always been a key activity. This activity is also reflected in the three following factors of corporate success:

- attracting knowledge creates know-how,

- open minds create superior products, and

- people value creates shareholder value.

The philosophy of the founders also characterizes the current organization. A maximum amount of enthusiasm for research and the motivation to create something new is supported by the best possible environment for all staff members.

## 13.2  Internal and external cooperation to create, acquire and share the best know-how

Knowledge management at Phonak is carried out consciously, but not explicitly. This conclusion, drawn by one of the top managers, reflects the approach quite well. The following guidelines apply to this idea:

- Interdisciplinary knowledge of hearing is the basis for developing the best possible hearing technology.

- If part of the necessary knowledge is not available internally, it has to be acquired externally. This guideline resulted in close cooperation with several colleges and research institutes. "If we don't know it, perhaps someone else does."

- Knowledge can and should be shared with experts (even if they develop competing products). Sharing knowledge is not regarded as dangerous; it is beneficial to all if an entire field advances. Only in the stage of implementation can we identify differences between suppliers.

When developing a new product, each project initially addresses the following questions:

- In which area do we identify the highest potential for innovation?

- Which resources do we need?

- Which resources are available internally?

- Which resources have to be acquired externally?

An idea that originated at Phonak may therefore be tested and further developed in cooperation with college physicists and engineers. If the result is promising, Phonak produces the solution. Tests of the new product then again occur in cooperation with external institutions, e.g., hospitals, audiologists, psychologists, and customers. Phonak now designs evaluation and diagnostics tools in close cooperation with external partners and clients. This close relation with customers is reflected in the high amount of time spend by R&D staff with clients inside or outside the company.

In this long process, Phonak plays the role of an interface between research and production, and between production and application. The most important goal of these partnerships is always to develop a common language that everybody understands and that results in the best possible solutions. This form of cooperation is profitable for all participants because they can jointly make advances in a certain field of study while they simultaneously pursue individual interests.

## 13.3 Corporate culture to foster cooperation and communication

Phonak's corporate culture begins with architecture. The headquarters in Stäfa reflects a philosophy of transparency, openness, and motion. Bright and open offices, isolated stairs, and few doors create an inviting and communicative atmosphere. Communication barriers are avoided wherever possible. The architecture clearly reflects the product of the company: hearing aids, or the intention to enable or improve communication.

Phonak's development from a pioneering company to a medium-sized corporation plays an important specific role. The close cooperation between staff members and appreciation for each individual even now provides Phonak with an internal and external image characterized as "more friendly, more human".

The knowledge that every staff person may ask anyone else questions is another remnant of the philosophy of the founders. This is why hierarchies are as lean as possible. Even managers are easily accessible.

In this sense, the bottom line is primarily understood as a result of successful internal and external cooperation – and only secondarily as a goal.

According to management people at Phonak, the corporate philosophy is best described with the so-called "Silicon Valley Spirit". This describes a certain subculture of many high-tech companies that is characterized by a highly innovative atmosphere. The company deliberately creates spaces and stimulation for thought, promotes creative and open internal and external discussions, supplies various opportunities to make suggestions, and tries and applies good ideas non-bureaucratically.

"A lot is talked about, and little is written down." Communication occurs directly and easily at that location where the exchange of knowledge is required. Written documents are reduced to the absolute minimum ("as many as necessary, and as few as possible"). However, rapid growth in the number of employees has put the company in a position in which it can no longer uphold this guideline. The functional "get principle" now has to be supported by the purposeful distribution of information. Therefore, Phonak plans to prepare more documentation to guarantee the successful exchange of information in the future.

The internal openness desired requires that staff members know how to deal with freedom. To get in touch with others actively, to be able to work in teams, and to be able to resolve disputes are the basis of successful projects. Staff members that cannot adjust to this style are – if necessary – asked to leave the company.

Phonak actively maintains a "culture of errors". The company has realized that errors are an essential factor in the process of learning in research and development. Errors are evaluated in the sense of "lessons learned", e.g., during debriefings (see below), and are then incorporated into future developments. "Errors can always be made, but please, not twice."

## 13.4  Management actions to support the exchange and generation of knowledge

The managerial structures also reflect that knowledge management at Phonak is conducted consciously, but not explicitly.

This begins with cooperation in project teams. Project teams correspond to the traditional form of cooperation. They are the result of new ideas, and are reorganized according to current requirements. Constantly changing contacts promote the exchange of knowledge and supply impulses for new ideas.

Phonak pays particular attention to the employment of staff members in individual projects. The guiding question is: "Who should be placed where and why?" Initially, staff members are obviously selected according to their qualifications. However, the managers also pay attention to whether the teams really consist of a new group of people. This is done to avoid "in-groups." Management also knows that Phonak's success during the past years may easily lead to laziness, and to "resting on what has proven to be reliable". Changing teams are to avoid this. For example, sometimes young staff members with completely different experiences are introduced into a team just to "create some movement".

Furthermore, the management pays attention to whether individual staff members are sole carriers of knowledge for a certain field. The company attempts to set up "know-how cells" of four to five staff members that are jointly responsible for a certain area of know-how. This reduces the danger of losing an entire field of knowledge if one individual leaves the firm.

The composition of committees is also planned carefully. New ideas are discussed and applied without unnecessary amounts of opposition.

Schmitz and Zucker[207] positioned the different measures at Phonak to support the generation and use of internal or external knowledge in the following Knowledge Quadrant. We have added the "Debriefing" and the "Off-Shore-Meetings into their scheme, because the Knowledge Quadrant reflects the essential aspects of knowledge management at Phonak well.

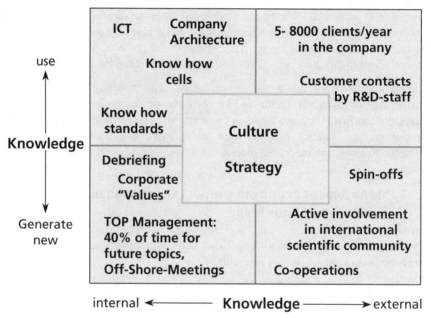

Fig. 13.2: Knowledge Quadrant of Phonak[208]

[207]  Schmitz, Zucker (1996).
[208]  edb.

### 13.4.1 Off-Shore meetings

Once or twice a year, as required, Phonak conducts"Off-Shore Meetings." A certain number of staff members (three to six) are selected to spend several days at another location to discuss new topics and develop ideas. This is easier if the participants are away from their daily job environment. It is easier to come up with new ideas if inherent necessities do not obstruct an individual's viewpoint and thoughts. This is the best possible space to come up with innovative ideas.

### 13.4.2 Debriefings

Debriefings are an important instrument to integrate identified errors into the continuous process of learning. Phonak has conducted these meetings regularly for ten years. The participants of the workshops evaluate in detail which aspects of a product are good and which should be improved, and why. A clear rule is: "Nobody is guilty!" An individual experience always results in a lesson learned for everybody. Good feedback is helpful for all participants. It also helps to conclude a project satisfactorily and consciously. At the end of these meetings there are clear proposals about how to avoid the same or similar errors in the future, and which measures should be applied to improve the process. Examples of possible improvements include the further education and qualification of staff members.

Debriefings are not scheduled according to formalized criteria. They are set up by managers if they find it necessary. A certain project volume, however, is required. In part, the meetings are moderated by a third party. To guarantee a structured meeting, the "key players" are asked in advance to prepare certain aspects of the discussion. The discussion may focus on the technological aspects of a project, or on problems within the team.

### 13.4.3 Expert meetings

Regular expert meetings that are open to all interested persons deal with new know-how, possibilities of the setting, and new solutions. Particularly young staff members get an opportunity to focus on the important aspects of the flood of daily information: "What do I need to know? What can be realized? Which inherent necessities are there?"

## 13.5 Summary and outlook

Phonak is an interesting example of a company that carriers out knowledge management activities at different points of the organization without stating it explicitly.

The key element of this approach is the company's traditional consciousness of the importance of exchanging and handling knowledge. This consciousness has implicitly led to an organizational design that promotes an intelligent management of knowledge. The company clearly focuses on promoting opportunities for direct communication, and on intensive partnerships with external experts and institutions. Furthermore this example underlines the importance of management actions to improve the use of knowledge. It shows the advantages small and medium-sized companies could gain, if their founders and managers act as promotors and actively model the supportive roles for knowledge management.

However, it is also obvious that the company is currently – due to its rapid increase in the number of staff members – undergoing radical changes. Measures that previously guaranteed sufficient flow of information and know how have now reached their limits. In the future, it will be necessary to develop a more explicit and more structured approach to knowledge management in order to channel information and know how sensibly.

# 14 Sharing Process Knowledge in Production Environments - Roche Diagnostics – Laboratory Systems

*Jens Vorbeck, Ina Finke*

The division Roche Diagnostics was created in 1998 after F. Hoffmann-La Roche Ltd. took over the Boehringer Mannheim group. Roche Diagnostics GmbH is divided into four business units: Molecular Biochemicals, Molecular Systems, Laboratory Systems and Patient Care.

http:// www.roche.de

| | |
|---|---|
| *Industry:* | **Chemicals and Pharmaceuticals** |
| *Business Process:* | **Produce and Deliver Products** |
| *Employees:* | **2.700 (Diagnostics -Laboratory Systems)** |
| *Sales:* | |
| *KM Best Practice:* | **Secure and distribute tacit knowledge** **Team specific culture** |

**Fig. 14.1: Company Overview - Roche Diagnostics - Laboratory Systems**

The main manufacturing centers of the new division are located in the German cities of Mannheim and Penzberg. At Penzberg, the company develops – among other products – product lines for the business unit Laboratory Systems. Especially immunological reagent components pass through a "scale-up" procedure that works closely with resident researchers. Components are later transferred to routine production sites. In Mannheim, Roche Diagnostics predominantly manufactures products for clinical-chemical analysis. Roche Diagnostics GmbH employs 6,500 people in Germany, from which 2,700 work in the business unit Laboratory Systems.

## 14.1 Knowledge management and organizational development: Two complementing efforts

The following approach to a new manufacturing concept - connected to team structures developed in the framework of the fractal factory - was initiated in 1995 by the division Laboratory Systems of Boehringer-Mannheim GmbH at the Mannheim and Penzberg locations.

To meet the increasing demands of markets and customers, the division Laboratory Systems implemented a new and integrated manufacturing concept.

194

The three factors technology, organization, and human resources were to be synchronized optimally to increase productivity on a long-term basis.

Comprehensive organizational development was based on the concept of the fractal factory. The goal of development was to create autonomous working units with clear goals and services.

The specific goals of the new manufacturing concept for the division Laboratory Systems were:

- produce quality products,

- produce cost-effectively and dynamically,

- establish simple and manageable structures and work flow, and

- use flexible technology and new organizational forms.

Units of fractal factories are characterized by a high degree of self-organization and self-optimization. Team structures are developed and established in as many areas of production as possible. The teams enjoy independence, pronounced autonomy, and flexibility. This places great demands on the employees' qualifications and learning capabilities. To encourage and support employees, the division Laboratory Systems initiated training sessions and team-specific CIP groups (Continuous Improvement Process).

Managers perform supervisory and strategic functions while they increasingly delegate responsibilities to teams. The encouragement of team autonomy results in teams that adopt typical management responsibilities. Managers therefore predominantly create and promote space to maneuver so that the staff members are best able to develop their creative abilities. Managers have to visibly support and live by the idea of teams.

Fig. 14.2 illustrates the integrated manufacturing concept and its guiding principle. The optimization of structures and processes also results in adequate spatial developments that integrate new technologies and team structures in the best possible way.

The attempt to create a 'vital' organizational structure that meets the requirements of permanent change connotes the realization of a learning organization.

At the beginning of the redesign of the manufacturing organization, the managers got a general idea of desirable standards in a goal setting workshop. While the product quality was to remain high, manufacturing costs and throughput times were to be reduced. Increasing integration of staff members was to result simultaneously in an increase in flexibility.

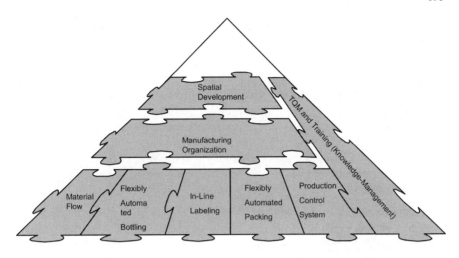

**Fig. 14.2:** **New Manufacturing Concept (Source Roche Laboratory Systems)**

Implementation initially occurred in pilot fractals. In the meantime, the concept has been integrated into the daily business operations of almost all manufacturing areas.

## 14.2 Team building and team empowerment as a basis for cultural change

In summary, Laboratory Systems has implemented knowledge management on the basis of an integrated manufacturing concept that is characterized to a great extent by new team structures.

The employees cooperate in manageable units with a high degree of self-management. On the level of teams, the traditional design of knowledge management fields are thus expressed by the fact that the teams manage themselves, and that they autonomously plan and control process sequences. The teams are responsible for sequence planning, operations scheduling, materials purchasing and disposal, documentation, etc.

The division Laboratory Systems placed great emphasis on open communication and the mutual assistance of staff members. The division regularly conducts team meetings to exchange information. The members are explicitly asked to become involved and participate in the meetings.

A further aspect is the transparency of processes. The motto, "We want a transparent company", is promoted and lived. This becomes particularly apparent in the spatial layout of the firm: Manufacturing areas and administrative offices are accessible and observable by everybody. Diagrams of processes and the continuous process of improvement visualize knowledge.

**Team Culture promotes Corporate Culture:** Cultural change may be accomplished with less effort if teams are used as promoting nuclei for the organization.

Corporate philosophy and visions, leadership, behavior of employees, communication and the structure of an organization constitute corporate culture. These issues are better approached on a team level than on a company-wide level.

Fig. 14.3: Best Practice - Team Culture

The division Laboratory Systems revived the original functions of management. The company primarily focuses on transferring responsibilities to employees, i.e., on cooperative management, the promotion of independence, and the creation of space to maneuver and make decisions. This requires a high degree of social competence.

The manager has to be prepared to pass on expertise, and thus to withdraw from the strictly operative level in order to increasingly act in consulting and coaching functions. The decisive aspect of this category is that managers have to live by team orientation consistently and convincingly.

To get rid of old fears, such as the loss of power through the surrender of responsibility, the division conducts training sessions on how to lead teams successfully.

## 14.3 It is not the technology that allows access to data but a trusting culture

Knowledge has to guide activities. For this to happen staff members need information on context and general conditions. At Laboratory Systems, all employees have access to all information on products, customers, goals, and index numbers (e.g., budgeting and performance data) that is relevant to their team. The data is accessible through a PC network. The knowledge and experience profiles of staff members are predominantly paper-based.

Corresponding to the consistent team structures, Laboratory Systems also organizes knowledge management in a self-organizing manner.

A single person performs the necessary conceptual coordinating function. This person holds a staff position that is also responsible for additional project management activities.

However, the decisive "promoters" and "multipliers" are the managers in their function as a coach and team manager. The uncoupling of traditional management tasks mentioned above creates room for managing knowledge in teams.

## 14.4   A company specific conceptual framework for the realization of knowledge management

Knowledge management at Laboratory Systems focuses on the development of the knowledge and experiences of staff members in production areas. The process illustrated in the following figure is an example of how core activities are put into action.

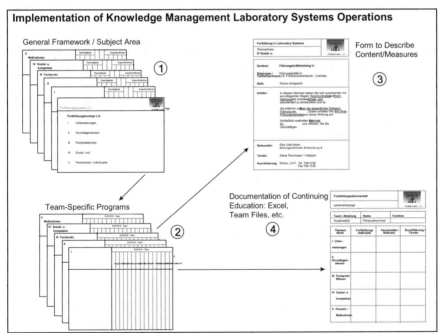

Fig. 14.4:   Implementation of Knowledge Management at Laboratory Systems Operations

A general framework (Fig. 14.4) (1.) is the starting point of knowledge goals and the identification of knowledge. There are also team-specific adjustments (2.) by the manager and the resulting educational measure (3.) that allows users to either store or spread knowledge (4.). This process – and others as well – are described in the following chapters in detail.

## 14.5 Informal interviews for the identification of knowledge and the setting of knowledge goals

To improve the knowledge of existing staff potential, the division Laboratory Systems approved a dissertation – submitted for a diploma – on "Knowledge Stock and Development Perspectives of Staff Members." During informal interviews, many employees on various hierarchical levels related their professional knowledge and their ideas of additional development perspectives, e.g., concerning multiple qualifications. Managers were asked about their opinions and wishes regarding opportunities for the development of individual staff members.

In teams, specific knowledge is visualized in tables. Each team member can indicate his or her individual competence so that this particular knowledge can be accessed quickly.

## 14.6 Continuing education as the basis for the creation, spread and storage of knowledge

The creation and the spread of knowledge at Laboratory Systems result from a highly structured and comprehensive continuing education concept. The program focuses on the following aspects:

- instructions (e.g., job safety, hygiene, etc.),

- basic knowledge (e.g., knowledge on products and customers, etc.),

- professional knowledge (e.g., knowledge on processes),

- social and methodical competence (successful teamwork, etc.),

- personal and individual measures.

The participants of each training session are to act as multipliers in their "home teams". They are expected to share newly acquired knowledge with their fellow team members.

An example of an interesting team measure is the "orientation rally" or "process rally" along the manufacturing process (Fig. 14.5). All staff members playfully learn about the entire process and all interfaces with neighboring processes.

The distribution of experiences occurs in team-specific "KVP groups." These groups focus on the process of continuous improvement. Problems are discussed and members introduce suggestions on how to improve certain processes. Usually, the groups nominate one member who is responsible for implementing ideas. The groups meet every two weeks.

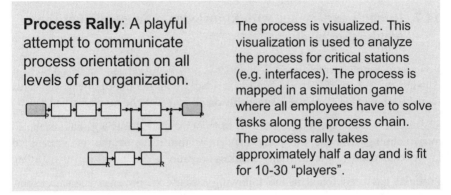

**Process Rally**: A playful attempt to communicate process orientation on all levels of an organization.

The process is visualized. This visualization is used to analyze the process for critical stations (e.g. interfaces). The process is mapped in a simulation game where all employees have to solve tasks along the process chain. The process rally takes approximately half a day and is fit for 10-30 "players".

**Fig. 14.5: Best Practice - Process Rally**

The various teams are connected by a "round table." Here, members from different teams meet to discuss professional problems. At the moment, teams meet once a month.

In addition, the company sets up bulletin boards to inform staff members about plans, on-going projects, and results.

The teams document their knowledge of staff competence and staff training in databases. Each team member can access the database.

Due to the rigid requirements of product and process documentation in the pharmaceutical industry, process parameters are recorded regularly. Interview partners in manufacturing areas use the "remark" field of the software to document their process-specific know-how. These "in-process remarks" enable staff members to turn their tacit knowledge into explicit knowledge that is then applicable by others. Professional know-how is thus accessible to all team members. This results in optimal manufacturing processes.

The central idea, however, is to store knowledge in the heads of the staff members and to illustrate to other staff members (team members) to which extent which knowledge is hidden in which brain.

At the beginning of 1999, the division Laboratory Systems introduce a team file that contains guidelines, goals, team-specific information, working time models, products, customers, specific measures, etc. Especially newcomers can use this file as an initial source of information.

The rigid documentation requirements force staff members to follow process records carefully. This guarantees that stored know-how is spread and applied.

The various methods to create and spread knowledge allow all team members to access knowledge easily. Knowledge can, therefore, be applied quickly.

## 14.7 Roche's experience with knowledge management at the production level

Long-term restructuring towards teamwork is now being carried out based on firm convictions and comparatively good experiences with the pilot project. Measures to make knowledge clear and manageable on all levels are being intensified.

The success of the first teams in Mannheim and Penzberg has been so overwhelming that the company may now move on to the integration of knowledge management into daily business operations.

Potential has been found in the following areas: content-based team networks, incorporation of new members into the team, and the re-qualification of managers for the new requirements.

The most important aspect is – according to our contacts – the re-orientation expected from managers.

Apart from many details and minor initiatives, there are four aspects that are remarkable:

The unity of the core process of knowledge management: Focusing knowledge management activities at the level of teams was one of the reasons why Laboratory Systems was able to conclude the core process successfully. In this context, it was noteworthy that the company took particularly important aspects of knowledge goals and the identification of knowledge into account.

Many companies are challenged by the fields "Culture", "HRM" (Human Resource Management), and "Management." The example of Laboratory Systems shows that these fields can be designed at the level of teams by providing appropriate general conditions. However, top managers must be committed to providing these conditions. At Laboratory Systems, this was the case.

As part of our second remark, we would like to point out how people at Laboratory Systems were willing to hand over responsibilities and to take staff problems seriously. For example, each team member is able to moderate and initiate the CIP process of his or her scope of work. The trust and confidence implied here results in highly motivated employees who are willing to take over responsibility.

The centralized coordination of all knowledge management activities in the form of the production management of a department attracts attention with creative and unusual ideas on how to create new knowledge or how to influence design fields in the teams. These ideas include the "process rally" mentioned above, outdoor events to promote team spirit, and other activities.

# 15 Measuring Knowledge and Generating Knowledge about the Future - Skandia AFS and Skandia Lebensversicherungen AG

*Peter Heisig, Oliver Diethert, Uwe Romanski*

Skandia is an international financial services and insurance group that was founded in Sweden in 1855. The company operates in 24 countries and has its head office in Stockholm. Today, Skandia is the fourth largest supplier of unit-linked insurance in the world. 3,000 of the firm's 11,000 employees work for Skandia AFS, the parent company of the German Skandia Lebensversicherung AG. Skandia operates with a universal fund management system that is adapted to country-specific conditions.

| Industry: | Insurance |
|---|---|
| Business Process: | Management of Financial and Intangible Assests |
| Employees: | 12,000 employees / AFS 2,600 employees |
| Sales: | |
| KM Best Practice: | Skandia Navigator Skandia Core People Skandia Future Centre |

http://www.skandia.se

**Fig. 15.1: Company Overview - Skandia AFS and Skandia Lebensversicherungen**

Skandia Lebensversicherung AG, the German subsidiary of Skandia AFS, was one of Germany's first unit-linked companies. Customers are able to select an individually optimized combination from 40 funds. In addition, they can modify the composition of their holdings on a daily basis. In Germany, Skandia competes with 40 other companies that offer similar products. Altogether, there are 720 insurance companies in Germany, 120 of which have specialized in life insurance. The decision to exclusively offer unit-linked life insurance was made because Skandia felt that this was an area in which it had core capabilities, and because this would give the company a unique and clearly demarcated position on the highly competitive insurance market.

Skandia Lebensversicherung AG has been active on the German market since 1991, and had initially focused on direct marketing. Due to the relatively complex product, however, Skandia soon took the traditional road via insurance agents. Therefore, there are nowadays 2,200 agents who represent the link between

Skandia and the customer in Germany. The rapidly growing number of agents is a constant challenge to the flow of knowledge within the corporation.

The increase in the number of internal staff members is quite impressive, too: In 1995, Skandia employed 34 staff members, and three field workers. Today, there are 135 staff members and 15 field workers. In the same period, the number of customers rose from 2,700 to 82,000. In this area too, the numbers indicate a need for permanent transfers of knowledge. This is because both the field workers and the agents are active in the entire Federal Republic of Germany.

## 15.1  Introduction of Intellectual Capital Management

In 1991, Skandia AFS began to deal with the problem of how to measure and portray the know-how of customers, products, and processes, i.e., the most important assets of a financial service provider. The firm planned to develop a range of tools that would allow them to convert and further develop knowledge into steady assets. Skandia realized that the future development and recognition of a company are triggered by today's knowledge and the experience of staff members.

The appointment of Leif Edvinsson to director of intellectual capital in 1991 came during a time of rapid growth. Within a few years, the company had become the number two in the USA, and the number three in the UK. In view of this growth, managing and localizing existing knowledge had become a decisive task.

Skandia AFS, as one of the pioneers in knowledge management, coined the term "Intellectual Capital Management" and distinguished it from "Knowledge Management" to indicate that the former term represents a more specific definition of knowledge management. On the basis of this understanding, Leif Edvinsson broke down the market value of Skandia (Fig. 15.2) to illustrate the significance and the components of the intellectual capital of a corporation.

The intellectual capital of a company can be understood as a bridge between the market value, e.g. represented by the stock market value, and the book value of its assets. The book value consists in part of the human capital, i.e., the employees and their knowledge. Assets additionally include the so-called structural capital, i.e., the knowledge that remains in the company even if staff members leave. This capital is stored in databases, documents, hardware, software, and organizational structures. The customer capital that belongs to the structural capital includes knowledge of and relations to customers. The other side of the structural capital is represented by the so-called organizational capital. This includes the innovation capital of a company, i.e., patents, licenses, etc., and the knowledge of processes, so-called process capital.

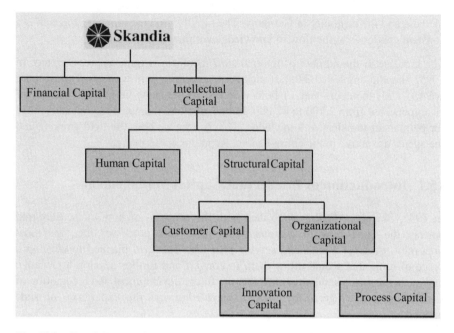

**Fig. 15.2:  Break Down of the Market Value of Skandia**

On the basis of the understanding of the market value of a company, Skandia recognized the necessity to transfer human capital into structural capital, and finally into financial capital. Because the knowledge and experience of staff members – the actual human capital – cannot be owned, only "rented" by a company, it is essential to integrate this knowledge into the corporate structure. This ensures that knowledge remains in the company, and is available on a long-term basis. For this purpose, Skandia developed a management tool to visualize and make this knowledge applicable.

## 15.2  Measuring knowledge: The Skandia Navigator

Skandia focused particularly on the management of existing knowledge. Leif Edvinsson contributed substantially to the development of the Skandia Navigator. This management tool is designed in such a way that it allows the company to control the development of human capital and to manage personnel development activities.

The typical focus on financial results and the flow of funds is supplemented at Skandia by a description of intellectual capital and its development. This supplement is based on the establishment of three main focal points: customers/agents, products, and growth and development. This expanded approach to record corporate value leads to a more systematic description of the capabilities and opportunities of a company, the Skandia Navigator.

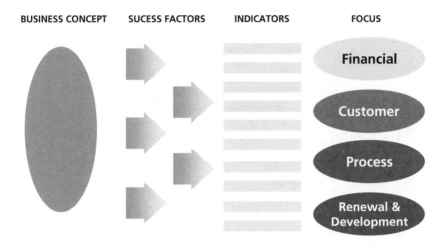

Fig. 15.3:  Skandia Navigator I

The Skandia Navigator contains financial and non-monetary values. It is shown as a house. The roof represents the financial capital, expressed by profits. Customers/agents and products form the walls. The foundation of the house is represented by the growth and the development of the company. Staff members who trigger the further development of the foundation represent the soul of the house.

Fig. 15.4:  Skandia Navigator II

Each of these fields is described by several indicators that enable the useful application of the navigator. Skandia Germany, for example, uses the following indicators (Fig. 15.5).

The indicators also illustrate the time-specific alignment of each focal point. While profit orientation is focused on the past, and the aspect "customer/agent" is focused on the present situation, the "foundation" of the house is oriented towards the development of the company in the future.

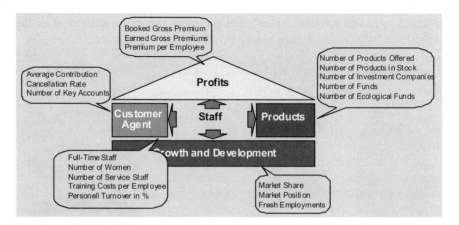

**Fig. 15.5: Skandia Navigator III**

The Skandia Navigator – an instrument to facilitate decisions – is increasingly used by the company. The possibility to supply a focal point with individual indicators allows the company to adjust the navigator to each department and to each situation that requires a decision. Further development and application of the navigator are strongly promoted by management because it allows the company to develop a common language, and because it represents a clear connection between corporate objectives and relevant indicators. In addition, the navigator is applicable for untrained users if the indicators per field are limited to from three to five.

## 15.3 The German branch: Skandia Lebensversicherung AG

The core process of knowledge management at Skandia AFS and its German subsidiary Skandia Lebensversicherung AG involves the application of knowledge about customers and their needs to the development of innovative financial services. In the language of the Skandia Navigator: Today's knowledge should strengthen the growth and development of the company, i.e., the foundation.

When visiting Skandia's German headquarters, attentive visitors immediately recognize that there are no locked offices and that the entire staff – including board members – are on a first name basis. Offices are separated from open-plan offices by glass walls. According to one board member, Skandia would have liked to replace all walls in the offices with glass. These glass walls should be understood as a symbol of the corporate philosophy. They indicate transparency, and imply that everyone is welcome everywhere, either in the offices of the staff or of board members.

### 15.3.1 Stimulation of the exchange of individual ideas, experiences and know how

This philosophy is also reflected in Skandia's "Best Idea" initiative in Germany. The initiative replaces an official employee suggestion plan that is regarded by the company as too formalized and thus leads to unnecessary internal barriers. The initiative asks each staff person to state problems. In contrast to traditional employee suggestion plans, this initiative explicitly does not ask for solutions. The problems are handled by a quality team – that includes the members of the board – within a few days, and are then fed back to the board. New solutions are applied immediately.

The involvement of the board in daily problems and questions keeps the glass walls transparent, and ensures that the board knows about all relevant events. It also allows the staff to realize that they are an important part of the company, and that improvements in the flow of information do indeed result in improvements.

The rapid growth of the headquarters in Berlin resulted in continuous hirings. Due to simultaneously rapid increases in work, new staff members were not trained sufficiently. They had to learn everything on the job. Management soon realized that this approach did not activate the true potential of new employees. Consequently, the company was soon faced with a new personnel shortage. In 1995, only 10% of the departmental and corporate objectives were achieved.

In 1995, Skandia initiated a program that focused on corporate objectives and the requirements of the core business. This was introduced to eliminate the problem mentioned above, to develop improvements, and to provide old and new staff members with a solid basis. The so-called "4U" program was used to sensitize staff members to the requirements of customers and to involve them in the development of corporate objectives. Skandia's "customers" include "internal" and "external" customers. Because Skandia hardly ever meets the actual customer, "external" customers are primarily represented by agents. The "internal" customers" include those departments with which each staff person cooperates on a daily basis.

The Four U's

- Unterstützung = Support: improving internal relations,

- Unverwechselbarkeit = Distinctiveness: realizing the importance of one's position and function,

- Unternehmergeist = Entrepreneurial Spirit: realizing the required intensity of consulting and services,

- Unwiderstehlichkeit = Irresistibility: Conveying fun to customer-oriented results.

During 4U sessions, each department is to determine how it can support the achievement of corporate objectives. In this context, it became apparent that poor departmental communication and coordination were the major barriers to attaining corporate objectives. During meetings, the departments therefore evaluated and weighted the preliminary work from other departments. The subsequent comparison of the evaluations revealed considerable potential for improvement in the area of communication. It also resulted in improved awareness of existing problems. Because the staff had regarded internal customer satisfaction highly, Skandia now conducts regular checks on internal customer satisfaction that are also applied to external customers.

### 15.3.2   Training sessions to make knowledge explicit and share it internally

As a further instrument to promote exchange between staff members, Skandia Germany has established short training sessions that are conducted by staff members for staff members. The meetings take place twice a month during lunch. Participation is completely voluntary. Staff members themselves suggest topics which are then collected by the personnel department. This department also organizes meetings and publishes dates in a catalogue of events months ahead of time. This allows staff members to hear about and select suitable internal training sessions early. The topics discussed include all areas from bookkeeping to IT networks. Some subjects require consultation by external experts.

Usually, there are approximately 20 staff members who learn about the newest developments and to ask questions. These events promote an intensive exchange of knowledge and allow staff members to establish informal internal networks. The employees also learn where to find experts on certain topics in the company.

### 15.3.3   A new incentive system to reward organizational improvements

To further improve the achievement of goals, Skandia in Berlin suggested a new incentive system. Developed in 1997, the system provided that employees are paid 10% of their annual income as an additional bonus if departmental and corporate objectives were attained. If only departmental objectives are attained, the staff receives a bonus of 5%. If goals are not attained, annual income is reduced by 1,5%. This model was based on the approval of all staff members. The headquarters in Berlin, therefore, asked all employees for their opinion.

Those staff members that expressed reservations about the system were regarded as important sources of information regarding improvement in the company. Usually, these people had a specific reason why they objected to the incentive system. Their opposition was not based on possible individual insufficiencies, but on their perception of organizational insufficiencies. By discussing these items intensively and constructively, management was able to identify appropriate "enablers" for improvements in attaining goals, and persuaded all staff members to accept the new incentive system. According to the participants, the open and trustful atmosphere at Skandia promoted the decision and the improvements decisively.

## 15.4 The international flow of experience and knowledge at Skandia AFS

In many publications we can read that Skandia AFS has reduced the time-to-market from seven years – typical for the industry – to seven months, and that this was due to the intensive exchange of knowledge and the intensive utilization of internal knowledge.

### 15.4.1 The knowledge champions: The Skandia core people

At Skandia, an important element of this drastic reduction of the time-to-market is a group of ca. 80 people who are called "core people". These people have distinguished themselves with specific skills or dynamics. They form a task force for specific jobs, and act additionally as an emergency team. They are on call at all times, and therefore make themselves indispensable in their home offices. These circumstances require a continuous exchange of knowledge among the core people and their environment.

If a branch office has a specific problem, e.g., caused by the absence of an important person, or if Skandia plans to open up a new branch office, the company relies on the "core people". Usually, it is enough if the branch effected calls headquarters and describes the problem in detail. Within hours, headquarters can then find the person who can solve the problem. For example, the director of accounting fell sick while preparing annual accounts in Germany. Within a couple of days, he was replaced by a Swedish staff person who was one of the "core people."

Even the German branch was founded by a person who had previously set up the Swiss branch. He was also responsible for the decision to initially market products directly. That this approach was later revealed as being inadequate did not disqualify the staff member. Quite the contrary: the corporation regarded his approach as an important experience in its attempt to market a complex product, such as unit-linked life insurance, directly – not through agents. The experience further qualified the staff person who was later assigned to establish a branch in Poland. Management was conscious of the fact that tolerating errors is an important aspect of learning, and thus one of the components of success. This approach also ensures that errors are made only once. This is illustrated by the fact that Skandia AFS became the number three in the UK and the number two in the USA within only nine years.

### 15.4.2    Ake Freij: One core person

Ake Freij is one of the eighty "core people." His "core competence" consists of being able to establish new international branches. During his college education he had accumulated know-how while working for various Swedish insurance companies. After receiving his Bachelor of Science from the University of Stockholm with a major in finance, investments and accounting, he worked in the accounting department of the Swedish headquarters of Skandia AFS in Stockholm. There he analyzed the business activities of individual branch offices. He thus became the company's leading expert in the establishment of international branches. In 1991, he founded the Swiss branch and in 1992, the German subsidiary. His experience in dealing with multi-national teams and his knowledge of information technology were essential aids. When setting up new branches, his areas of responsibility include the key functions of corporation: accounting, customer service, human resources, and strategic IT decisions. While establishing the German subsidiary, he decisively contributed to the development of the organizational structure. The decision to make inroads into the German market as a direct insurer proved to wrong, but was a part of Ake Freij's process of learning. Therefore, he will not repeat this mistake in future projects. Currently, Ake Freij applies his international experience to the preparation of Skandia AFS's entry into US American financial markets.

### 15.4.3    International meetings to share knowledge and benchmark achievements

To keep the exchange of knowledge between subsidiaries on national and international levels going, Skandia organizes meetings with responsible managers several times a year. There are annual meetings of the different branch managers to exchange experiences, and to promote new concepts. These meetings last three to five days and take place in a different country each time. They are structured rigidly, and focus on mutual learning according to the principles of benchmarking. At each of these meetings, each branch presents its present level of development. The participants are asked to hand in their presentations beforehand so that the organizing subsidiary can put together a manual in advance. This approach ensures that all participants arrive well prepared. Even though the meetings are also used to cultivate informal relations, and establish networks, the rigid organization ensures that the meetings focus on the purposeful exchange of information, and do not lapse into a purely social event.

Apart from these annual exchange meetings, Skandia also promotes the organization of annual regional meetings. For example, at these meetings the German offices adjust their approaches, and learn from each other. There are particular needs for adjustment in countries that are notclearly separated by different languages, e.g., in Austria, Germany or Switzerland. In this case, the meetings focus on avoiding competition by developing uniform rates.

## 15.5 Generating knowledge about the future: The Skandia Future Centre

The Skandia Future Centre[209], founded in 1996, is one of the most innovative concepts. The introduction of the centre was based on the ideas of Björn Wolrath, for sixteen years the president and CEO of Skandia, who was convinced that a company must regard the future as an asset if it wishes to survive competition.

The Future Centre is situated in an old mansion on one of the many small islands east of Stockholm. This is where the Skandia Future Team meets every three months for three days. The team consists of one staff member per country. It now comprises of 25 people. The members of the Future Team are of different age groups, from different personal, educational, and professional backgrounds. They thus form something like a microcosm of Skandia. This ensures a multitude of different views and opinions, which is necessary since the team is to develop visions of the future. The team is not tied to any orders, and can operate freely. Apart from "free" ideas, it also discusses future scenarios and policy issues. Topics are taken from current publications, e.g., from the Club of Rome. To maintain the dynamics of the Future Centre and to continuously include new views, members are changed every two years.

---

[209] The concept of Future Centre has also been adopted by ABB in 1999.

# 16 Secure Tacit and External Knowledge in the Insurance Industry - Thomas Miller & Co. Ltd.

*Peter Heisig*

Thomas Miller & Co. Ltd. was founded 116 years ago. Its headquarters are located in London. The company focuses on the management of mutual insurance companies. Each fund is operated as a mutual insurance association (or club) with individual rights and shared risks. Most business is conducted in the transportation industry, particularly in the shipping industry. The owners of about 50% of the global tonnage are insured in some respect by clubs managed by Thomas Miller. In addition insurance is provided to many of the world's leading container ports, freight forwarders and ship agents.

| | |
|---|---|
| *Industry:* | **Insurance** |
| *Business Process:* | **Produce and Deliver Services** |
| *Employees:* | **450 in London and 150 agents world-wide** |
| *Sales:* | |
| *KM Best Practice:* | **Secure and distribute tacit knowledge** |
| | **Integrating and structure external know how** |

http://www.thomasmiller.com

**Fig. 16.1: Company Overview - Thomas Miller & Co. Ltd.**

Thomas Miller & Co. Ltd. employs approximately 450 staff members in London, and 150 staff members in more than 15 overseas locations. The company also has correspondents in more than 100 countries, including one in each of the major harbors around the world.

## 16.1 Knowledge management: content and learning

The insurance business is controlled by contractual regulations. If claims are made for damages, these contracts have to withstand every legal review. Business processes are therefore dominated by lawyers and their tools of the trade, i.e., legal regulations, laws, contracts, and interpretations. In this context, the written word is particularly important. Written communication can be advantageous because expert opinions, memorandums, etc. become an integral part of daily business operations. However, the legal significance of words also results in cautious wordings and limited spoken communication. This was regarded as one of the cultural barriers that oppose the implementation of knowledge management.

Knowledge management at Thomas Miller & Co. Ltd. began to take shape during the development of a vision for the utilization of information technologies in the early nineties. The implementation of this vision gained fresh impetus through the arrival of a new Chairman in 1994. He focused knowledge management activities on content and learning, rather than on technical aspects. The technologies to be employed include a document management system, e-mail, and later, groupware and expert system applications (pilot application GUIDE – underwriting system).

These thoughts led to the following two strategies of knowledge management. One strategy focused on the development of a structured knowledge basis for core business operations. The second strategy concerned cultural change. This idea focused on the development of a learning organization in which sharing knowledge and experiences is especially important.

## 16.2 From library to Business Intelligence Center

To illustrate the new importance of information within the company, Thomas Miller & Co. Ltd. created the "Business Intelligence Centre" as a central location for pooling and structuring information. For this purpose, two existing libraries were combined. The goal was not only to combine the libraries organizationally, but also to develop a new identity. The image of a library, as it had previously been oriented towards books and other hardcopy materials, was to be dismantled. The two librarians were now called "information officers." The center focused on three jobs:

- Identify and make available external knowledge and information (business libraries, suppliers of information, online databases): "If they don't have the answers themselves, they at least know who – internally or externally – can supply the demanded information," was the motto for conceiving and implementing this strategy.

- Development of a regular, continuous supply of information, e.g., daily e-mails with the most important press clippings from the Financial Times or Lloyds List sent to all employees worldwide. Another example of an appropriate information medium is the internal electronic weekly "Miller News".

- Management of the Lotus Notes database to ensure coherent structure.

In addition to central knowledge resources, the center can now also supply secondary information, e.g., good restaurants for important business lunch appointments. These services that are helpful in daily business operations led to a change in the reputation of the former library. Evidence of this is the increase in inquiries (ca. 2,500 inquiries per year). Personnel-wise, the library was staffed with five people, instead of three as before. Two teleworkers handle inquiries, two others edit the information, and one staff member is responsible for the Lotus Notes database.

There are various knowledge bases maintained under Lotus Notes:

- Main topics in three categories: insurance market, customers, and suppliers;

- the "Miller Encyclopedia": an Internet encyclopedia with information on all topics that are relevant to the transport industry;

- Yellow Pages of all staff members with photographs, position, job description, language skills, and voluntary information on hobbies;

- Notes from conferences, meetings and discussions with customers, suppliers, and competitors;

- Internet directory with important links to external WWW pages.

### 16.2.1 The Miller Online Encyclopedia: Secure, structure and deliver knowledge

One important issue in knowledge management is the question how to structure the knowledge and how to assure high quality. The solution found by Thomas Miller & Co. Ltd. was called the "Miller Encyclopedia". This application was not only designed to structure knowledge about the transport industry relevant for the insurance business, but also to set a standard and to secure the knowledge of suppliers and clients.

The "Miller Encyclopedia" is an Internet application with three access levels. The highest level is accessible by any Internet user, provided he has registered on the site. A second level offers all customers relevant information, and the third level contains specific customers claim records. These two last levels are used like newsgroups or/and discussion groups to poll the knowledge that offers the best solutions to members.

20% of the staff volunteered to contribute to the development of the modules of the "Miller Encyclopedia". This was due to actions undertaken to promote internal direct communication and the exchange of information and knowledge. Another factor was the e-mail culture at Thomas Miller & Co. Ltd. For years the exchange of information between headquarters in London and offices, customers, and suppliers overseas had been handled through e-mail.

### 16.2.2 Workflow application integrates lessons learned approach

For the settlement of insurance transactions, it is fairly easy to determine certain processes that can be supported by appropriate workflow systems. When specifying these systems, the persons responsible at Thomas Miller & Co. Ltd. did not forget to determine "lessons learned." For example, a project can only be concluded if the respective person in charge enters his or her lessons learned during the case in the system. A Case studies' database with legal cases and experiences was achieved with just one additional work step. Full text search capabilities allow each staff member to access the company's know-how that has been electronically recorded.

The transition from sequential task processing to parallel processing combined with more efficient document management improved the generation of insurance policies considerably. In the past the preparation of a 100-page policy used to take three weeks; today, this is accomplished within just a few hours.

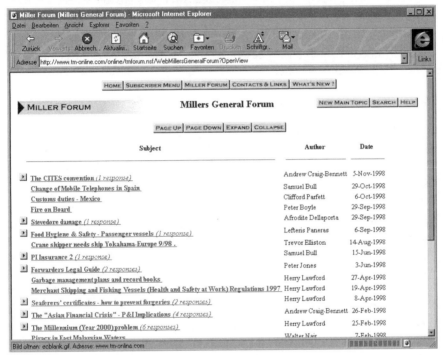

**Fig. 16.2: The Miller Forum**

### 16.2.3  New forms of learning

In 1995, the company introduced the position of Director of Learning. This job includes the initiation of cultural change to help employees to pass on experiences and knowledge. To identify, store, and spread knowledge, Thomas Miller & Co. Ltd. created different platforms.

- One platform for promoting knowledge and the sharing of experiences is the weekly or monthly soapbox (= "standing on the soapbox"). In the style of the speaker's corner in Hyde Park, a director or senior manager shares his or her insights on a current topic, or explains the current development of the company. These statements are also recorded on video. This pragmatic approach is further illustrated by the use of the lunch break (with sandwiches!) for this kind of event.

- A second way consists of monthly priority programs ("flavour of the month"). During a certain month, there are several training sessions, workshops, and videos on one certain topic.

- As required, the company also organizes informal lunch-workshops ("lunch bytes") with question-and-answer sessions on selected current topics.

- A further form is a so-called "safari." This means that a staff member works for six to eight weeks in another department or in the company of a customer or supplier.

## 16.2.4  Secure tacit knowledge

One important barrier for knowledge management is the lack of time to make tacit knowledge explicit for experts and document it. Experts usually have little time. The best practice solution Thomas Miller found is very interesting because of its clear focus, easy handling and low investment. The solution is 'in-a-nutshell' videos that present expert knowledge.

The focus of these expert videos is knowledge that was acquired within the company itself. Knowledge which could be learned at the university or other training courses was not recorded. Therefore some interview guidelines were worked out by the Director of Learning. Two experts are invited to talk about their experiences and tips & tricks during 15 to 30 minutes. The video is then edited and copied externally, and sent to all offices worldwide.

When organizing these various offers, the company pays particular attention to the contents of learning and knowledge that are almost exclusively covered by internal experts and knowledge workers. Examples of this procedure are so-called "cultural briefings", which attempt to brief staff members on specific cultural practices, standards, and the habits of a certain customer. For example, Greek shipowners who live in London should be treated differently than Greek shipowners who operate from New York City or one of the Greek islands. In insurance businesses, which rely heavily on trust and commitment, the exchange of knowledge is very important.

## 16.3 Achievements

There are hardly any examples of successful knowledge management in insurance businesses. The solutions of the medium-sized company Thomas Miller & Co. Ltd. may encourage even the large companies of this industry.

With its focus on structured document management through workflow applications on one hand and the promotion of know-how exchange in direct communication on the other, Thomas Miller & Co. Ltd. combines the most important aspects of knowledge in the service industry. The first focus makes sure that knowledge processes and explicit knowledge are managed adequately, and are accessible at all times, while the second focus accesses part of the tacit knowledge, the "tips and tricks" of how to do it best. At the same time, central know-how modules are stored, copied and spread globally by low-cost technologies (video).

**Lessons Learned at Thomas Miller & Co. Ltd.**

The following aspects were decisive for the success of knowledge management from the point of view of the people in charge of the initiative:

- Keeping it simple like using video-tapes to store experiences from experts,
- building on existing processes like the underwriting process and the existing e-mail culture,
- internal branding and naming metaphors for internal marketing and achieving the commitment of staff people,
- senior management support,
- success as a success factor,
- external recognition helps internal coordination,
- IT director business-focused and business process-oriented.

Part IV

**KM in Europe**

# 17 European Landscape of Knowledge Management

The multidisciplinary understanding of knowledge management has arisen the interest of a wide range of academic disciplines. We found contribution from accountants, anthropologists[210], architects[211], researchers in business administration, computer scientists, economists, engineers, journalists, library scientists, multimedia designers[212], psychologists, and sociologists.

The European Landscape of Knowledge Management is aimed to become a European-wide platform for exchange and collaboration between the leading European institutes and universities. We have asked fifteen colleagues from different European countries if they could briefly describe their knowledge management approach with a graphic and give a brief outlook on the future of knowledge management. The results are shown below.

If you like to become part of this European Landscape of Knowledge Management, you could register on our Web-page:

**www.km-in-europe.org**

---

[210]  Jordan (1994).
[211]  Henn (1996); Streitz et al. (1999).
[212]  Wurmann (1996).

## 17.1 Knowledge management at the Cranfield School of Management

The Cranfield approach towards KM is to consider it as an Organizational Competence, because this links KM and business strategy. Thinking about KM this way also supports competitiveness since competences are what distinguish businesses in their market place. An organization must be competent in the supply of knowledge, the exploitation of knowledge, and have a strategy for the use of its knowledge assets. This way of thinking about KM also accords with Resource-Based theory. In the latter everything that an organization has is classed as resource not just plant, money, and people – but also brands, credibility, knowledge etc. It is the role of managers to integrate resources into competences. A further combining of competences and resources at the strategic level delivers a capability and it is this capability that the market place recognizes and puts a value on. Thus for example a brand is a resource; being able to extend a brand or develop new ones is a competence; and how it is exploited in the market place would be a capability. The assertion is that the knowledge of how to do this (ie combine and integrate in a way that appeals to the market) is one of an organization's most crucial assets.

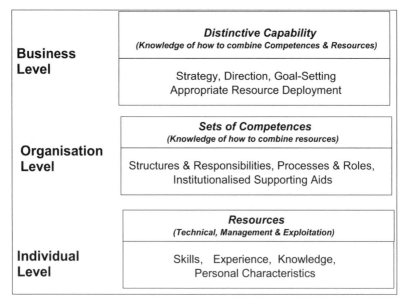

**Fig. 17.1: Knowledge Management as Organisational Competence**

## Future Trends

The future trend in KM is likely to be one where organizations having invested in knowledge supply, will realize that the demand side needs senior executive attention, and that this itself needs locating in the business's plans and strategies. Only this way will it be truly treated as an organizational asset.

## Address:

Cranfield School of Management
IS Research Center
Peter Murray
Cranfield
Bedford
MK43 0AL
Great Britain

Phone: 0044 - 1234 - 75 11 22
http://www.cranfield.ac.uk/som/

## 17.2 Organisational knowledge creation in technology-intensive companies

### KM-Approach at the Eindhoven University of Technology

The purpose of our research is to obtain understanding in mechanisms of knowledge generation, knowledge dissemination and knowledge application (in short: knowledge processes) as well as how to manage these processes.

In our research we consider the organization as a distributed cognitive system with a knowledge structure.

Furthermore, we rely on three primitive assumptions:

-   Knowledge cannot exist outside an individual.

-   Knowledge is the capacity that enables a person to perform a task.

-   Knowledge is a function of (task related) *i*nformation, *e*xperience, *s*kills and *a*ttitude at a given moment in time; $K = f(I*ESA)$.

The focus of the research is on technology-intensive organizations and three ontological levels are considered: the interaction (small group) level, the organization level and the alliance level.

Important research questions are:

•   How do knowledge processes work on interaction level in interplay with the knowledge structure?

•   How do control mechanisms of management influence knowledge processes?

•   How does the alliance setting influence knowledge processes?

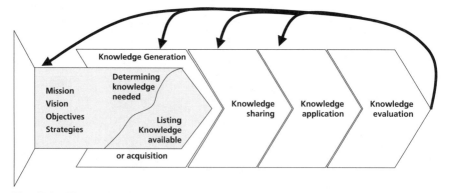

**Fig. 17.2:   Knowledge Value Chain with Knowledge Processes**

**Future trends in KM**

- Knowledge Infrastructure Engineering: the synergetic application of relevant concepts from the areas of workplace design, ICT, human talent development and knowledge management.

- The increasing application in knowledge intensive organizations of hypertext structures, fuzzy structures and web structures (or knowledge based network structures).

- The revival of master-mate work relations to share (tacit) knowledge, especially in those domains/disciplines where the half-life of knowledge has decreased substantially.

**Address:**

Eindhoven University of Technology
Faculty of Technology Management
Department of Organization Sciences
Prof.dr.ir. M.C.D.P. Weggeman
P.O. Box 513
5600 MB Eindhoven

e-mail: m.c.d.p.weggeman@tm.tue.nl

226

## 17.3  A balanced approach between the knowledge and learning perspectives

**By EKD Spain**

From the knowledge perspective an organization can be simplified as a core business system which inputs information –such as requirements, specifications, expectations, needs, and aspirations- and outputs added value. This business system is governed by the strategy and uses knowledge as the main mechanism to produce value.

In this schema we can consider that Knowledge Management –within a given business system- is a business process to create, share and apply the knowledge required to produce the desired added value. This process should incorporate the appropriate technology to manage content; or knowledge in its explicit form.

On the other hand, learning takes place when the knowledge derived from the comparison between objectives and results is fed back to modify and improve the actions and the governing values of the organization.

The learning perspective has to do with the way the knowledge flows, is renewed and absorbed; with the way people socialize, align a common vision, share different points of view and mental models, and agree on simplified representations of a complex reality.

In order to manage its knowledge properly an organization should integrate both perspectives –in a very specific and unique fashion- and make them gradually part of their own culture.

In the near future KM will concentrate on:

- Eliminating individual and organizational barriers which prevent learning.
- Defining adequate operative processes to manage knowledge.
- Bringing down technologies to the level of day to day activities.
- Developing knowledge maps, taxonomies and indexes to navigate, filter and distribute content.

**Address:**

Federation for Enterprise Knowledge Development EKD Spain
Víctor Furundarena
Parque Tecnologico de Zamudio
edif. 206
48170  Zamudio, Vizcaya
Spain

Phone: 0034 94 420 95 30
Email: charo@fend.es
http://www.fend.es/home/

228

## 17.4 Putting knowledge to action: intelligent ways of organizing knowledge work through knowledge media

### mcm-institute St.Gallen, Competence Center Enterprise Knowledge Medium

The competence center Enterprise Knowledge Medium has conducted research and industry projects in the area of knowledge management since 1994. During these six years, the center has worked with more than a dozen companies in improving the way that individuals, teams, organizations and inter-organizational networks develop, share, and use knowledge to foster innovation, learn more about customers, or generally improve know-how-intensive processes and projects.

### Our Approach

The main focus of this research has always been the question of *how knowledge media can improve the collaboration of knowledge workers.* We view knowledge media as socio-technological platforms for the development and exchange of knowledge in and between communities. Communities in this context are groups of people who are bound together through common interests, common norms and terms, and through a common way of interaction. A knowledge medium should provide services that assist the community in its implementation tasks (e..g, completing know-how-intensive projects or processes). Knowledge media are based on an IT-infrastructure, but also go beyond mere information technology solutions by incorporating new forms of interaction, such as team debriefings or mapping sessions (to foster the transfer and elicitation of implicit knowledge). The following diagram illustrates this approach through the knowledge media reference model.

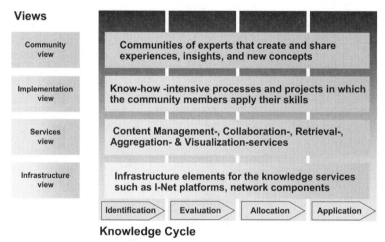

**Fig. 17.3: The Knowledge Media Reference Model**

## Knowledge Management Trends

We see the following four major trends in Knowledge Management:

1.  A closer linkage to project management: knowledge management tools become integrated aspects of most project management methods and approaches as projects become increasingly know-how intensive.
2.  A closer linkage to e-commerce and concepts such as customer relationship management as E-Business becomes one of the most know-how intensive business areas.
3.  A stronger focus on team knowledge management and personal knowledge in comparison to the organizational management of knowledge, as knowledge work is more and more organized around teams and individual experts that collaborate (e.g., e-lancers).
4.  The emergence of new socialization forms that provide rich and systematic contexts for the transfer of implicit knowledge and the integration of knowledge management systems to improve the transfer of explicit knowledge.

**Address:**

mcm institute
Competence Center Enterprise Knowledge Medium
Dr. Martin J. Eppler or Oliver Sukowski
Müller-Friedbergstr. 8
9000 St. Gallen
Switzerland

http://www.knowledgemedia.org

230

## 17.5  THESEUS knowledge management competence center

The THESEUS Knowledge Management Competence Center ($KMC^2$) was established in 1997 and has concentrated on understanding and structuring this emerging field.  It conducts applied research with companies and academic centers around the world, with a research portfolio that embraces STRATEGIC ALLIANCES, VIRTUAL SOCIAL CAPITAL, CONTEXTS IN KM, and CROSS-CULTURAL DIFFERENCES.   Despres and Chauvel will publish *Knowledge Horizons: The Present and the Promise of Knowledge Management* (Butterworth-Hienemann) in September 2000.

$KMC^2$ is a think tank rather than a consulting unit: its goals are non-commercial and aimed at the pursuit and publication of new KM knowledge. An illustration is the TAXONOMY OF APPLIED KNOWLEDGE MANAGEMENT, which it developed to "make sense" of the many, often divergent approaches that managers encounter (Figure). This taxonomy claims that all current KM practices and products can be located in a four-dimensional space, formed by Time, Type, Level and Context.

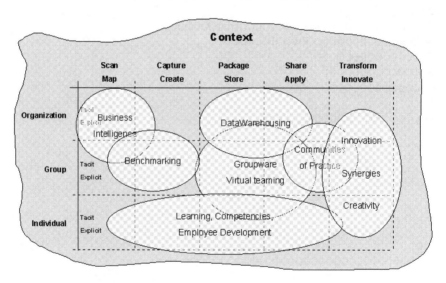

**Fig. 17.4:  Taxonomy of Applied Knowledge Management**

Our work indicates that "Knowledge Management" is moving away from the fragmented perspectives that were its recent hallmark, toward a second phase of that is characterized by (1) a developing mainstream of thought that is (2) orbited by various fringe elements, (3) textbooks and journals that treat KM concepts as social facts, (4) professions and positions that turn around this literature, and (5) emerging standards for behavior and thinking.

**Address:**

THESEUS Knowledge Management Competence Center
Charles Despres, Daniele Chauvel
Sophia Antipolis
France

e-mail: (despres@mail.esc-marseille.fr) / (chauvel@theseus.fr)

## 17.6   The knowledge source at University of St. Gallen

**Approach on Knowledge Management:**

> "Knowledge has become the most crucial component in the struggle for sustainable competitive advantage"

The KnowledgeSource is a research center organized jointly by the Institute for Information Management and the Institute of Management at the University of St. Gallen, Switzerland. As a joint research venture, the KnowledgeSource draws on resources from Information and Communication Management, Strategic Management, our Corporate and Academic Partners and International Academic Relations. This unique, interdisciplinary setup enables us to incorporate into our research a variety of perspectives on Knowledge. In a number of projects involving corporate partners, we are able to implement the results of our academic research, while receiving immediate feedback. The overall aim of the KnowledgeSource is to develop and adopt a framework of values, guidelines and methods in order to contribute to deal with the complexity of knowledge management and setting directions for the field of Knowledge Management in academia and in practice.

**The KnowledgeSource view on Future Trends in Knowledge Management**

> „Most important, in an age of rapidly proliferating knowledge, the central domain is a social network that absorbs, creates, transforms, buys, sells, and communicates knowledge. Its stronghold is the knowledge embedded in a dense web of social, economic, contractual, and administrative relationships" (Badaracco 1991).

Knowledge has become the most crucial component in the struggle for competitiveness. Especially the ability to generate constantly new knowledge and transfer it to the development of new products and services is seen as critical, i.e. the ability to create knowledge and move it from one part of the organization to another is the basis for competitive advantage. Parallel to this, a large body of theoretical and empirical research has suggested a significantly increased importance of the phenomenon network structures in recent years. Taking this transformation of relatively well-structured and manageable systems into intertwined networks with no clear boundaries, one can assume that knowledge management will rather be pursued in the context of these networks than with traditional organizational structures.

**Address:**

University of St. Gallen
Institute for Information Management
Prof. Dr. Andrea Bach
Institute of Management
Prof. Georg von Krogh
Dufourstraße 48
9000  St. Gallen
Switzerland

Email: georg.vonkrogh@unisg.ch
http://www.knowledgesource.org

234

## 17.7 Managing knowledge: The building blocks for success

**KM-Approach at the University of Geneva, Switzerland (Gilbert J. B. Probst, Nicole Pauli, Michel Binggeli)**

Due to the complex nature of knowledge, Knowledge Management (KM) has to build on a holistic approach and be integrated into day-to-day management activities. Only KM that is part of the company processes has been recognized as successful by our research.

Our model relies on eight building blocks, which provide a useful frame for tailoring innovative KM applications to individual company needs. It starts with the definition of knowledge goals to provide strategic direction for the KM initiative. Identifying existing knowledge, and achieving internal transparency are necessary steps for understanding possible knowledge gaps and guiding external acquisition as well as internal development of skills and competencies. Further steps include knowledge sharing as the most important building block, preservation, and use. As a final step, we propose effective measurement as a way to support the evolution of the knowledge system.

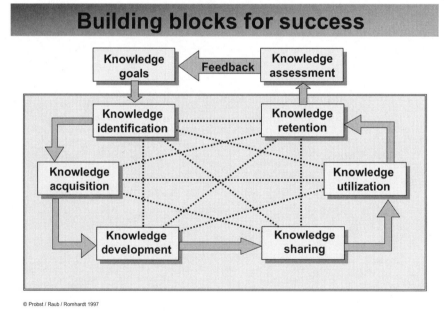

© Probst / Raub / Romhardt 1997

**Fig. 17.5:  Building Blocks for Success**

Each step is related to a set of particular activities including human resources and process-oriented approaches as well as IT. Eventually, all KM activities have to center around the human being. We firmly believe that a true KM solution has to go beyond the mere implementation of IT systems - which by definition is Information Management.

## Future Trends

KM will move from its purely operational level to *Knowledge Strategy* where the knowledge & learning requirements of the environment have to be linked with the corresponding capabilities of the organization. Only the fusion of consistent Knowledge Strategy and effective KM will finally lead to the overall goal of a *Learning Organization.*

## Address:

Université de Genève - Hautes Ètudes Commerciales
Prof. Gilbert Probst
102 boulevard Carl-Vogt
CH - 1211  Genève 4
Switzerland

Phone: 0041 - 22- 705 8103
Email: gilbert.probst@hec.unige.ch

## 17.8 The Fraunhofer IPK reference model for knowledge management

**The Competence Center Knowledge Management at Fraunhofer IPK**

The developments and services of the Competence Center Knowledge Management at Fraunhofer IPK are based on proved methods and empirical data from a wide-range of projects since the beginning of the 90ies (Figure). A powerful team of scientists from business administration, engineering, computer science, psychology and social science are working together to provide a customized knowledge management solution for clients from service and manufacturing industry as well as from public administration and associations world-wide.

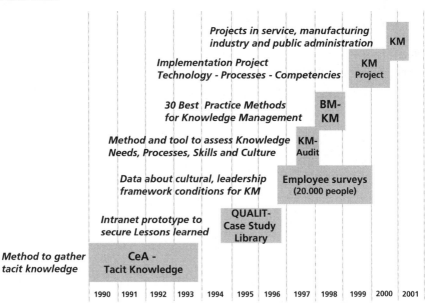

**Fig. 17.6: Selected Research and Development Projects on Knowledge Management**

The "heart and the soul" of the Fraunhofer IPK reference model for knowledge management are the business processes which an organization has to carry out to achieve their organizational goals. The core process of knowledge management consisting of four integrated core activities has to be linked to the operational tasks of the business processes. Measure in the six design fields have to be undertaken in order to speed up the wheel of knowledge management. The core activities and design fields are based on survey results from European companies and the evaluation of experiences of the pioneers in knowledge management.

## Future Trends

The development of knowledge management will focus on the integration of operational methods and tools into existing processes. Skills for knowledge management have to be defined, training modules have to be developed and implemented. Knowledge management technologies will become more and more standard and increasingly integrated. The potential of new emerging information technology applications will only be realized when user-friendly software tools are integrated into existing processes and fed by available sources. Measurements have to be developed and tested by practitioners.

**Address:**

Competence Center Knowledge Management at
Fraunhofer IPK
Mr. Peter Heisig
Pascalstrasse 8-9
D – 10587 Berlin
Germany

Phone: +49 / 30 / 39006 – 171
Fax: +49 / 30 / 393 25 03

e-mail: Peter.Heisig@ipk.fhg.de
http://www.um.ipk.fhg.de/ccwm/index.htm
http://www.um.ipk.fhg.de/ccwm/indexenglish/indexEng.htm

# Table of Figures

240

# Recommended Literature

## Journals and Newsletters

These Journals and Newsletters are especially dedicated to Knowledge Management and related fields of interest such as Intellectual Capital and Process Management.

These journals mainly address the **scientific community**:

- **Journal of Intellectual Capital**

- **Journal of Knowledge Management**

- **Knowledge Management Review**

- **Knowledge Organisation** – Official Quarterly Journal of the International Society for Knowledge Organisation. International Journal devoted to Concept Theory, Classification, Indexing and Knowledge Representation

- **Knowledge and Process Management** – The Journal of Corporate Transformation. The Official Journal of The Institute of Business Process Re-Engineering

  **www.interscience.wiley.com**

These magazine are specially addressed to **business communities**:

- **Knowledge Management** – The Magazine for Knowledge enabled Enterprise
  **www.knowledge-management.co.uk**

- **Knowledge Management**
  published by arkgroup

- **Wissensmanagement** – Das Magazin für Führungskräfte
  **www.wissensmanagement.net**

This newsletter provides a short update of award winners, companies, methods, tools, events and news from the world-wide **knowledge management community**:

- **The International Knowledge Management Newsletter**

## Special Issues on Knowledge Management:

- Wiig, K., de Hoog, R., et al. (1997): Knowledge Management (special issue) Expert Systems with Applications, 13 (1)
- Cole R. E. (1998): Special Issue on Knowledge and the Firm. California Management Review, 40 (3)

## Reprints

The special series "Resources for the Knowledge-Based Economy" provides a selection of articles from different journals and authors.

- Cross, R., Israelit, S. (2000): Strategic Learning in a Knowledge Economy. Butterworth- Heinemann, Boston, Oxford
- Klein, D.A. (1998): The Strategic Management of Intellectual Capital. Butterworth- Heinemann, Boston, Oxford
- Myers, P.S. (1996): Knowledge Management and Organizational Design. Butterworth- Heinemann, Boston, Oxford
- Prusak, L. (1998): Knowledge in Organizations. Butterworth- Heinemann, Boston, Oxford

244

- Ruggles, R. L. (1997): Knowledge Management Tools. Butterworth-Heinemann, Boston, Oxford

## Studies on Knowledge Management

- APQC (1996): Knowledge Management. Consortium Benchmarking Study. Final Report. Houston, American Productivity & Quality Center

- Ashton, C. (1998): Managing Best Practices. Transforming business performance by identifying, disseminating and managing best practice. London, Business Intelligence

- Bullinger, H.-J., Wörner, K., Prieto, J. (1997): Wissensmanagement heute. Daten, Fakten, Trends. Fraunhofer IAO, Stuttgart

- Chase, R. L. (1998): Creating a Knowledge Management Business Strategy. Delivering Bottom-Line Results. Lavendon. Management Trends International

- Cranfield School of Management, Information Strategy, The Document Company Xerox (1998): Europe's State of the Art in Knowledge Management, November Cranfield

- EFQM, APQC, KMN (1997): Knowledge Management and the Learning Organisation. Results of a joint EFQM/APQC/KMN Benchmarking Study Project. Brussels, Houston, Utrecht

- ILOI (1997): Knowledge Management. Ein empirisch gestützter Leitfaden zum Management des Faktors Wissen. München, Internationales Institut für Lernende Organisation und Innovation

- Skyrme, D.J., Amidon, D.M. (1997): Creating the Knowledge-Based Business. Key lessons from an international study of best practice. London, Business Intelligence

- Skyrme, D.J. (1998): Measuring the Value of Knowledge. Metrics for knowledge based business. London, Business Intelligence

- The Economist Intelligence Unit (1996): The Learning Organisation. Managing knowledge for business success. Written in Co-operation with the IBM Consulting Group. New York, The Economist Intelligence Unit, Research Report

# Further Readings

The following books are recommended to achieve a deeper insight into the subject:

- Allee, V. (1997): The Knowledge Evolution- Expanding Organizational Intelligence. Butterworth-Heinemann, Boston

- Boisot, M.H. (1998): Knowledge Assets- Securing Competitive Advantages in the Information Economy. Oxford University Press

- Bukowitz, W.R., Williams, R.L. (1999): The Knowledge Management Fieldbook. Pearson Education Limited Financial Times, Prentice Hall

- Davenport, T.H., Prusak, L. (1998): Working Knowledge. How Organizations Manage what they Know. Harvard Business School Press

- Gentsch, P. (1999): Wissen managen mit innovativer Informationstechnologie. Gabler, Wiesbaden

- Kluge, A. (1999): Erfahrungsmanagement in lernenden Organisationen. Verlag für angewandte Psychologie, Göttingen

- Van Krogh, G., Roos, J. et al. (Eds.) (1998): Knowing in Firms. Understanding, Managing and Measuring Knowledge. Sage Publications, London

- Probst, G., Raub, St., Romhardt, K. (1998): Wissen managen. Wie Unternehmen ihre wertvollste Ressource optimal nutzen. 2. Aufl. Frankfurt Allgemeine Zeitung GmbH, Gabler Verlag, Frankfurt/Main, Wiesbaden

- Schmidt, M.P. (2000): Knowledge Communities. Addison-Wesley, München, Boston

- Skills for Knowledge Management: Building a Knowledge Economy: A Report by TFPL Ltd., September 1999

- Skyrme, D.J. (1999): Knowledge Networking. Butterworth-Heinemann, Oxford, Auckland

- Sullivan, P.H. (1998): Profiting from Intellectual Capital. Extracting Value from Innovation. John Wiley & Sons, Inc., New York

- Sveiby, K.E. (1997): The New Organizational Wealth. German: Wissenskapital- das unentdeckte Vermögen. Berrett-Koehler Publishers, Inc., San Francisco

- Tiwana, A. (2000): The Knowledge Management Toolkit. Practical Techniques for Building a Knowledge Management System. Prentice Hall, Inc., Upper Saddle River

- Wenger, E. (1998): Communities of Practice, Learning, Meaning and Identity. Cambridge University Press

## Studies on Knowledge Management Tools

Knowledge Management has been enabled by Information Technology. The development of new technologies continues a fast growing market. Some technologies will merge to provide the user with better results. The following studies are helpful about information technologies.

- Bottomley, A. (1998): Enterprise Knowledge Management Technologies. An Investment Perspective. London, Durlacher Research Ltd. April 1998

- Mühlbauer, S., Versteegen, G. (2000): Wissensmanagement. Empirische Untersuchung, beste Pratiken und Evaluierung von Werkzeugen. Edited by it Research GmbH, Höhenkirchen

- Seifried, P., Eppler, M.J. (2000): Evaluation führender Knowledge Management Suites. Wissensplattformen im Vergleich. Benchmarking Studie. St. Gallen, NetAcedemy Press

- Woods, E., Sheina, M. (1998): Knowledge Management. Applications, Market and Technologies. London, Ovum

# References

- Allweyer, Th. (1998): Modellbasiertes Wissensmanagement. In: Information Management, 1, 37-45

- American Library Association (1989): Report of the Presidential Committee on Information Literacy. Chicago: American Library Association cited in the web: www.ucalgary.ca/library/ILG/litdef.html

- Bach, V., Vogler, P., Österle, H. (Ed.) (1999): Business Knowledge Management. Praxiserfahrungen mit Intranet-basierten Lösungen. Springer, Berlin, Heidelberg, New York

- Bair, J.H., O'Connor, E. (1998): The state of the product in knowledge management. Journal of Knowledge Management, 2, (2), 20-27

- Bair, J: Developing a Scaleable Knowledge Management Architecture and IT Strategy. In: Building the Knowledge Management Framework. The New IT Imperative. 1st & 2nd July 1998, Business Intelligence, London

- Barchan, M. (1998): Capturing Knowledge for Business Growth. How Celimi ensures strategic gains by measuring intangible assets. Knowledge Management Review 4, 12-15

- Baumert, A. (1999): Recherchegespräche. Das Interview in der Informationsbeschaffung. Doculine-Verlag, Reutlingen

- Benchmark, British Aerospace plc: BEST

- Bertels, T., Savage, Ch. M. (1998): Tough Questions on Knowledge Management. In: von Krogh, G., Roos, J., Kleine, D. (Eds.): Knowing in Firms. Understanding, Managing and Measuring Knowledge. SAGE Publications, London New Delhi

- Blumberg, M. (1988): Towards a new theory of job design. In: Karwowski, W., Parsaei, H.R.,Wilhelm M.R. (Eds.): Ergonomics of Hybrid Automated Systems I. Elsevier, Amsterdam, 53-59

- Borghoff, U.M., Pareschi,R. (Eds.) (1998): Information Technology for Knowledge Management. Springer, Berlin Heidelberg New York

- Bottomley, A. (1998): Enterprise Knowledge Management Technologies: An Investment Perspective 1998. Durlacher Research Ltd.

- British Aerospace Annual Report 1997

- British Aerospace Virtual University: Achievement through Knowledge (April 1998)

- British Aerospace Virtual University: Prospectus (April 1998)

- British Aerospace: Our Value Plan, Issue 2, 1998

- Bromme, R. (1992): Der Lehrer als Experte. Zur Psychologie des professionellen Wissens. Verlag Hans Huber, Bern, Göttingen, Toronto

- Brooking, A. (1997): Intellectual Capital. Core Asset for the Third Millenium Enterprise. 2nd Edition. Thomson, London Boston

- Bullinger, H.-J., Wörner, K., Prieto, J. (1997): Wissensmanagement heute. Daten, Fakten, Trends. Fraunhofer IAO, Stuttgart

- Burnhein, R. (1992): Information literacy – a core competency. Australian Academic and Research Libraries. 23(4), 188-96

- Camp, R. C. (1995) Business Process Benchmarking. Finding and Implementing Best Practices. ASQC Quality Press, Milwaukee

- Carbon, M., Heisig, P. (1993): Verbesserung der Prozeßtransparenz durch konstruktive Veränderungen. In: Bolte, A., Martin, H. (Ed.): Flexibilität durch Erfahrung. Computergestützte erfahrungsgeleitete Arbeit in der Produktion. Verlag Institut für Arbeitswissenschaft, Kassel, 71-77

- Club Intelect (December 1998): Medición Del Capital Intelectual. Modelo Intelect. Euroforum, Madrid.

- Cranfield School of Management, Information Strategy, The Document Company Xerox (1998): Europe's State of the Art in Knowledge Management, November Cranfield

- Davenport, Th. H., Prusak, L. (1998): Working Knowledge. How Organizations Manage What They Know. Harvard Business School Press, Boston.
  German: Wenn Sie wüßten, was Sie wissen. Verlag Moderne Industrie, Landsberg/Lech 1999

- Davenport, Th.H., Jarvenpaa, S.L., Beers, M.C. (1996): Improving Knowledge Work Processes. Sloan Management Review, Summer, 53-65

- De Hoog, R. (1997): CommonKADS: Knowledge Acquisition and Design Support Methodology for Structuring the KBS Integration Process. In: Leibowitz J., Wilcox, L.C. (ed.): Knowledge Management and Its Integrative Elements. CRC Press, Boca Raton, New York, 129-141

- Diebold Deutschland GmbH (1993): Geschäftsprozesse im Zentrum der modernen Unternehmensführung. Diebold Deutschland GmbH, Eschborn

- Doyle, C. (1992): Outcome measures for information literacy within the national education goals of 1990. Final report to National Forum on Information Literacy. Summary of findings. Syracuse, NY: ERIC

Clearinghouse on Information Resources. (ED 351033) cited in the web: www.ucalgary.ca/library/ILG/litdef.html

- Eck, C.D. (1997): Wissen – ein neues Paradigma des Managements. Die Unternehmung, 3, 155 - 179

- Edvinson, L., Brünig, G. (2000): Aktivposten Wissenskapital. Gabler, Wiesbaden

- Edvinsson, L. (1998): Managing Intellectual Capital at Skandia. In: Sullivan, P.H. (Ed.): Profiting from Intellectual Capital. Extracting Value from Innovation. John Wiley & Sons, New York

- Edvinsson, L. (2000): Some perspectives on intangibles and intellectual capital 2000. Journal of Intellectual Capital, 1 (1), 12-16

- Eppler, M., Röpnack, A., Seifried, P. (1999): Improving Knowledge Intensive Processes through an Enterprise Knowledge Medium, in: Proceedings of THE 1999 ACM SIGCPR Conference, Managing Organizational Knowledge for Strategic Advantage. The Key Role of Information Technology and Personnel

- Finke, I., Scholz, C. (2000). Interne Kommunikation und Transactive Memory in Organisationen – Eine Fallstudie. Unveröff. Diplomarbeit an der Humboldt-Universität zu Berlin

- Fleig, J., Schneider, R. (1995): Erfahrung und Technik in der Produktion. Springer Verlag, Berlin, Heidelberg, New York

- Föcker, E., Goesmann, T., Striemer, R. . (1999): Wissensmanagement zur Unterstützung von Geschäftsprozessen. HMD Praxis der Wirtschaftsinformatik 208, 36-43

- Forkel, M. (1994): Kognitive Werkzeuge – ein Ansatz zur Unterstützung des Problemlösens. Hanser Verlag, München

- Frei, F. (1996): Die kompetente Organisation: Qualifizierende Arbeitsgestaltung- die europäische Alternative. Schäffer-Poeschel, Stuttgart

- Gentsch, P. (1999): Wissen managen mit innovativer Informationstechnologie. Gabler, Wiesbaden

- Göber, Th. (1992): Modellbasierte Wissensakquisition zur rechnerunterstützten Wissensbereitstellung für den Anwendungsbereich Entwicklung und Konstruktion. Hanser Verlag, München

- Gödicke, P. (1992): Wissensmanagement – aktuelle Aufgaben und Probleme. in: io Management Zeitschrift, 61, (4), 67-70

- Häcker, H., Stapf, K. H. (Eds.) (1998): Dorsch Psychologisches Wörterbuch, 13. Auflage. Hans Huber Verlag, Bern

- Hammer, M., Champy, J. (1993): Reengineering the Corporation., New York 1993

- Hansen, M.T., Nohria, N., Tierney, T. (1999): What's your Strategy for Knowledge Management. In: Harvard Business Review, March-April, 106-116

- Hedlund, G. (1994): A Model of Knowledge Management and the N-Form Corporation. Strategic Management Journal 15, 73-90

- Heilmann, H. (1999): Wissensmanagement – ein neues Paradigma? HMD Praxis der Wirtschaftsinformatik 36, 7-23

- Heisig, P. (1998): Knowledge Management and Kaizen. Proceedings 2nd International EuroCINet Conference on Continuous Improvement: from idea to reality. Enschede, The Netherlands, 14-15 September1998, (Eds.: Harry Boer and José Gieskes)

- Heisig, P. (1998a): KVP und Wissensmanagement. In: Howaldt, J., Winther, M.: KVP: Der Motor der lernenden Organisation. Wirtschaftsverlag Bachem, Köln, 214 – 229

- Heisig, P. (1998b): Erfahrung sichern und Wissen transferieren: Wissensmanagement im Projektmanagement. Projektmanagement, 9. Jahrgang, (4), 3-10

- Heisig, P. (1999): Geschäftsprozessorientiertes Wissensmanagement. In: Bläsing, J.P., Heimann, D., Högle, E. (Eds.): Total Business Knowledge. Spitzenleistung durch Kernkompetenz. Vom Qualitätsmanagement zum Wissensmanagement. TQU Verlag, Ulm, 27-42

- Heisig, P. (2000): Benchmarking Knowledge Management und wissensorientierte Gestaltung von Geschäftsprozessen. Bühner, R. (Ed.): Organisation. Schlank – Schnell – Flexibel. Verlag moderne industrie, Landsberg/Lech, 1 – 38

- Henn, G. (1996): Das Büro als Wissensbörse. Sonderdruck aus AIT 4/1996

- Hess, Th., Brecht, L. (1995): State of the Art des Business Process Redesign. Darstellung und Vergleich bestehender Methoden. Gabler, Wiesbaden

- Huang, K.-T. (1998): Capitalizing Collective Knowledge for Winning, Execution and Teamwork. Unpublished IBM Working Paper

- Intellectual Capital. Supplement to Skandia's 1996 Interim Report: Power of Innovation.

- Jordan, B. (1994): Ethnographic Workplace Studies and Computer Supported Cooperative Work. IRL Report No. IRL94-0026

- Kaiser, Th. M., Vogler, P. (1999): PROMET®I-NET: Methode für Intranet-basiertes Wissensmanagement. In: Bach, V., Vogler, P., Österle, H. (Ed.):

Business Knowledge Management. Praxiserfahrungen mit Intranet-basierten Lösungen. Springer, Berlin, Heidelberg, New York, 117-129

- Kaplan, R., Norton, D. (1996): The Balanced Scorecard. Translating Strategy into Action. Harvard Business School Press, Boston

- Kenney-Wallace; G. (1999): The Virtual University. In: Defence Management Journal 3, (1)

- Klein, D. A. (1998): The Strategic Management of Intellectual Capital: An Introduction. In: Idem (Ed.): The Strategic Management of Intellectual Capital. Butterworth-Heinemann, Boston

- Krogh, G.v., Venzin, M. (1995): Anhaltende Wettbewerbsvorteile durch Knowledge Management. Die Unternehmung, 49, (6), 417-436

- Liedtke, P., Roessiger, U. Spur, G., Albrecht, R., Heisig, P. (1995): Gestaltung ganzheitlicher Arbeitsabläufe. Management von Teamarbeit durch integrative Planung und Qualifizierung. ZWF Zeitschrift für wirtschaftlichen Fabrikbetrieb 90, (3), 104 – 107

- Luhn, G. (1999): Implizites Wissen und technisches Handeln am Beispiel der Elektronikproduktion. Meisenbach Verlag, Bamberg

- Lullies, V., Bollinger, H., Weltz, F. (1993): Wissenslogistik. Über den betrieblichen Umgang mit Wissen bei Entwicklungsvorhaben. Campus Verlag, Frankfurt/Main, New York

- Mandl, H., Spada, H. (1988): Wissenspsychologie. PVU, München

- Martin, H. (1995): CeA – Computergestützte erfahrungsgeleitete Arbeit. Springer, Berlin, Heidelberg, New York

- McCracken,C. (2000): Information Retrieval. Knowledge Management, March, 28-30

- Mertins, K., Jochem, R. (1999): Quality-oriented design of business processes. Dordrecht, Norwell

- Mertins,K., Schallock,B., Carbon,M., Heisig, P. (1993): Erfahrungswissen bei der kurzfristigen Auftragssteuerung. Zeitschrift für wirtschaftliche Fertigung 88, (2), 78 - 80.

- Ministry of Economic Affairs (October 1999): Intangible Assets. Balancing accounts with knowledge. The Hague

- Mroß, M.D. (2000): Knowledge Management oder Personalentwicklung? – Brauchen Unternehmen ein Management ihres Wissens? Zeitschrift für Unternehmensentwicklung und Industrial Engineering 49, (1), 34-38

- Nonaka, I., Takeuchi, H. (1995): The Knowledge-Creating Company. Oxford University Press, Oxford
  German: Die Organisation des Wissens. Wie japanische Unternehmen eine brachliegende Ressource nutzbar machen. Campus Verlag, Frankfurt/Main, New York 1997

- North, K. (1998): Wissensorientierte Unternehmensführung: Wertschöpfung durch Wissen. Gabler, Wiesbaden

- Pawlowsky, P. (1994): Wissensmanagement in der lernenden Organisation. Unveröffentlichte Habilitationsschrift Universität Paderborn

- Picot, A., Reichwald, R. Wigand, R.T. (1998): Die grenzenlose Unternehmung. Information, Organisation und Management. Lehrbuch zur Unternehmensführung im Informationszeitalter, 3. Auflage. Gabler, Wiesbaden

- Platon (1981): Theätet. Reclam Verlag, Ditzingen

- Probst, G., Raub, St., Romhardt, K. (1998): Wissen managen. Wie Unternehmen ihre wertvollste Ressource optimal nutzen. 2. Aufl. Frankfurt Allgemeine Zeitung GmbH, Gabler Verlag, Frankfurt/Main, Wiesbaden

- Prusak, L (1998): Why Knowledge, Why Now? In: Klein, D.A. (Ed.): The Strategic Management of Intellectual Capital. Butterworth-Heinemann, Boston.

- Rao,R. Sprague, R.H. jr., (1998): Natural Technologies for Knowledge Work: Information Visualization and Knowledge Extraction. Journal of Knowledge Management, 2, (2), 70-80

- Rehäuser, J., Krcmar, H. (1996): Wissensmanagement in Unternehmen. In: Schreyögg, G., Conrad, P. (Eds.): Managementforschung 6: Wissensmanagement. Walter de Gruyter, Berlin, New York, 1-40

- Reinmann-Rothmeier, G., Mandl, H. (1999): Individuelles Wissensmanagement: Strategien für den persönlichen Umgang mit Information und Wissen am Arbeitsplatz (Praxisbericht 15), Ludwig-Maximilians-Universität München, Institut für Pädagogische Psychologie und Empirische Pädagogik, München

- Romhardt, K. (1998): Die Organisation aus der Wissensperspektive. Möglichkeiten und Grenzen der Intervention. Gabler Verlag, Wiesbaden

- Roos, J., Roos, G., Dragonetti, N.C., Edvinsson, L. (1997): Intellectual Capital. Navigating the New Business Landscape. Macmillan, Houndmills London

- Ruggles,R.L. (1997): Knowledge Management Tools. Butterworth-Heinemann, Boston, Oxford

- Sattelberger, T. (1999): Wissenskapitalisten oder Söldner? Personalarbeit in Unternehmensnetzwerken des 21. Jahrhunderts. Gabler, Wiesbaden

- Schmitz, C., Zucker, B. (1996): Wissen gewinnt: Knowledge-Flow Management. Metropolitan Verlag GmbH, Düsseldorf, München

- Schreiber A.Th., Hoog, R., Akkermans, H., Anjewierden, A., Shadbolt, N., Velde W. (2000): Knowledge Engineering and Management. The CommonKADS Methodology. The MIT Press, Cambridge, London

- Schuller, F. (1998): Wissensaufbau erfordert eine offene Lernkultur. Personalwirtschaft, 5, 27-30

- Schüppel, J. (1996): Wissensmanagement. Gabler Edition Wissenschaft, Wiesbaden

- Schütte, S. (2000): Kaufhaus des Wissens. Wirtschaft & Weiterbildung. Mai, 14-19

- Sheina, M. (2000): Knowledge Portals: Avoiding a Bloodbath. Knowledge Management, February , 32-33

- Skyrme, D.J. (1998): Measuring the Value of Knowledge. Metrics for the Knowledge-based Business. Business Intelligence, London.

- Skyrme, D.J., Amidon, D.M. (1997): Creating the Knowledge-Based Business. Business Intelligence, London, New York

- Snowden, D. (1998): A Framework for Creating a Sustainable Programme. In: Rock, S. (Ed.): Knowledge Management. A Real Business Guide. Caspian Publishing Ltd., London

- Spur, G., Mertins, K., Jochem, R. (1993): Integrierte Unternehmensmodellierung. Beuth Verlag, Berlin, Wien, Zürich

- Stewart, Th. A. (1998): Der vierte Produktionsfaktor. Wachstum und Wettbewerbsvorteile durch Wissensmanagement. Hanser, München Wien. English edition (1997): Intellectual Capital – The New Wealth of Organizations, Nicholas Brealey Publishing, London

- Streitz, N., Remmers, B., Pietzcker, M., Grundmann, R. (1999) Arbeitswelten im Wandel – fit für die Zukunft?: Menschen, Organisationen, Technologien und Architektur an der Schwelle zum 21. Jahrhundert. Deutsche Verlags-Anstalt, Stuttgart

- Sullivan, P.H. (Ed.) (1998): Profiting from Intellectual Capital. Extracting Value from Innovation. John Wiley & Sons, New York.

- Sveiby, K.E. (1997): The New Organizational Wealth, Berrett-Koehler Publishers, Inc., San Francisco

254

- Sveiby, K.E. (1997): Wissenskapital – das unentdeckte Vermögen. Immaterielle Vermögenswerte aufspüren, messen und steigern. Verlag Moderne Industrie, Landsberg/Lech

- Syed, J.R. (1998): An adaptive framework for knowledge work. Journal of Knowledge Management 2, (2), 59-69

- Tampoe, M. (1996): Motivating Knowledge Workers – The Challenge for the 1990s. In: Myers, P.S. (Eds.): Knowledge Management and Organizational Design. Butterworth-Heinemann, Newton, MA, 179-189

- Tebbutt, D. (2000): KM intranet. In Knowledge Management, February, 28-30

- TFPL Ltd. (1999): Skills für knowledge management – building a knowledge economy. TFPL Ltd., London

- The Danish Trade and Industry Development Council. Memorandum (May 1997): Intellectual Capital Accounts. Reporting and managing intellectual capital

- The International Knowledge Management Newsletter (July 2000). Published by David Watts, Management Trends International

- Thiesse, F., Bach, V. (1999): State-of-the-Art des Wissensmanagements, Universität St. Gallen, Hochschule für Wirtschafts-, Rechts- und Sozialwissenschaften (HSG)

- Tiwana, A. (2000): The Knowledge Management Toolkit. Prentice-Hall, Upper Saddle River

- Tünschel, L., Hille, T. Jochem, R. (1998): Geschäftsprozessmodellierung – Werkzeug für das Management des Wandels. io Management, 5, 66-74

- Ulich, E. (1998): Arbeitspsychologie (4., neu überarb. und erw. Aufl.). Schäffer-Poeschel, Stuttgart

- Versteegen, G., Mühlbauer, S. (2000): Wissensmanagement. Empirische Untersuchung, beste Praktiken und Evaluierung von Werkzeugen. IT Research GmbH, Höhenkirchen

- Victor, B., Boynton, A.C. (1998): Invented Here. Maximizing Your Organization's Internal Growth and Profitability. Harvard Business School Press, Boston

- Vogel, E. (1999): Wissensmanagement bei den Helvetia Patria Versicherungen – Ein Vorgehen zur Bewertung des Ist-Stands und zur Entwicklung eines Grobkonzepts. In: 21. Online-Tagung der DGI: Aufbruch ins Wissensmanagement; Frankfurt am Main, 18. bis 20. Mia 1999, Proceedings / Ralph Schmidt (Hrsg) – Frankfurt am Main: Deutsche Gesellschaft für Informationswissenschaft und Informationspraxis (DGI), 117 – 128

- von Krogh, G. M. Venzin (1995): Anhaltende Wettbewerbsvorteile durch Wissensmanagement, Die Unternehmung, 417 - 436

- Warnecke, G., Gissler, A., Stammwitz, G. (1998): Referenzmodell Wissensmanagement – Ein Ansatz zur modellbasierten Gestaltung wissensorientierter Prozesse. Information Management 1, 24-29

- Weggeman, M. (1998): Kenntnismanagement. Inrichtig en besturing van kennisintensieve organisaties. Scrptum, Schiedom German: Wissens-management – Der richtige Umgang mit der wichtigsten Ressource des Unternehmens. MITP-Verlag, Bonn 1999

- Weinert, F.E. (1997): Wissen und Denken. In: Clar, G.,Doré, J., Mohr, H. (Eds.): Humankapital und Wissen: Grundlagen einer nachhaltigen Entwicklung. Springer, Berlin, 31-32

- Wenger, E.C. (1998): Communities of Practice. Learning, meaning, and identity. Cambridge University Press, Cambridge

- Wenger, E.C., Snyder, W.M. (2000): Communities of Practice: The Organizational Frontier. In: Harvard Business Review, 78, (1), 139-146

- Wiig, K.M. (1995): Knowledge Management Methods. Practical Approaches to Managing Knowledge. Vol. 3. Schema Press, Arlington

- Wiig, K.M. (1997): Knowledge Management: Where did it come from and where will it go? Expert Systems with Applications, 13, (1), 1-14

- Willke, H. (1998): Systemisches Wissensmanagement. Lucius und Lucius, Stuttgart

- Woods, M.S.(1998): Knowledge Management, Applications, Markets and Technologies, Ovum Ltd., London

- Wurman, R.S. (1996): Information Architets. Graphis Press Corp., Zurich

- Yakhlef, A., Salzer-Mörling, M. (2000): Intellectual Capital: Managing by Numbers. In: Prichard, C., Hull, R., Chumer, M., Willmott, H.(Eds.): Managing Knowledge. Critical Investigations of Work and Learning. Macmillan, Houndmills London

# The Editors

## Prof. Dr.-Ing. Kai Mertins

Prof. Dr.-Ing. Kai Mertins has been the Director for Corporate Management at the Fraunhofer Institute for Production Systems and Design Technology (IPK), Berlin/Germany since 1988. After completing Control Theory studies in Hamburg as well as Economy and Production Technology at the Technical University of Berlin, he became a member of the scientific staff at the University Institute for Machine Tool and Manufacturing Technology. He has held a Ph.D. in production technology since 1984 and has more than 20 years experience in the design, planning, simulation and control of flexible manufacturing systems (FMS), manufacturing control systems (MCS), computer integrated manufacturing (CIM), business reengineering and enterprise modelling. He was General Project manager in several international industrial projects and gives lectures and seminars at the Technical University Berlin and several other universities. His special field of interest is manufacturing strategy development, modelling and planning for production systems, shop floor control, simulation and BPR. Kai Mertins is a member of the editorial board of the journal „Production Planning and Control" and of the „Business Process Management Journal".

Professor Mertins is responsible for the Representative Office of the Fraunhofer Society (FhG) in Jakarta. He has led several projects in Indonesia since 1985.

## Peter Heisig

Peter Heisig is Head of the Competence Center Knowledge Management at Fraunhofer IPK. He studied Social Sciences at the Universities of Göttingen, Vienna and Bilbao, and has carried out research projects in Spain and Argentina . He started applied research at Fraunhofer IPK in 1990 with a project on the tacit knowledge of experienced workers and designers in metal companies. He was responsible for several projects in cooperation with industrial companies, in the fields of factory planning and business process engineering, teamwork, continuous improvement, benchmarking and knowledge management. In 1996 he assumed responsibility for the Information Center Benchmarking (IZB). Since summer 1997 he has been in charge of the area of knowledge management at the Fraunhofer IPK. In autumn 1997 he initiated the first German consortium-benchmarking study on knowledge management. He is the Vice-Chairman of the Global Benchmarking Network (GBN). He is researching the integration of knowledge management into daily business tasks and processes. He has been invited to over 30 conferences and workshops about Knowledge Management in

Germany, Sweden, Switzerland, Spain, United Kingdom and Mexico since autumn 1998.

## Jens Vorbeck

Jens Vorbeck was senior researcher at the Fraunhofer IPK, Berlin/Germany from 1997 until 2000. He studied Psychology at the Technical University of Berlin and the Business School of Dublin City University and Information Sciences at the Freie Universität Berlin. During the past years he has conducted several national and international projects in the fields of knowledge management, benchmarking and business process engineering. His special fields of interest are the issues of motivation, corporate culture and leadership in the context of knowledge management. Furthermore, he is involved in the development of the benchmarking method, business process modelling and the development and application of the balanced scorecard approach.

Since autumn 2000 Jens Vorbeck has continued his work as a consultant with the IBM consulting group *IBM Unternehmensberatung GmbH (UBG)*.

# Contributors

*Christian Berg*
  Director of R&D
  Phonak AG
  Laubisrütistrasse 28
  CH-8712 Stäfa
  Switzerland


*Robert C. Camp, PhD, PE*
  Chairman Global Benchmarking Network (GBN)
  Best Practice Institute™,
  625 Panorama Trail
  Suite 1-200
  Rochester, NY, USA


*Oliver Diethert*
  Fraunhofer Institute IPK
  Pascalstr. 8-9
  D-10587 Berlin
  Germany


*Peter Drtina*
  Coordinator of Knowledge Management & IPR
  Phonak AG
  Laubisrütistrasse 28
  CH-8712 Stäfa
  Switzerland


*Ina Finke*
  Fraunhofer Institute IPK
  Pascalstr. 8-9
  D-10587 Berlin
  Germany

*Dr. Rolf W. Habbel*
Vice President & Partner
Booz Allen & Hamilton
Lenbachplatz 3
D-80333 München
Germany

*Dr. Christoph Haxel*
Head of Henkel InfoCenter
Henkel KGaA, Düsseldorf
Henkelstraße 67
D-40191 Düsseldorf
Germany

*Peter Heisig*
Head of Competence Center Knowledge Management
Vice-Chairman Global Benchmarking Network (GBN)
Fraunhofer Institute IPK
Pascalstr. 8-9
D-10587 Berlin
Germany

*Ingo Hoffmann*
Fraunhofer Institute IPK
Pascalstr. 8-9
D-10587 Berlin
Germany

*Andrea Martin*
IBM Deutschland Informationssysteme GmbH
Anziger Straße 29
D-81671 München
Germany

*Prof. Dr. Ing. Kai Mertins*
Head of Division Corporate Management
Fraunhofer Institute IPK
Pascalstr. 8-9
D-10587 Berlin
Germany

*Johannes Niebuhr*
  Fraunhofer Institute IPK
  Pascalstr. 8-9
  D-10587 Berlin
  Germany

*Janet Runeson*
  Celemi
  Box 577
  SE – 20125 Malmö
  Sweden

*Dr. Peter Schütt*
  IBM Global Services
  Pascalstr. 100
  D-70548 Stuttgart
  Germany

*Frank Spellerberg*
  Manager Europe, Knowledge Research & Information Services
  Arthur D. Little International, Inc.
  Gustav-Stesemann-Ring 1
  D-65189 Wiesbaden
  Germany

*Dr. Andreas Spielvogel*
  Director Development Processes & Tools
  Business Unit Original Equipment
  Continental AG
  Vahrenwalder Str. 9
  D-30165 Hannover
  Germany

*Jens Vorbeck*
  Fraunhofer Institute IPK
  Pascalstr. 8-9
  D-10587 Berlin
  Germany

# Index

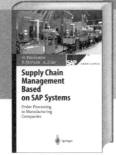

Druck:           Strauss Offsetdruck, Mörlenbach
Verarbeitung:    Schäffer, Grünstadt